Outlines of
Shakespeare's Plays

OUTLINES OF
Shakespeare's Plays

by HOMER A. WATT
Late of New York University

KARL J. HOLZKNECHT
Late Head, Department of English
Graduate School of Arts and Science
New York University

RAYMOND ROSS
Department of Speech
Washington Square College
New York University

HarperPerennial
A Division of HarperCollins*Publishers*

Reprinted, 1970

L. C. Catalogue Card Number: 57-8496

Manufactured in the United States of America

98 99 RRD H   30

Foreword

No PLAY SYNOPSIS, it need hardly be said, can take the place of its original; and this little volume is not presented as a substitute for the dramas themselves. To be appreciated and understood, Shakespeare's plays must be read carefully in full—not in the dilution of outlines or abridgments. In preparing this book, therefore, the authors had in mind only to provide student and lay reader with a convenient device for reviewing plays previously read, and for acquiring some general facts about Shakespeare's life and times and some simple suggestions and aids for studying his dramas.

The order of the play synopses in this book is, by type, the traditional one established by the First Folio of 1623: *Comedies, Histories,* and *Tragedies*. Within these divisions, however, the non-significant order of tradition has been abandoned in favor of one which seems to the authors to fulfill better the objectives of the volume. In the divisions of *Comedies* and *Tragedies* the order is that in which Shakespeare wrote the plays, as these are listed, with dates of composition, on page 14. The *Histories* have been arranged in the chronological order of the reigns of the kings; by this plan the full significance of the relationship of the plays of the double tetralogy (second to ninth *History* inclusive) becomes apparent.

The plot or story synopses have all been carefully constructed on very definite principles. In the first place, of course, an attempt has been made to give in each synopsis the story of the play being summarized. No episode or detail essential to a complete understanding of the plot has been omitted, and there are no broken story threads. Omissions have been restricted to scenes and parts of scenes which are in no wise essential to a complete understanding of the development of the narrative from the initial instability of the situation, through the unraveling of the tangled skein of events, to the climax.

i

In the synopses the division into acts follows scrupulously that of the original play with no transfer whatever of any episode from one act to another. Inasmuch, however, as the division into scenes in Shakespeare's plays is often of no narrative significance, the order of events in the synopses has frequently been altered within the act from that of the plays. One reason for these alterations is that the synopses might have a continuity of narration and a smoothness of flow which they might not otherwise possess. By careful linking of sentences and acts, by references to events past and sometimes to events to come, and by other compositional devices to secure coherence, an attempt has been made to avoid the libretto-like effect which appears in synopses made scene by scene.

But in addition to giving a complete and smoothly told story of the play, the authors have tried to reflect in their synopses something of the art of Shakespeare which is analyzed briefly in the section of the introductory material which deals with the reading of the plays. For example, the synopses reveal the dramatist's skilful use of related parallel plots and of contrasting characters or *foils,* care having been taken to make these artistic devices readily apparent even in these brief summaries. With this purpose in mind, the authors have even included some subplots or general situations which do not ordinarily appear in similar play outlines, such, for example, as the Fortinbras subplot in *Hamlet,* which marches with solemn and ominous tread behind the story of the Danish prince and merges with it at the end.

The nature and limitations of a brief synopsis preclude its suggesting much of the flavor of its dramatic original. Wherever possible, however, actual quotations from the play have been woven into the narrative, quoted accurately and with square brackets setting off the non-Shakespearean words and phrases which the structure of the sentence sometimes requires. In selecting these quotations the authors have had in mind both the significance of the passage quoted in explaining action or character and its beauty, vigor, concreteness, adaptability, or familiarity.

In preparing the *dramatis personæ* the authors believe that they have hit upon an original and compendious device for pre-

senting the characters to the reader. Arranging the characters
"in the order of their appearance" would mean nothing in such
a book as this. Moreover, the old arrangement, followed, apparently without thought of change, from the first editions of the
plays to the present time, does not seem to have any especial
significance. Nothing but tradition, indeed, justifies the listing of
characters, regardless of their relative importance, in the strict
order of social rank and with a sharp and curious division between
male and female. In the *dramatis personæ* preceding each synopsis
here the general plan has been to list the characters in the order
of their importance without distinction of social rank or sex.
An attempt has been made, furthermore, to place together those
characters which represent obvious contrasts or *foils,* or which
are related in some other important way. Finally, no character,
no matter how insignificant, has been named without some indi-
cation of his part in the action; thus the meaningless inclusion of
dozens of mere names has been entirely avoided.

Following somewhat the method of modern plays, the authors
have described briefly but carefully each major figure in the
dramatis personæ; furthermore, characters not essential to an
understanding of the plot but nevertheless worth knowing for
themselves—like the worthy Launcelot Gobbo—have been similarly characterized. All these analyses have been necessarily brief,
but the authors believe that this brevity is more than compensated
by the fact that as far as possible the descriptive phrases employed
have been taken from the plays themselves, which were read
carefully with this purpose definitely in mind. Moreover, the
characterizations taken from the plays were selected for their
general applicability to the characters, and those discolored by
rage, hate, or other emotions were excluded. The quotations are
accurate with letters, words, and phrases not directly quoted
included in square brackets. It is perhaps not too much to say
that often a single vivid phrase from the play is worth more
as a characterization than pages of flat and wordy "character
analysis."

The introductory material, finally, was designed not to be
complete but generally helpful to the average lay reader. Care has

been taken to make it scrupulously accurate, but it is not meant to take the place of books on Shakespeare's life, times, and workmanship. Every section, however, was included because of the authors' conviction that it contains some information or suggestion which will make the reading of Shakespeare's plays more understandable and more enjoyable. Nevertheless, this *Foreword* must end as it began: for the reading of the dramas themselves there is no substitute.

Table of Contents

Introduction

Shakespeare's Life 1
Shakespeare's Theatre 5
The Sequence of Shakespeare's Plays 12
Shakespeare's Sources 15
Suggestions on Reading Shakespeare 25

Synopses

COMEDIES:

  Love's Labor's Lost 40
  The Comedy of Errors 43
  The Two Gentlemen of Verona 47
  A Midsummer Night's Dream 50
  The Merchant of Venice 54
  The Taming of the Shrew 58
  The Merry Wives of Windsor 62
  Much Ado About Nothing 66
  As You Like It 70
  Twelfth Night: or, What You Will 74
  All's Well That Ends Well 77
  Measure for Measure 80
  Pericles, Prince of Tyre 84
  Cymbeline 87
  The Winter's Tale 92
  The Tempest 96

HISTORIES:

  Shakespeare's History Plays 103
  King John 106
  Richard II 110
  Henry IV: Part I 113
  Henry IV: Part II 117

Henry V 121
Henry VI: Part I 125
Henry VI: Part II 129
Henry VI: Part III 133
Richard III 137
Henry VIII 142

TRAGEDIES:

Titus Andronicus 148
Romeo and Juliet 151
Julius Caesar 154
Hamlet, Prince of Denmark 158
Troilus and Cressida 162
Othello, the Moor of Venice 166
King Lear 170
Macbeth 174
Antony and Cleopatra 178
Timon of Athens 183
Coriolanus 187

Appendices

Everyday Expressions from Shakespeare 190
Book-titles from Shakespeare 192
Bibliography 198
An Index of Characters and Places in Shakespeare's Plays . . . 204

Illustrations and Maps

The Theatres of Shakespeare's London 5
New York University Model of a Typical Elizabethan Theatre 6
New York University Model Showing Stage 8
Interior of the Swan Theatre (from a contemporary drawing) . 9
Ben Jonson's Verses Printed Opposite the Title-Page
   of the First Folio, 1623 36
Title-Page of the First Folio 37
England and Northern France in Shakespeare's Plays . . . 102
The London of Shakespeare's Plays 104

Outlines of
Shakespeare's Plays

Shakespeare's Life

IN VIEW OF THE FACT that William Shakespeare was a man of no social standing who lived nearly four hundred years ago, it is remarkable that so much is definitely known about him. Not only can his existence be proved by documents and records to the satisfaction of any law court, but the outlines of his career are also by no means shadowy. One must not look for romance or mystery or excitement in Shakespeare's biography, however, for his was the commonplace decent life of a busy man who kept out of trouble.

What we know of his personal affairs may be briefly summarized. Born at Stratford in central England about April 23, 1564, he sprang from honest, hard-working, middle-class stock. His father, John Shakespeare, was a tanner and glover by trade who owned considerable property and held important civic offices in Stratford, including those of alderman and high bailiff, or mayor. His mother, Mary Arden, was the daughter of a "gentleman of worship" and of somewhat higher social standing than her husband. Nothing is known of William's education, except the tradition that he attended a free school, and such evidences of learning as his plays exhibit. His formal schooling was probably not unusually long in duration, because John Shakespeare suffered financial reverses about 1577, and William, like others of his class, married early. While still in his teens, on November 28, 1582, he was contracted to Anne Hathaway, a Shottery girl several years his senior, and soon found himself with the responsibilities of a family. A daughter, Susanna, was born in the following May, and twins, Hamnet and Judith, in February, 1585. Many conjectures have been made as to the happiness or unhappiness of Shakespeare's married life, but they are entirely unsupported by evidence of any kind. Significant at least is the fact that as soon as he was able, in 1597, he purchased New Place, a large house in

1

Stratford, as a residence; improved his social standing by acquiring a coat of arms and the privilege of writing himself "gentleman;" and retired to his native town at the close of his life.

Precisely when Shakespeare left Stratford for London is not known. There is a familiar romantic tradition that he was driven from his native city because of a poaching escapade on Sir Thomas Lucy's game preserves; another that he was a butcher's apprentice who ran away from his master to join a troupe of actors; and a third that he was for a time a country schoolmaster. All these traditions are late, and none has the support of any corroborative evidence. Whatever the immediate reason, it was probably to provide for his increasing family that Shakespeare turned to London and its theatres, inspired by the same high hopes with which young men of to-day look to Hollywood or to Broadway. Like the adventurous young blades of his own plays, he knew that "home-keeping youth have ever homely wits" and resolved "to seek his fortune farther than at home, where small experience grows." Perhaps it was not the theatre alone which at first lured him from Stratford; London has at all times been a powerful magnet to the provincial Englishman. At any rate, when he is first heard of, he has already overcome the indifference with which the big city discourages the newcomer and made a name for himself as an actor. By 1592 he had aroused the resentment of Robert Greene, a university man, who called him an "upstart crow" and warned his fellow dramatists against the whole race of actors, but especially against this "absolute Johannes factotum" who in his own conceit was the "only Shakescene in the country." Perhaps Shakespeare had already tried his hand at refurbishing old plays. An epidemic of plague closed the theatres soon after, and the first definite news from Shakespeare shows him writing narrative poetry and seeking a patron. In 1593 *Venus and Adonis* appeared, and was followed the next year by *The Rape of Lucrece,* both dedicated to the young Earl of Southampton. But, if Shakespeare had ever seriously contemplated a literary career, he soon abandoned it, and we next hear of him back in the theatre.

There is some evidence for believing that Shakespeare's earliest stage connections were with the Earl of Pembroke's company of players and that he served an apprenticeship in playmaking under Christopher Marlowe, their chief writer. Now in 1594, when we have definite knowledge of his new connections, he is associated as a "sharer" in the Lord Chamberlain's company, one of the best of troupes, and has as his fellows Richard Burbage, the greatest tragedian of his day, and Will Kempe, a famous low comedian. To this company Shakespeare devoted his talents as actor and author to the end of his career. In December, 1594, he is mentioned as one of the actors who took part in several plays before the Queen, and in the same month his own *Comedy of Errors* was performed before the law students at Gray's Inn. By this time, then, Shakespeare was established as both an actor and a playwright.

The rest of the story of his professional career may be simply told. In 1597 his name appeared for the first time on printed plays; in 1598 a critic pointed to him as the best author of both comedy and tragedy for the stage; and in 1599 his name had sufficient renown for a dishonest publisher to appropriate it for the title page of a book he was issuing. His company prospered and in 1599 erected the famous Globe Theatre in which Shakespeare was one of the stockholders, and here his greatest plays were probably produced. With the coming of King James in 1603, the Lord Chamberlain's company passed under royal patronage and became the King's Men, and Shakespeare and his fellow actors became Grooms of the Chamber, i.e., minor court officers. About this time also Shakespeare apparently gave up acting and devoted his energies entirely to playwriting. In 1608 his company acquired the right to open another theatre in Blackfriars, and in this venture Shakespeare was again a stockholder. The *Sonnets*, which he had been writing for years and had circulated in manuscript among his friends, appeared in print in 1609. About 1611 or 1612, having written the whole, or at least the major part, of thirty-seven plays, he retired to Stratford, which, tradition says, he had visited once a year, to spend the rest of his days in "ease, retirement, and the conversation of his friends."

Records in Stratford, London, and elsewhere add a number of facts to fill in this outline of a busy life. His only son died in

1596, his father in 1601, and his mother in 1608. His daughters married. He made further investments, some of them substantial in both Stratford and London; and as his reputation as a man of means increased, he was even touched for loans by his fellow townsmen. His business affairs involved him in various petty law-suits in Stratford, which are interesting only as they indicate his continued connection with his home city. In London he was called as a witness in a dowry suit against one Christopher Mountjoy, a Huguenot merchant, with whom, as the testimony showed, Shakespeare had been lodging about 1604. He was the recipient of small bequests from a fellow actor and a Stratford friend. All of these details have little significance to those who wish to know the plays, but they make Shakespeare the man very real to us.

Practically nothing is known of Shakespeare's closing years. The Globe Theatre burned to the ground in 1613 during a performance of *Henry VIII,* and Shakespeare probably assisted his fellows in making plans for a new building. At least he visited London about this time. In March 1616 he revised his will, leaving the bulk of his estate to his elder daughter, Susanna, wife of Dr. John Hall, and to his wife, "the second best bed, with the furniture," thus providing his modern biographers with something to worry over. On April 23 he died and was buried in the chancel of the Church of the Holy Trinity in Stratford, where his sculptured monument, with a portrait bust, may still be seen.

Those who knew Shakespeare personally testify, to a man, to his honorable and genial character. One tradition says that he was "a handsome well-shaped man, very good company, and of a ready and pleasant smooth wit." Another notes that though naturally inclined to festivity he could be solemn and serious on occasion. A contemporary remarks that he was "excellent in the quality he professes," meaning that he acted and wrote well. Ben Jonson said "he was indeed honest, [i.e., honorable] and of an open and free nature;" and the adjective most frequently used by his contemporaries in describing him is "gentle," implying that Shakespeare in his daily life displayed the qualities of a man of breeding. Nothing could be more thoroughly in line with what we should expect from his plays.

Shakespeare's Theatre

WHEN SHAKESPEARE came up to London, sometime in the late 1580's, there were already in existence two fairly well-defined theatre districts. Both were outside the city limits, because of the opposition to such godless entertainment on the part of the Lord Mayor and the civic council. The first of these districts was Finsbury Field, a holiday section north of the city just outside Bishopsgate, where picnics, athletic contests, and other innocent pastimes were held. Here the Theatre (1576) and the Curtain (1577), the first structures in England expressly erected for

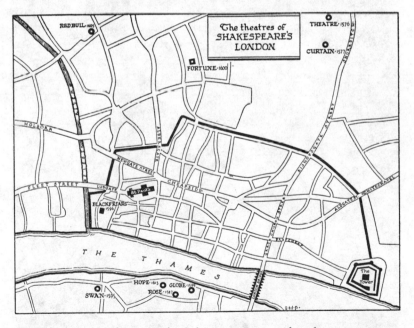

theatrical entertainment, had been set up only about ten or a dozen years before. The second theatre district was the Bankside, across the Thames south of the city, and long notorious as a pleasure resort of a less innocent kind. Here the Rose (1587) had been erected, and as the inaccessibility of the earlier theatre section caused it to decline in popularity, here new playhouses, such as the Swan (1595) and the celebrated Globe (1599), were built. In addition, during Shakespeare's lifetime there were scattered about the suburbs close to London several other playhouses, like the Fortune (1600) and the Red Bull (1605), and within the city, Blackfriars, which, under the guise of a "private" theatre, managed to evade the civic ordinances against playhouses. Shakespeare's company controlled the Theatre, the Globe, and after

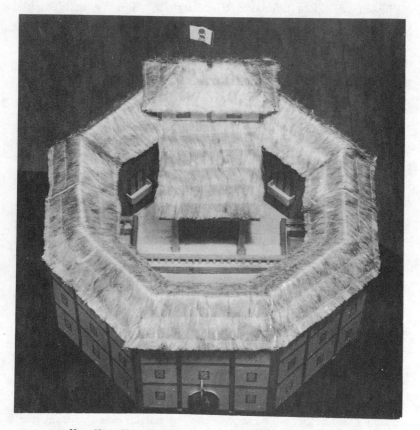

New York University Model of a Typical Elizabethan Theatre

6

1608, Blackfriars, which they used as a winter house. It was at these three theatres that Shakespeare's plays were first produced.

The Elizabethan playhouse for which Shakespeare wrote had little in common with the theatre of to-day. To the modern play-goer, familiar with the seating arrangements and the picture-frame stage of the present, Shakespeare's playhouse would seem more like a stadium than a theatre. His theatre was a circular or polygonal wooden structure of galleries surrounding an open court into the middle of which projected a covered platform. About this platform most of the audience stood, rather than sat, though some of the more affluent found seats in the galleries or even on the stage itself. Most of the action of an Elizabethan play took place upon the platform, which had no front curtain and was backed on each side by the "tiring-house" or actors' dressing-rooms, so constructed as to give the illusion of a house fronting a street, for which the platform often stood. In the center of this back wall and between the entrance doors were two annexes to the platform which could be brought into use when necessary—an inner stage for propertied interiors, such as studies, tents, caves, cells, or shops; and directly above this alcove, an upper stage for scenes requiring elevation. Both the inner and the upper stages were fitted with traverse curtains which could be closed when the annexes were not in use, and which created the illusion of a tapestried wall when the platform represented a hall in a castle.

Naturally, painted scenery and properties in the modern sense were used only sparingly in the theatre of Shakespeare's day, the object being not so much completely to realize a setting as to suggest or symbolize it. Little in the way of artificial lighting was possible, yet spectacular effects of no mean kind were obtained by the pageantry of mass scenes and by rich costumes, for which actors were famous from very early times.

To many readers of Shakespeare who do not take the trouble to understand his stage, the conditions under which he and his contemporaries worked seem not only primitive but decidedly limiting to the playwright as well. Yet, taken as a whole, Shakespeare's theatre was adequate for his needs and a far more resourceful and flexible place than is sometimes supposed. Change of scene could

7

be effected quickly without loss of continuity, and consequently the action of a play could be rapid and continuous. Drama under such conditions was essentially a narrative art, play-construction was looser than it is to-day, and as a result the technique of the average Elizabethan play was more like that of the movie than that of the modern drama. On the other hand, the absence of a front curtain, painted scenery, and artificial lighting made certain modern stage effects impossible. Hence, there is little attempt at local color in the average Elizabethan play and a disarming informality about the precise location or time of every scene. The producer simply used the built-in scenery at his disposal in combinations that pleased him. His stage was a setting—no more—and he permitted the audience

New York University Model Showing Stage.

to concentrate its attention upon the play. Whenever place or time mattered, some references to them could be introduced into the dialogue, and if special atmosphere or dramatic effects were needed, they could be created by the poet's pen. Hence, it is to the Elizabethan stage that we are indebted in great measure for the exquisite descriptive poetry of Shakespeare. Such conditions, moreover, encouraged a greater imaginative cooperation on the part of the audience in the production of a play, and this active participation was further increased by the informality of the platform stage. With such intimacy, soliloquies, asides, and long set speeches are natural and not absurd as they are in the modern theatre. These are but a few of the ways in which the physical conditions of the theatre and the characteristics of the Elizabethan

Interior of the Swan Theatre
(from a contemporary drawing)

drama explain one another, yet they should make clear that Elizabethan theatrical conditions begot a whole code of conventions which Shakespeare accepted—just as he would accept those of the modern theatre, were he writing to-day. On his stage he was a king of infinite space, though to our eyes he may seem to have been bounded by a nutshell.

For prestige, and to a certain extent for protection against the harsh laws regulating the theatrical profession, Elizabethan actors sought the patronage of some nobleman who was willing to sponsor them before the world, but who was in no way expected to maintain them. The company thus formed merely adopted his name and livery, and sought its own fortune, either by travelling through rural England or by establishing itself in one of the permanent playhouses in London. In both personnel and organization these Elizabethan troupes differed from the companies of to-day. They were more like joint stock companies than anything else in the modern theatre, except that the better companies of Shakespeare's time were much more stable than such organizations to-day. The Shakespearean troupe, for example, has a continuous history from its organization in 1574 to the closing of the theatres by government edict in 1642; and there were others with comparable records, just as there were some which sprang up and died quickly.

The secret of this stability lay perhaps in the fact that most of the companies were organized upon a profit-sharing basis, and this was especially true of the Chamberlain's-King's company, to which Shakespeare was attached. In this troupe the leading actors shared in the profits of the aggregation, and a select group of the members were also the joint owners of the playhouse in which they acted. The younger actors receiving wages looked forward to being admitted some day as full members of the company or as "housekeepers." Moreover, the leading dramatists were not free-lances, but were attached more or less permanently to one of the better troupes, and hence thoroughly familiar with the talents and the eccentricities of each of the actors who would play the rôles he was creating. Most difficult for us to understand is the circumstance that the Elizabethans never saw an actress on the stage. All of the women's parts in plays were acted by boys, whose lithe figures and unchanged voices made them suitable for their rôles. They were not rank amateurs, but the apprentices to the individual actors in the company, and, as the understudies and potential successors of their masters, were as well trained as many an actress to-day. Indeed, some private theatre companies which grew up around the royal singing schools, were composed entirely of boys and enjoyed immense popularity with the court and the London social set. As a result of this ladder-like organization, producing plays for an Elizabethan troupe must have been more like writing for a team of actors than for a modern company. At least it is pleasant to think of Shakespeare's plays as having been tailor-made for a troupe of stagers who had worked together for a period of years and whose physical, mental, and professional peculiarities he knew perfectly and made dramatic capital of.

It must not be supposed that Shakespeare has had to wait until our enlightened day to be properly appreciated. At no time have his works ever been neglected either in the theatre or in the library. To the greatest popular favor of his time was added as well the applause of the court. In a day, too, when plays had not as yet attained the double character of pieces to be seen in the theatre and books to be read in the library, it is extraordinary evidence of Shakespeare's fame that during his lifetime nearly half of his plays "escaped into print" in one way or another, some of them running into many editions. Shortly after his death, too, Shakespeare's fellow-actors paid him the unusual tribute, in 1623, of collecting his work into a large, expensive volume, the famous First Folio, which went into a second edition less than ten years later and was republished twice more before the end of the seventeenth century. Since that time editions of his work have been innumerable, and the rôles he created have been the goal of achievement for the greatest actors.

The Sequence of Shakespeare's Plays

OBVIOUSLY, IF THE READER wishes to observe the development of Shakespeare's style and the growth of his powers as an artist, the most satisfactory order in which to read his plays would be that in which they were composed. Yet, important as the matter is, the arrangement of Shakespeare's work in chronological order is one of the most difficult of scholarly problems. In many cases it is quite impossible to determine the order of succession, many of the dates usually assigned to plays are conjectural, and those who know most about Shakespeare are the least willing to suggest a definite order or to be dogmatic concerning the exact year in which an individual play was written. In the case of a modern author, information to answer questions of this kind is readily accessible; in Shakespeare's case it is almost wholly lacking. The traditional order of the First Folio, which classifies the plays as Comedies, Histories, and Tragedies, and places *The Tempest* first and *Cymbeline* last, is still adhered to in many modern editions, but scholars universally reject this arrangement as having no chronological basis. The character of the evidence upon which they attempt a rearrangement will be clear from a few examples. The sources of information are six in number:

(a) Records of Performance:

These are few in number and usually furnish a date *before* which a play was composed, without any information as to how long before. Thus, an account of the revels of the law students at Gray's Inn on December 28, 1594, mentions a performance of *The Comedy of Errors;* one John Manningham, a student at the Middle Temple, in his diary mentions seeing *Twelfth Night* there on February 2, 1602; a foreign visitor to London, Thomas Platter, records in his diary seeing *Julius Caesar* on September 21, 1599; the first edition of *Love's Labor's Lost* (1598) mentions a performance at court the previous Christmas; and an account of the burning of the Globe Theatre June 29, 1613, refers to *Henry VIII* as a new play.

(b) Literary Allusions:

Of these the most important is Francis Meres' praise of Shakespeare in *Palladis Tamia* (1598) and his specific mention of twelve plays then written: *The Two Gentlemen of Verona, The Comedy of Errors, Love's Labor's Lost, Love's Labor's Won* (unidentified), *A Midsummer Night's Dream, The Merchant of Venice, Richard II, Richard III, Henry IV, King John, Titus*

SEQUENCE OF SHAKESPEARE'S PLAYS

Andronicus, and *Romeo and Juliet.* There is also an allusion to Talbot, a character in *1 Henry VI,* in Thomas Nashe's *Pierce Pennilesse* (1592); a quotation from *Julius Caesar* in Jonson's *Every Man Out of His Humor* (1599); and a note about *Hamlet,* made by Gabriel Harvey sometime between 1598 and 1601. Like the notices of performances, these allusions are usually indefinite and furnish only a terminal date.

(c) *References in the Plays to Datable Historical Events:*

Shakespeare, again, is sparing in "topical allusions," and passages thought to refer to current events or controversies require caution on the part of the interpreter. Yet, the chorus before the fifth act of *Henry V* contains a clear allusion to the campaign of the Earl of Essex in Ireland, and fixes the date of the performance at which that prologue was used between March 27 and September 28, 1599. There are also allusions in *Hamlet* to the revival of the boy actors (1599); in *Macbeth,* to the house of Stuart; and perhaps, in *A Midsummer Night's Dream,* to the baptism ceremonies of Prince Henry of Scotland (1594).

(d) *Links between Plays themselves:*

The most marked of these is the continuity of *Richard II, 1* and *2 Henry IV,* and the author's promise at the end of the last-named play of continuing the story in *Henry V,* which establish the chronological sequence of four plays. The pointed allusion of Robin Goodfellow in *A Midsummer Night's Dream* that this time "naught shall go ill, Jack shall have Jill," likewise seems to be a link with *Love's Labor's Lost,* which "doth not end like an old play, Jack hath not Jill." If so, it establishes the order of composition, though not a definite date.

(e) *Dates of Publication:*

Dates on title pages or dates of registration in the books of the Stationers' Company are less valuable than might at first be supposed because in Shakespeare's time plays were almost never written for publication, and those which "escaped into print" usually did so after their popularity on the stage had declined. Yet, for several of Shakespeare's plays no other reliable information exists, among them *Richard III* (1597), *Romeo and Juliet* (1597), *Richard II* (1597), *1 Henry IV* (1598), *Much Ado* (1600), and *The Merry Wives* (1602). *Antony and Cleopatra* was entered for publication in 1608 and *As You Like It* in 1600, though neither appeared in print before 1623; *Troilus and Cressida* was registered in 1603, though no edition earlier than 1609 is known. The date of licensing or of publication, therefore, at least gives a terminal date, and is sometimes a valuable clue.

(f) *Variations of Style and Versification:*

This is the least reliable type of evidence, and great caution must be exercised in drawing inferences from it. The assumption is that as Shakespeare grew in experience, his style of writing reflected his intellectual development, his character study deepened, his taste improved, and his technique became more and more individual. Especially singled out have been the variations of Shakespeare's blank verse and its growth from a stereotyped to a flexible medium. Certain broad features of Shakespeare's development as an artist are of course recognizable, but obviously also a detailed literary and psychological analysis is possible only *after* the proper order of the plays has been established, and not *before.* Subject matter and mood, too, determine to a large extent the style of writing, and allowance must also be made for experiment or for passing influences. Yet, taken as a whole, this "internal evidence," when tactfully and objectively used, is

13

valuable, if only as a check upon other evidence. In the case of some plays, notably *The Taming of the Shrew, All's Well, Coriolanus, Cymbeline,* and *Timon of Athens,* little or no other evidence exists as to the date of composition.

If, therefore, the absolute chronology of Shakespeare's plays is far from certain, students have found it necessary to establish at least a working order. The following sequence represents a consensus of opinion of the leading modern scholars and should serve as a guide to the reader.

DATE	COMEDIES	HISTORIES	TRAGEDIES
1590-2	Love's Labor's Lost	1, 2, 3 Henry VI	
1592-4	Comedy of Errors Two Gentlemen of Verona		
1593-4		Richard III	Titus Andronicus
1594-6	Midsummer Night's Dream Merchant of Venice	King John Richard II	
1594-7	Taming of the Shrew		Romeo and Juliet
1597-8		1, 2 Henry IV	
1598-9		Henry V	Julius Caesar
1597-1600	Merry Wives of Windsor		
1598-1600	Much Ado About Nothing		
1599-1600	As You Like It		
1599-1601	Twelfth Night		
1600-1			Hamlet
1600-4	All's Well that Ends Well		
1601-3			Troilus and Cressida
1603-4	Measure for Measure		
1604-5			Othello
1605-6			King Lear Macbeth
1607-8	Pericles		Antony and Cleopatra Timon of Athens
1608-10			Coriolanus
1609-10	Cymbeline		
1610-11	Winter's Tale		
1611-12	Tempest		
1612-13		Henry VIII	

Shakespeare's Sources

SHAKESPEARE'S ORIGINALITY lies not in the novelty of his plots but in the fresh vigor and effectiveness of his dramatic art. He seemed content, as one critic has said, to "pour his new wine into old bottles" by dramatizing stories sad and gay for his tragedies and comedies and borrowing freely for his histories from chronicles and biographies. Writing an average of two plays a year, he levied upon an amazingly wide variety of sources. For the romantic comedies he usually put under conscription one of the artificial but highly popular *novelle* which had emigrated to England from Italy or France, and which he served up on the stage with a seasoning of his own realism. He drew also upon the poems of Ovid, the plays of Plautus, and contemporary travel-books filled with tales of wonder from the brave new worlds which the Elizabethan sea-dogs were discovering. For his tragedies there were many "sad stories of the death of kings," some, like the tale of the jealous Moor, from the Italian story books, some from chronicle and history, still others from biography or from older plays. For his histories he could always draw upon the chronicles, even if he could find in the library of his acting company no yellow-paged play in manuscript or quarto to which he might give permanent life. Only a single drama of Shakespeare's—*Love's Labor's Lost* —cannot be traced to at least one definite source; the other six and thirty may all be studied in comparison with the originals which he has transmuted into higher forms of art. And the careful comparison of any one of Shakespeare's plays with its original is at once fascinating and profitable, for such a study reveals, as hardly any other can, his dramatic theories and practices.

When Shakespeare attempted to weave a drama out of the raw materials of his sources, what, then, caused the originals to

"suffer a sea-change
Into something rich and strange"?

15

First, it must be remembered that excepting where the source was itself a drama, and this was relatively seldom, the original was written to be read, whereas Shakespeare's product was composed for the stage,—it was, in other words, made dramatic. Thus what was originally narrative, historical, lyrical, or expository became not only dialogue but dialogue involving passion, suspense, climax, and other elements presented not in cold type but in the vivid mimicry of life. It cannot be said that Shakespeare's respect for his sources very often checked his expression of his sense for the dramatic. He did not hesitate, therefore, to combine details from plots originally unrelated or to change episodes by re-emphasizing them or altering them completely. Furthermore, he often changed the proportions of the original story, he expanded scenes from the barest of hints, he reversed a conclusion, he even added episodes from another story or from his own fertile brain. He sometimes introduced realism to contrast with romance or a bit of clowning to dull the bitter edge of grief. The mood of the material he often changed, sentimentality becoming sentiment, the cynical becoming the wholesome, the immoral, the moral. For the original geographical setting, moreover, he had no respect if it stood in the way of his higher purposes. With his characters he was just as free; he frequently retained both name and characteristics of a figure in his original or, on the contrary, he changed both. Where his sense of dramatic economy dictated, he dropped a character out entirely, or he added one or more not in the original. These and a dozen more liberties with his sources will be found in any extended comparisons of the plays and their originals. Such pleasant study reveals Shakespeare as a man of wide reading and keen powers of observation, who was bold enough to take what he wanted and to change the borrowed materials as he wished.

Since it is impossible to do more in this brief section than suggest how Shakespeare transmuted his originals into drama, a glimpse of his methods can be given in only three plays, a comedy, a history, and a tragedy, and only a paragraph may be devoted to each. In the chart of his sources which follows, however, there are enough suggestions to provide a much fuller study of this aspect of the dramatist's art.

Shakespeare dramatized *As You Like It* from Thomas Lodge's *Rosalynde,* an English prose romance of the usual artificial type which was popular with the Elizabethans. This story is sentimental and extravagant, with language and lyrics that are totally lacking in reality. To the general plot Shakespeare adhered rather closely; two or three changes, however, he made in the interest of better drama. In the original the exiled ruler and the usurper are unrelated; Shakespeare made them brothers so that their story might parallel that of Orlando and Oliver. Shakespeare's banished ladies are, therefore, cousins; in Lodge's story they are merely friends. In the original the usurper is killed in a great battle with the rightful king; in Shakespeare's play he is converted by "an old religious man" and retires to a monastery. This happier disposal of the tyrant leaves no sad daughter, and there is, therefore, no discord in the merry weddings which conclude the play. Shakespeare changed the names of some of the characters but not of others; thus the Duke Senior, Frederick, Oliver, Orlando, Silvius, and Celia of the play are respectively Gerismond, Torismond, Saladin, Rosader, Montanus, and Alinda in Lodge's story, but Rosalind and Phebe are the same. Perhaps the most important change of all is Shakespeare's introduction into the play of realistic characters who do not appear at all in the original, the melancholy Jaques, the witty Touchstone, the bucolic morons, William and Audrey, and the hedge-priest. This entertaining group provide for the courtiers and their ladies and for the Dresden-china shepherds and shepherdesses that realistic contrast with romance which is so characteristic an element in Shakespeare's comedies. This realism and the lively movement of the main plots does much to break down in the comedy the stiff artificiality of the prose romance. Shakespeare retained many of the lyrical elements of his original, but he rewrote the songs, and through the mouths of his two truth-tellers, Jaques and Touchstone, he poked gentle fun at the artificialities and pretenses of the court characters and the pastoral lovers.

Shakespeare's plays of Prince Hal (*Henry IV,* Parts 1 and 2), have a double source, Holinshed's *Chronicle,* from which he derived so much of his material for other plays, and *The Famous*

Victories of Henry the Fifth, acted 1588. Holinshed is the chief source, but from the crude old history play the dramatist drew some hints for the realistic tavern scenes in the *Henry IV* pair of dramas. The reader who believes that he can learn his English history from Shakespeare's plays needs to be reminded that the dramatist was a playwright and not an historian, and that he did not hesitate to play at ducks and drakes with historical fact where fact seemed to interfere with dramatic effect. In his history plays there is, therefore, much compression, and often an actual change in the sequence of events. But his chief effort is always to make good drama, and since drama means contrast and conflict, his modification of characters and events is often very considerable. In *1 Henry IV,* to illustrate merely from one play, the dramatic opposition is provided by an apparently fun-loving, irresponsible prince, roistering in a London tavern, and a fiery young warrior of the North Country whose chair of state is not the cushion of a tap-room but the hard saddle of his charger. These two are of the same age, and their stars ascend until at the great battle of Shrewsbury they come face to face, and the impetuous Percy dies under the sword of the silken Crown Prince. Thus it is in Shakespeare, for he must have foils and opposites, contestants of equal age, and a grand climax toward which all earlier episodes obviously converge. But it is not thus in Holinshed. Historically, Prince Hal was only sixteen when, in 1403, he fought against the proud and angry northern rebels, and Hotspur was thirty-nine—or three years older than Prince Hal's father, represented in Shakespeare as an aged monarch who was rescued by the son whose riots he despised. Furthermore, the Henry Monmouth of history, though the boy fought bravely at Shrewsbury and was wounded, did not encounter Hotspur; that ambitious nobleman died by an unknown hand. In all these changes, it will be observed, history has yielded to drama, and the playwright has eclipsed the historian.

Shakespeare took his *Julius Caesar* from Sir Thomas North's translation of Plutarch's *Lives of the Noble Grecians and Romans* (stories of Caesar, Brutus, and Antony), 1579. Jean Paul Richter has called Plutarch "the biographical Shakespeare of universal history," and North's translation of the Greek biographer was so dignified and moving that often Shakespeare did little more than transmute his language into blank verse. A single example of the occasional closeness of North and Shakespeare must suffice:

> *Plutarch*: "Antonius, I dare assure thee, that no enemy hath taken or shall Marcus Brutus alive; and I beseech God keep him from that fortune; for wheresoever he be found, alive or dead, he will be found like himself."

> *Shakespeare*: (Lucilius to Antony)
> "Safe, Antony; Brutus is safe enough;
> I dare assure thee that no enemy
> Shall ever take alive the noble Brutus:
> The gods defend him from so great a shame!
> When you do find him, or alive or dead,
> He will be found like Brutus, like himself."
> (V, iv, 21-25)

In his plot construction Shakespeare tended to condense his original, as he did so frequently when he reworked history and biography into the more compressed form of drama. Thus he combined the *two* quarrels of Brutus and Cassius into one (IV, iii) and similarly telescoped the *two* battles of Philippi into a single day's engagement whereas they really occurred twenty days apart. Again he restricted to one day the triumphs of Caesar and the Feast of the Lupercalia; and he has the funeral orations of Brutus and Antony follow immediately after the assassination of Caesar; in Plutarch these respective events are separated. He transferred Portia's suicide to a place *before* the quarrel of the two generals; in the original it follows. Perhaps the change that shows best how in a single touch he could make an episode dramatic is his creation of "the ghost of Caesar," which appears to Brutus, out of the "wonderful strange and monstrous shape of a body coming toward him." This change was a stroke of genius, for by making it the dramatist forced his audience to realize that though Caesar was dead in the flesh, his vengeful spirit was abroad turning the swords of the conspirators into their "own proper entrails."

PRINCIPAL SOURCES OF SHAKESPEARE PLAYS
Comedies
LOVE'S LABOR'S LOST:

> No literary source has been identified. Contemporary events, particularly court gossip and Anglo-French diplomatic relations, probably gave this play a great deal more "point" for an Elizabethan audience than for the modern.

The Comedy of Errors:

Menaechmi, or The Twins, a Latin farce by Plautus, adapted to the Elizabethan romantic formula and to Elizabethan social conditions, is the main source, direct or indirect. The parallel of twin servants and twin masters, and the barring-out scene (III, i) probably were suggested by *Amphitruo,* also by Plautus.

The Two Gentlemen of Verona:

The Proteus-Julia story is most closely related to that of Felix and Felismena in Jorge de Montemayor's *Diana Enamorada,* a Spanish romance translated by Bartholomew Yonge about 1582, but not published until 1598. For the rest of the play no satisfactory parallel has been found; but the conflict of love and friendship, together with the contrast of a loyal and a faithless friend, is a common one in Renaissance literature.

A Midsummer Night's Dream:

No single source has been identified for this play, but the various elements which compose it were well-known materials. The nucleus story of Theseus and Hippolyta is found in Chaucer's *Knight's Tale,* as well as in Plutarch's *Lives.* The romantic main plot of the unsmooth "course of true love" follows a common Elizabethan dramatic formula. The fairy element draws upon both folk-lore and early fairy literature. Finally, the "tragical comedy" of Pyramus and Thisby is a *reductio ad absurdum* of a popular classical tale from Ovid's *Metamorphoses,* retold in Chaucer's *Legend of Good Women.* Analogues to details in the action are numerous, but the unification of these diverse materials is a peculiarly Shakespearean feat.

The Merchant of Venice:

The various stories which make up this play come from scattered sources. (a) The Bond, or Pound of Flesh, story is a folk-tale, possibly of Oriental origin, of which there were several English versions in prose and in ballad form in Shakespeare's time, some of which may have contributed details to Shakespeare's story. The analogue nearest to Shakespeare's play, however, is an Italian *novella* in Ser Giovanni Fiorentino's *Il Pecorone,* written c. 1378. It includes the wooing episode (on a much less delicate plane), the usurous Jew, the newly-wedded wife disguised as a lawyer, and the stratagem of the ring. (b) The Casket theme, also of Oriental origin, was likewise well-known in Italian and English, but the version most nearly like Shakespeare's, in the *Gesta Romanorum,* a popular collection of medieval sermon stories, shows a princess as the chooser. That these two main themes had already been blended in an earlier drama is suggested by an allusion in Stephen Gosson's *School of Abuse* (1579) to a play called *The Jew* which represented "the greediness of worldly choosers, and bloody minds of usurers." But it is lost. (c) The Elopement theme (Lorenzo and Jessica) has also several analogues, the most interesting of which appears in the *novelle* of Massuccio di Salerno.

The Taming of the Shrew:

The relation of *The Taming of the Shrew* to an earlier anonymous play, *A Pleasant Conceited History called the Taming of A Shrew* (1594), is in dispute. Most scholars believe that it is the direct source of Shakespeare's play; others that it represents a badly garbled version of it. All of the various plot elements are common to both *A Shrew* and *The Shrew.* The induction dealing with the transformed drunkard is a folk-tale which is as old at least as *The Arabian Nights,* and analogues are common. The theme of the shrewish wife is also widespread in popular literature, an Elizabethan example being

A Merry Jest of a Shrewd and Curst Wife Lapped in Morel's Skin for her Good Behavior. (c. 1560). The sub-plot of romantic wooing bears a resemblance to Ariosto's *I Suppositi*, translated by George Gascoigne as *Supposes* (1566).

THE MERRY WIVES OF WINDSOR:

This farce, written, according to tradition, that Queen Elizabeth might see Falstaff in love, is a mosaic of popular comic devices. The jealous husband, the merry wife (usually not honest), and the lover concealed in household stuff, are commonplaces of Renaissance literature, English and Italian. The themes of the "tricker tricked" and the "boy-bride" derive ultimately from Plautus and Italian comedy. Although numerous analogues to the play exist, no single source can be identified.

MUCH ADO ABOUT NOTHING:

The main plot of malicious slander involving Claudio and Hero is adapted directly or indirectly from the sentimental tale of Don Timbreo and Fenicia in Bandello's *Novelle,* itself a version of a very old story. Some details of the deception episode may have been suggested by a simliar story of Ariodante and Genevra in Ariosto's *Orlando Furioso,* translated by Sir John Harington (1591) and adapted by Spenser in the *Faerie Queene* (Book II, Canto 4). No satisfactory literary source has been found for the contrasting parallel plot of "honest" slander involving Benedick and Beatrice, or for the low comedy of Dogberry and the watch.

AS YOU LIKE IT:

The source is Thomas Lodge's pastoral romance *Rosalynde: Euphues Golden Legacie* (1590), conceived in a different spirit with some significant additions and parallels.

TWELFTH NIGHT: OR, WHAT YOU WILL:

The sentimental main plot involving Orsino, Olivia, Viola (Cesario), and Sebastian is a loose adaptation of the tale of Apolonius and Silla retold from Bandello's *Novelle* by Barnabie Riche in his *Farewell to Military Profession* (1581). Bandello in turn based upon an Italian comedy called *Gl'Ingannati* (*The Deceived*) (1537), of which a Latin translation, entitled *Laelia* after the heroine, was performed at Queen's College, Cambridge, in 1590 and again in 1598.

ALL'S WELL THAT ENDS WELL:

The source is the story of Giletta of Narbonne from Boccaccio's *Decameron* as retold by William Painter in *The Palace of Pleasure* (1566).

MEASURE FOR MEASURE:

The main source, considerably modified, is George Whetstone's play *Promos and Cassandra* (before 1578) and a novel version in the same author's *Heptameron of Civil Discourses* (1582), both based upon a story in Giraldi Cinthio's *Hecatommithi* (1565), which that author had dramatized as *Epitia.* Shakespeare's principal modification is the creation of Mariana, which establishes certain parallel dramatic patterns and necessitates the introduction of the "substitute bride" theme, common in folk stories and already utilized in *All's Well.*

PERICLES, PRINCE OF TYRE:

This very old story, which is found in all European languages, was "gathered into English" in Shakespeare's day by Lawrence Twine in a prose novel, *The Pattern of Painful Adventures* (1576, reprinted 1607). Earlier English versions appear in John Gower's *Confessio Amantis* (c. 1390), the *Gesta Romanorum,* and *Apollonius of Tyre.* A novel called *The Painful Adventures of Pericles Prince of Tyre,* by George Wilkins, (1608), mentions the play and was probably written after it, though the relation between the play and the novel is obscure. Shakespeare's principal sources seem to have been Twine and Gower.

CYMBELINE:

The historical background is freely adapted from Holinshed's *Chronicle,* and the romantic theme of the wager involving Posthumus, Imogen, and Iachimo is a folk theme, derived directly or indirectly from the story of Bernabo of Genoa in Boccaccio's *Decameron.* The kidnapped princes, the cruel stepmother, the wrongly accused wife, and the sleeping-draught are commonplaces in romantic literature. One situation is similar to the tale of Schneewitchen and the Dwarfs.

THE WINTER'S TALE:

The main source is a pastoral romance by Robert Greene, *Pandosto: The Triumph of Time, or the History of Dorastus and Fawnia* (1588, reprinted 1607), but considerably modified to the extent of keeping the wronged queen alive, discarding the unpleasant incestuous attraction of the king to his new-found daughter, and preserving him from suicide at the end. The episode of the statue coming to life may have been suggested by the Pygmalion or the Alcestis myths, and the character of the rogue Autolycus by the coney-catching pamphlets also written by Greene.

THE TEMPEST:

No satisfactory literary source is known, but the character of the main story and the existence of analogues to it in Italian literature and elsewhere suggest the possibility of a source now lost. Travellers' tales and contemporary pamphlets, particularly two describing the wreck of a ship-load of colonists on the Bermudas in 1609, may have contributed the background and some of the details of the play. Passages in the drama suggest a number of minor sources, notably Montaigne's *Essais,* translated by John Florio (1603), which seem to have suggested the character of Caliban and Gonzalo's description of an ideal commonwealth (II, i).

Histories

1, 2, 3, HENRY VI:

All three of these plays are probably revisions of earlier works. The principal sources of the historical matter are Raphael Holinshed's *Chronicle of England, Scotland, and Ireland,* second and enlarged edition, 1586-7; and Edward Halle's *The Union of the Two Noble and Illustrious Families of Lancaster and York* (1547). There is no unanimity of opinion among scholars as to the relation between *2* and *3 Henry VI* and two other plays covering the same material: *The First Part of the Contention betwixt the Two Famous Houses of York and Lancaster* (1594), and *The True Tragedy of Richard Duke of York* (1595). An edition of both of these plays in 1619 bears Shakespeare's name on the title-page. Some hold (a) that *The Contention* and *The True Tragedy* are crude, unrevised sources of *2 and 3 Henry VI;* others (b) that *2* and *3 Henry VI* are the originals as Shakespeare wrote them and that *The Contention* and *True Tragedy* are piratically printed and mutilated copies.

RICHARD III:

Holinshed and Halle furnish the historical materials. Whether or not Shakespeare knew earlier dramatic versions of the story cannot be determined.

SHAKESPEARE'S SOURCES

KING JOHN:

The relation of *King John* to *The Troublesome Reign of King John*, an anonymous two-part play printed in 1591 and republished in 1611 and 1622 as "written by W. Shakespeare," is not clear. Some scholars believe that both plays are of Shakespearean authorship, *King John* representing a late rewriting. Most believe that *The Troublesome Reign* is the source of *King John*. *King John* follows the older drama fairly closely as regards events, but the strong nationalistic and Protestant bias is modified and redirected considerably.

RICHARD II:

The basis is again Holinshed.

1, 2 HENRY IV:

HENRY V:

Holinshed's *Chronicle* furnishes the historical material; a popular, crude play, *The Famous Victories of Henry the Fifth* (acted before 1588 and printed in 1594), suggests several incidents and the possibilities of a realistic, comic sub-plot.

HENRY VIII:

Holinshed's *Chronicle* supplies most of the material; the scenes dealing with Cranmer (V, i, ii, iii) are derived from Foxe's *Book of Martyrs* (1563).

Tragedies

TITUS ANDRONICUS:

This legend of an imaginary Roman emperor had some currency in Shakespeare's England, but the immediate source of his play, which was also the basis of a Dutch and two German versions, is lost. The existence of a unique copy of an eighteenth century chapbook entitled *The History of Titus Andronicus, the Renowned Roman General*, which professes to be a translation from Italian, and which tells the story with some variations from the Shakespearean version, suggests that the source of the play was an earlier edition of this prose version, now lost.

ROMEO AND JULIET:

The direct source is *Tragical History of Romeus and Juliet*, a poem by Arthur Brooke (1562), which in turn was a redaction of a famous story that appears in a number of forms in Italian. One version, deriving from Bandello, appears in translation in Painter's *The Palace of Pleasure* (1566). Brooke also mentions having seen the story "set forth on the stage," but the version, if it existed, is lost.

JULIUS CAESAR:

The material for this play is derived mainly from the *Lives* of Julius Caesar, Marcus Brutus, and Marcus Antonius in Plutarch's *Lives of the Noble Grecians and Romans Compared* as translated into English by Sir Thomas North (1579) from the French version of Jacques Amyot (1559).

HAMLET, PRINCE OF DENMARK:

This tragedy is a redaction of an older lost play, conjecturally attributed to Thomas Kyd, which was based upon a legend retold in French in Belleforest's *Histoires Tragiques* (1570), which in turn is derived from the *Historia Danica* by Saxo Grammaticus, a twelfth century Danish historian.

Outlines of Shakespeare's Plays

Troilus and Cressida:

Chaucer's narrative poem, *Troilus and Criseyde,* modified as to Cressida's character by sixteenth century redactions and continuations of the tale, is the basis for the love-story. The background of the Trojan War is derived probably, either from John Lydgate's *Siege of Troy* (c. 1420) or from Caxton's *Recuyell of the Histories of Troy,* and from Homer. The story had been told many times, and there was already a stage tradition in Shakespeare's time.

Othello, The Moor of Venice:

The story of the Moor, his Ensign, and his wife, Disdemona, appears in Giraldi Cinthio's *Hecatommithi* (1565). There was no English translation in Shakespeare's time.

King Lear:

The main plot is a free adaptation of an anonymous earlier play which 'has a happy ending and is called *The True Chronicle History of King Lear and his Three Daughters* (published in 1605, but written about 1594). Shakespeare seems to have been familiar also with the story as originally told in Geoffrey of Monmouth's and Holinshed's chronicles; in the *Mirror for Magistrates* (1574), an Elizabethan narrative of the falls of princes; in Spenser's *Faerie Queene* (Book II, Canto 10); and in Warner's *Albion's England* (1586), a popular historical poem. The parallel story of Gloucester and his sons is not in the old play or in any other version, but is derived from the story of the Paphlagonian unkind king in Sidney's *Arcadia* (1590).

Macbeth:

This tragedy derives from Holinshed's *Chronicle* and is a blend of two stories. Added to the account of Macbeth's usurpation are details borrowed from the story of King Duff and Donwald, which records a similar murder of a king by his thane, and in which the thane's wife is the evil counsellor.

Antony and Cleopatra:

The source, closely followed, is Plutarch's *Life of Marcus Antonius* as translated by North.

Timon of Athens:

A brief story of Timon the man-hater appears incidentally in Plutarch's *Life of Marcus Antonius* from which a free rendering in Painter's *Palace of Pleasure* is derived. There is reason to believe that certain details in the play, such as the faithful steward and the mock-banquet of warm water, came to Shakespeare from some intermediary source, possibly derived from Lucian's *Misanthropos.* The contrasting parallel plot is based upon Plutarch's *Life of Alcibiades,* which also refers to Timon.

Coriolanus:

The direct source is Plutarch's *Life of Coriolanus* in North's translation.

Suggestions on Reading Shakespeare

SHAKESPEARE'S PLAYS are not difficult to read if it be remembered that they were written originally not to be read but to be played, that they contain a great deal of poetry, and, finally, that because they were composed more than three hundred years ago, they have some allusions with which we are not familiar and some words which we no longer use. Apart from these difficulties they may be read like modern plays for the story, the characters, and the philosophy of life which Shakespeare has packed into them. A careful reading for a complete understanding will demand, of course, frequent references to a glossary of Shakespearean words, but this necessity is no different from that of consulting a dictionary for unfamiliar words in a modern play. A careful reading, too, will demand close attention to the ideas expressed in the blank verse and other verse forms which Shakespeare used. Here practice will make the reading easy, and the poetic conventions employed by the playwright will soon become familiar. But even if an occasional word or allusion is lost, and an occasional bit of poetical dialogue remains obscure, the reader may get the cream of the play if only he adopt the right attitude of mind toward it. He must know something of what Shakespeare has tried to do in the play, and something also of his methods of work. He must know, too, what to look for so that his reading will not drift but will have a definite objective. In the following paragraphs are a few suggestions to guide him in his reading.

To Shakespeare, a play was not a few printed pages of dialogue for the isolated reader but a vivid mimetic presentation of human conflict by impersonators on the open platform of the Elizabethan theatre for an alert audience of imaginative Londoners. As explained above, he made no attempt, moreover, to insist upon a complete *physical* representation of every detail of his play; on the contrary, in the burlesque of the craftsmen in *A Midsummer Night's Dream* he pokes glorious fun at the amateur Thespians who do insist that moonshine, wall, and lion must be physically presented. The men and women who flocked to the Globe Theatre formed an *audience,* not a crowd of *spectators;* they came to hear as well as to see, and Shakespeare used their ears to suggest to their imaginations much that could not be physically represented, as he does, for example in the *Prologue* to *Henry V*:

> "Piece out our imperfections with your thoughts;
> Into a thousand parts divide one man,
> And make imaginary puissance;
> Think, when we talk of horses, that you see them
> Printing their proud hoofs i' the receiving earth."

Shakespeare staged his plays, that is, not only on the platform of the theatre but also in the lively minds of the men and women in his audience; to them he gave the symbols of life and conflict, and they expanded these symbols into full being. "The best in this kind," said Duke Theseus of the players, "are but shadows; and the worst are no worse, if imagination amend them."

To *read* a play of Shakespeare's well, it is really necessary to go a step beyond the practice of the man in the Globe audience, and to create in our own minds the whole of the play. To read a play vividly we must recreate on the stage of our imaginations the whole setting and atmosphere, the action, and the characters. Dialogue between two characters must be more than words divided into statement and response; it must be the vivid interchange of ideas between two distinct individuals whom we see, as Hamlet carried the image of his father, in our "mind's eye." Moreover, we must be alert for every verbal suggestion that can help us to make our reconstruction of the play. So when the gentle King Duncan, coming to the castle of Macbeth, remarks,

> "This castle hath a pleasant seat; the air
> Nimbly and sweetly recommends itself
> Unto our gentle senses,"

lo, the castle must rise in our imaginations as vividly as ever it did on theatrical canvas. Similarly, when Macbeth demands angrily of the frightened servant who has come to report that the English soldiers are advancing against the stronghold,

> "The devil damn thee black, thou cream-faced loon!
> Where gott'st thou that goose look?"

we must realize with the eye and the ear of the mind the desperate, raging king and the trembling servant, "whey-faced" with terror. To read a play of Shakespeare's effectively, therefore, is actually to stage it on the platforms of our imaginations; only thus will the dramatic conflict be more than a faint and far-off thing and the characters more than bloodless and impersonal wraiths. When we pick up our Shakespeares we must not read "words, words, words;" we must recreate ideas, images, backgrounds, characters, conflicts, life.

Fortunately, Shakespeare did more than most modern dramatists to help his reader make this dramatic reconstruction. In fact, from one point of view his plays are very easy to read; he has taken his audience so completely into his confidence that they can follow his play-story as easily as though it were a fairy-tale. For the audience there are no mysteries or surprises in the play; the characters may be fooled and puzzled, but the members of the audience never are. For the reader the disguise is never complete; when Julia and Rosalind and Viola put on male garb, they may disappear from the knowledge of their lovers, but the reader knows that a girl's heart is beating beneath the doublet of the page or the smock of the shepherd. Similarly, *Hamlet* and *Macbeth* are not murder mysteries, nor is the villainy of Iago or of Iachimo kept dark from the audience. In the practical jokes of the comedies the reader always shares as a participant; Malvolio may be trapped, fat Falstaff may be derided by the merry wives, and Benedick and Beatrice may be tricked into matrimony, but the audience is invariably "in" on these jests and derives its delight from laughing at the blind folly of the poor dupes. Thus Shakespeare's plots are always open and easy to reconstruct on the stage of the imagination.

Even the simplest of Shakespeare's plays will repay a double reading. It is best to read the play rapidly once for the story and a second time for plot structure, characterization, and other elements which an honest reader will want to consider. The first reading should be done in the manner indicated, reproducing the play in the imagination. The play, in other words, should be read *as a drama,* not as a novel or an essay. The second reading may be done more slowly and more methodically with the attention alert for whatever technique of playwrighting and other elements are to be noted. This study-reading should be done, of course, with pencil in hand to make annotations on a convenient pad or even in the margin of the book and to underline passages that seem significant for any reason. For what in this closer reading should the student look? A few of the most essential elements follow.

The reader may determine first what manner or type of play he is reading, for in Shakespeare's day the distinctions were kept rather carefully in mind although Shakespeare tended more than did most of his contemporary playwrights to mix his forms. The basic division into comedy, tragedy, and history is made by the conventional grouping in the usual editions. But such division does not go far enough. *Henry V* and *Richard II,* for example, are both history plays, but the first is epic and the second tragic in character. Again, *As You Like It* and *Twelfth Night* are both romantic comedies, but the first is, in addition, a pastoral comedy, whereas the second is not. *The Taming of the Shrew* is a farce; *Love's Labor's Lost* is a court comedy of a social type. Shakespeare was essentially a romanticist; that is, most of his plays deal with events in a romantic and vague past and in a foreign country— often Greece, Rome, Italy, France. But the plays contain, nevertheless, much that is realistic. His dukes are not really Athenian, or Italian, or French, but English; his mobs are not Roman, or Italian, but London; and in many of his plays he ignores the early date of the action by bringing in contemporary episodes, backgrounds, and characters, as he does in the Boar's-Head Tavern scenes in *Henry IV*. All of these pastoral, romantic, and realistic elements the reader may wish to note before turning his attention particularly to plot, characters, and background.

Shakespeare's plots, as has been said above, are not particularly complicated or difficult to follow; on the contrary, they are usually simple and compact. A few of the history plays like *King John* and *Henry V* seem to have no particular climax that results from the issue of a conflict between individuals; and a few of his romances, like *Cymbeline* and *Pericles,* are straggling and loose in structure. But these are exceptions; the majority of the plays follow a rather definite pattern which is easily discernible. One might suppose that since Shakespeare seldom took the trouble to make his own basic plots but borrowed here and there from histories, prose romances, old plays, and even poems, his plots would invariably be what their originals are. This is not, however, true; he did not hesitate to change, add, and omit details and characters to suit his sense of craftsmanship with the result that he often made an excellent drama out of conventional and unpromising materials. It is good fun for the reader to compare a play of Shakespeare's with its source, but such comparison is not necessary for an understanding of the play, and at most it gives a sense of the facility with which the dramatist erected his striking structures on old foundations. Thus in *Henry IV* he makes Prince Hal and Hotspur—the grand rivals—of the same age, whereas Hotspur was actually some years older than the Prince's father; in *As You Like It,* again, he has the usurping duke reformed instead of killed in battle with his abused brother; in *Othello* Desdemona is strangled to death by her own husband instead of being struck down with a sand-filled stocking in the hands of the villainous ensign. Shakespeare is always quite original, therefore, in *dramatizing* his materials.

The simplicity of the plots consists ordinarily in their following a simple formula. Like all good drama, the plays have their bases in human conflict—in tragedy, a losing conflict, in comedy, a less serious one which has a happy conclusion. At the beginning of the play the audience is presented with an unstable condition which has existed for some time, and which continues to prevail in various aspects until it reaches its climax either in a tragic crash or in a happy and harmonious stability. In tragedy, the conflict has its poisonous roots in one or more of the grand passions which tear the hearts of kings, princes, and great generals—vaulting ambition, hate, greed, and other vultures of the soul which rest not until they have destroyed their victim. In comedy, the conflict is milder—a love tilt, perhaps; the turn of Fortune's wheel that restores a banished duke to his throne; the chance that puts twin brothers into the same city to be a source of confusion to their friends and relations. In comedy, the play usually begins with a number of separations, husband and wife, two brothers, brother and sister, two lovers, parents and child; it concludes with happy unions and reunions. It is not easy to reduce all of Shakespeare's plays to a single formula, but if we omit certain of the history plays, the rest may be said to present—often with considerable irony—to an audience wise as the gods, the spectacle of blind humanity forced to grope through a fog of uncertainty to a pre-destined doom in the tragedies or to light and happiness in the comedies. The tragedy ends with death; the comedy usually with marriage. The death-knell is as characteristic of one as the wedding-bell is of the other. The reader of the plays will readily note these essential features and patterns, for even play synopses will reveal them.

A play synopsis may not reveal, however, Shakespeare's frequent device of developing sub-plots, side-plots, and parallel plots in such a way as to strengthen the reader's understanding and emotional appreciation of the main plot. These secondary plots are never in Shakespeare's plays, as they are often in those of his contemporary playwrights, simply appendages to the main action; they are invariably and economically welded into it so that the total effect is that of one play and not that of two or more plays in one. The reader will want to note, of course, just what these various plots are, and by what methods they are woven into the texture of the whole. An illustration or two may make clearer this particular structural device. The story of *As You Like It* has to do with the disagreements of two sets of brothers,—in the main plot, older men, of whom one has exiled the duke, his brother, and, in the parallel plot, younger men, of whom the older has driven the younger into banishment. The two exiled brothers are ultimately followed into their place of banishment by the two villains, but both oppressors have a change of heart so that the banished men return home in happiness. The main plot is linked to the secondary plot not only by this obvious parallelism but further by the fact that the two brothers in the minor plot marry respectively the two daughters of the royal brothers of the major plot. In tragedy there are similar plot parallels. *King Lear,* for example, may be characterized as a tragedy of filial ingratitude. In the main plot, Lear disinherits his youngest daughter in favor of her two hypocritical sisters, who turn him out of doors as soon as they have come safely into full possession of his kingdom. In the minor plot, the Earl of Gloucester is tricked into disinheriting his loyal and legitimate son for a bastard son, who turns upon his father. The link in these two plots comes with the tiger queens' abuse of Gloucester and with their lust for the wicked bastard. In reading Shakespeare's plays the various plot-lines of the story and their relationship one to another must be carefully considered.

Shakespeare's plots, as has been frequently pointed out, have their roots in his characters. That is to say, in spite of the intervention of the Goddess of Chance, the events grow out of the moods and emotions of the main characters. Thus there is a dramatic harmony between persons and events so that things happen as they do because characters are what they are. It is amusing fun to shift characters from play to play, and to try to determine what would happen with the new actors in the plot. Just how, for example, would Rosalind act in Viola's place, and what would happen to the King of Denmark if Macbeth or Othello were in Hamlet's black doublet and hose? The outcome of these fancies is to realize that the action is exactly what might be expected with the characters in any given play what they are. A knowledge of the main characters is, therefore, highly important for an understanding of the action. How may the characters be analyzed?

Human beings reveal themselves in numerous ways. We know them by what they say, by their manner of saying it, and, often enough, by their silences or failure to say anything under given circumstances. We know them, too, by their actions, and even by their failure to act on occasions. We know them from what others say about them in statements which reveal both the speaker and the object of his comments. They are revealed to us, finally, by the device of contrasting them with others, by what is known technically as the use of character *foils*.

The first mentioned of these methods of revelation hardly needs elaboration. Shakespeare has often been called coarse because some of his characters are frank in their language. Actually he is only logical; he would have his hostlers, his prostitutes, his innkeepers, his rogues use the speech of their breeding and their trade and not that of ladies and gentlemen of the court. Similarly, his pedants talk like pedants, his soldiers like soldiers, his kings and queens like royalty. Beyond these group indications, however, the individual characteristics of his men and women are revealed by their speech. We could hardly understand the soul of Hamlet without his self-revealing soliloquies or his almost equally revealing conversations with his friend Horatio. Indeed, Shakespeare has a trick of providing many of his major characters—Portia, for instance—with confidants into whose ears they may pour their secrets. And as they speak so do they act or fail to act, the gentlemen like gentlemen, the rascals like rascals, kings royally if sometimes criminally, commoners according to their light and training. Again, characters are frequently characterized by those who speak about them. "These tedious old fools," says Hamlet of the boresome Polonius; and he stigmatizes Rosencrantz and Guildenstern as "adders fang'd." He is himself described in one of his distracted moods by Ophelia,

> "with his doublet all unbraced;
> No hat upon his head; his stockings fouled,
> Ungartered and down-gyved to his ankle;
> Pale as his shirt; his knees knocking each other;
> And with a look so piteous in purport
> As if it had been loosed out of hell
> To speak of horrors."

So Portia describes her lovers; Enobarbus, his emperor and "the serpent of the Nile;" and Macduff, the "hell-hound" usurper. All these characterizations the careful reader will wish to note, even though they may be as short as the epithet just quoted.

To one method of characterization Shakespeare seemed to have been especially partial; it is that of providing his major characters with contrasting opposites or *foils* designed to set them off. Sometimes the contrast is physical; Falstaff is fat, Shallow is thin; Hermia is short and dark, Helena is tall and fair. Usually, however, the contrast is one of temperament. Thus Claudio is reserved and cold, Benedick is alert and mercurial; Adriana is impatient and shrewish, her sister is calm and cool-headed. Occasionally the foils are of great importance and are carried throughout the entire play. Thus it is in *Hamlet,* where three men of different temperaments are all faced with the problem of avenging the death of a father. For fear that the audience may miss the comparison, indeed, Shakespeare has Prince Hamlet himself point out the resemblance of his own situation to that of Fortinbras and of Laertes. The question is this: How will each man solve the same problem? Hamlet himself, the man who thinks without acting, delays; Laertes, the man who acts without thinking, plunges; and the two tragic figures perish on the same poisoned sword, leaving the kingdom to Fortinbras, the cool-headed, balanced Norwegian who plans and acts in due proportion and at appropriate times for each. To drop Fortinbras from the play, as is done in most modern productions, is like knocking one leg from a tripod.

The background of the play, as has been said in an earlier section, cannot be secured from any elaborate description of the setting such as those which embellish many modern printed plays. Locale and atmosphere come out of the mouths of the speakers and must be reconstructed from the dialogue. An assembling of these allusions and longer descriptions will reveal the essential appropriateness of the setting and the care with which the background has been made to harmonize with plot and characters. The blasted heath for the witches, the gloomy castle of Elsinore for the lone sentinel and the ghost in armor, the furious storm on the moor for the maddened King Lear and his ragged followers, the pleasant Forest of Arden for the exiles, Olivia's garden for Toby and Aguecheck—these and others too numerous to mention should be studied for their contribution to the whole and for their share in the structural unity which is one of Shakespeare's essential characteristics.

A profound study of the plays of the dramatist would demand many more considerations than those which have been too briefly outlined here. But for the reader asking only a layman's, and not a specialist's, knowledge of the plays, and for a student engaged in review, it may be enough to read the play once for the story and general acquaintance with the main characters, and once again, more slowly, for a consideration of the technique of plot, characters, and background, which is so markedly characteristic of Shakespeare's art.

Title Page of
the First Folio

To the Reader.

This Figure, that thou here feeſt put,
    It vvas for gentle Shakeſpeare cut;
Wherein the Grauer had a ſtrife
    with Nature, to out-doo the life :
O, could he but haue dravvne his vvit
    As vvell in braſſe, as he hath hit
His face ; the Print vvould then ſurpaſſe
    All, that vvas euer vvrit in braſſe.
But, ſince he cannot, Reader, looke
    Not on his Picture, but his Booke.

B. I.

Mr. WILLIAM
SHAKESPEARES

COMEDIES,
HISTORIES, &
TRAGEDIES.

Published according to the True Originall Copies.

Martin Droeshout sculpsit London.

LONDON
Printed by Isaac Iaggard, and Ed. Blount. 1623.

Comedies

Love's Labor's Lost

Dramatis Personæ

FERDINAND, King of Navarre, who is determined to make his court "a little Academe, still and contemplative in living art."

BIRON, whose "eye begets occasion for his wit," "not a word with him but a jest,"

LONGAVILLE, "a man of sovereign parts," "few taller are so young,"

DUMAIN, "a well-accomplish'd youth," with "wit to make an ill shape good, and shape to win grace though he had no wit,"

the "vow-fellows with this virtuous Duke," all "merry mad-cap lords," ordinarily given to wit and mockery.

THE PRINCESS OF FRANCE, a "maid of grace and complete majesty" on an embassy to the court of Navarre, one whose "conceits have wings fleeter than arrows, bullets, wind, thought, swifter things."

ROSALINE, "a wightly wanton with a velvet brow with two pitch-balls stuck in her face for eyes,"

MARIA, a "heavenly love,"

KATHERINE "an amber-colored raven," "fair as a text B in a copy-book;" ("O that [her] face were not so full of O's,")

her ladies-in-waiting.

BOYET, "monsieur the nice," "wit's pedler," "an old love-monger" and an "ape of form," court usher in the Princess' suite. "This gallant pins the wenches on his sleeve;" "the stairs, as he treads on them, kiss his feet."

MERCADE, a messenger.

COSTARD, an "unlettered small-knowing soul," "a most simple clown."

JAQUENETTA, a country wench.

ANTHONY DULL, an unimaginative constable who "hath never fed of the dainties that are bred in a book; he hath not eat paper, as it were; he hath not drunk ink; his intellect is not replenished; he is only an animal."

DON ADRIANO DE ARMADO, "fashion's own knight," a fantastical Spaniard who "speaks not like a man of God's making" and "draweth out the thread of his verbosity finer than the staple of his argument;" "one that makes sport to the Prince and his bookmates."

MOTH, a "handful of wit," a "pigeon-egg of discretion," Armado's "pretty knavish page."

SIR NATHANIEL, a hedge-priest,
HOLOFERNES, the village pedant,
two "arts-men" who "have been at a great feast of languages and stolen the scraps."

A Forester, Lords, Attendants.

Scene of the Action: Navarre.

Act I

Instead of following the usual round of courtly pleasure, King Ferdinand and his friends, Biron, Longaville, and Dumain, resolve to make Navarre a little academe. Defying Biron's prophecy that they will be forsworn three thousand times, they bind themselves by oath to spend three years in studying, fasting, sleeping but three hours a night, and, above all, speaking to no woman. Their only recreation is to be the conversation of Costard, a yokel, and Don Armado, an affected military Spaniard—"one who the music of his own vain tongue doth ravish like enchanting harmony." Reality is not long in asserting itself in this ideal commonwealth. In their zeal, the gentlemen of Navarre have completely forgotten the Princess of France, who, with her train of three vivacious ladies, is already on her way to Navarre on a diplomatic mission. The first violation of the edict is reported by Don Armado, who has taken Costard with Jaquenetta, a country wench with whom Armado himself is so enamored that he has not only fallen into melancholy, but even been driven into versifying. Costard is condemned into Armado's keeping for a week's fasting on bran and water.

Act II

Unable, because of his absurd vows, to entertain the Princess and her ladies, Rosaline, Maria, and Katherine, in his palace, Ferdinand makes them as comfortable as possible in a tent in the park outside his gates. During the conduct of his diplomatic business with the Princess, the King is much attracted to her, and each of his lords pairs off with one of the ladies.

Act III

Armado's love having inspired him to literary composition, he releases Costard from jail to deliver a love-letter to Jaquenetta, and Biron, meeting the messenger by accident, also entrusts him with a note to Rosaline.

Act IV

Costard stupidly gets the letters mixed. He delivers Armado's absurd rhetoric to Rosaline and thus affords much amusement to the ladies, and Biron's poetical effusion to Jaquenetta, who, being unable to read it, asks help of the village schoolmaster, Holofernes. The pedant perceives that the verses are the composition of one of the King's votaries and dispatches Jaquenetta with them in haste to the King. Meanwhile, love has turned all of the gentlemen into sonneteers. Biron, in hiding, overhears his King composing verses to the Princess; both overhear Longaville reading a sonnet which he has written to Maria, and all three hear the ode Dumain has been concocting to the "most divine Kate." Longaville steps from hiding to reprove Dumain, the King reproves Longaville, and while Biron is virtuously chiding his companions with their inconstancy and their shattered vow, Costard and Jaquenetta appear with the evidence of his own treason. Perceiving that "young blood doth not obey an old decree," all conclude that, after all, women are "the books, the arts, the academes, that show, contain, and nourish all the world." Hence, they plan revels, masques, and dances with which to woo their loves, but with some misgivings, however, that "light wenches may prove plagues to men forsworn."

Act V

Having sent presents to their sweethearts, the gentlemen disguise as Muscovites to visit the pavilion of the Princess, but the merry ladies find out that they are coming, mask, and exchange favors, so that each gentleman woos the wrong girl. "The tongues of mocking wenches are as keen as is the razor's edge invisible," and the Muscovites are routed. When the courtiers return in their own guise, the ladies disdainfully describe the absurd "mess of Russians" who have lately been there, and the joke is revealed. Meanwhile, the village schoolmaster and the curate have likewise prepared an entertainment, and the presentation of a pageant of the Nine Worthies with Costard, Moth, and Armado as actors before the sophisticated ladies and gentlemen yields riotous amusement. Into the midst of this merriment, a messenger from France arrives with the news that the Princess' father is dead, and she is obliged to return home with all speed. Ferdinand, therefore, pleads openly for the hands of the ladies for himself and his courtiers, but the gentlemen are still attainted with perjury for breaking their vow, and the "wooing doth not end like an old play." The ladies assign suitable penances and postpone their answers for a year and a day.

The Comedy of Errors

Dramatis Personæ

SOLINUS, Duke of Ephesus, who tempers justice with mercy.

AEGEON, aged merchant from Syracuse.

AEMILIA, abbess at Ephesus, discovered to be the wife of Aegeon.

ANTIPHOLUS OF EPHESUS,
ANTIPHOLUS OF SYRACUSE, } identical twin brothers, sons of Aegeon and Aemilia.

DROMIO OF EPHESUS, } identical twin brothers, personal servants of the two Anti-
DROMIO OF SYRACUSE, } pholuses; "trusty villains" who jest with their masters.

ADRIANA, impatient wife of Antipholus of Ephesus, a "fond fool" who "serves mad jealousy" and indulges in "venom clamors."

LUCIANA, her unmarried and placid sister who preaches patience; foil to Adriana. She is "possess'd with such a sovereign grace."

PINCH, a schoolmaster; "a hungry lean-faced villain, . . . a mountebank, . . . a fortune-teller, a needy, hollow-eyed, sharp-looking wretch, a living dead man."

BALTHAZAR, a merchant.

ANGELO, a goldsmith.

A COURTEZAN, "of excellent discourse, pretty and witty, wild, and yet, too, gentle."

LUCE, a serving-woman of Adriana's.

Jailer, Officers, Merchants, and various Attendants upon the Duke.

Scene of the Action: Ephesus.

Act I

Because of the enmity between the cities of Ephesus and Syracuse, Aegeon, an aged merchant from Syracuse, is apprehended in Ephesus and condemned to death by the Duke Solinus. Aegeon moves the ruler's compassion by the sad story of his life. A quarter of a century before, while he and his wife were in Epidamnum, they became the parents of twin sons, and to attend his children he bought from "a meaner woman" her twin sons born "that very hour." On the return voyage their ship was wrecked, he escaped with one infant son and one little slave, but was separated from his wife, who was lashed to a spar with the other two babies. The father and his charges were picked up and taken to Epidaurus but not before he had seen his wife and the other children carried

43

away by a Corinthian fishing-boat. Eighteen years later his son obtained his permission to leave Syracuse, accompanied by his slave to search for his lost brother. When he did not return, the father set out after him and wandered for five years in a vain search only to be arrested and condemned to death in Ephesus on his way home. Duke Solinus can not remit the sentence but is moved to grant the old man one day in which to secure his ransom.

Unknown to his father Aegeon, Antipholus of Syracuse has just come to Ephesus with his slave Dromio, and to escape the law against Syracusians has given out that he is from Epidamnum. The younger traveler is unaware of his father's fate, nor does he know that the twin brother whom he has sought for so many years is living in Ephesus with a wife, Adriana, and his life-long slave, the other Dromio. And Antipholus of Ephesus and his household are also unaware of the presence in the city of the visiting twins. When, therefore, Antipholus of Syracuse, after having sent his Dromio to the inn with money, is invited to come home to dinner by the Ephesian Dromio, who mistakes him for his master, he is at first astounded, then angered, and beats the slave heartily.

Act II

Poor Dromio of Ephesus, bearing the physical marks of his error, returns to his mistress Adriana only to be upbraided by her for not having brought his master home. In the meantime Dromio of Syracuse, returned from the inn, is being beaten by *his* master for denying that he ever invited that angry gentleman to go home to his wife and dinner. But both master and man are convinced that the city is full of witchcraft when Adriana and her sister Luciana appear, call them by name, chide them for their delay, and hale them off to eat at the home of Antipholus of Ephesus.

Act III

While Antipholus of Syracuse is dining with his brother's wife, with Dromio guarding the door, the real owner of the house approaches with the other Dromio and with Angelo and Balthazar whom he has invited to dinner. To their amazement they find the door locked and hear themselves ordered away. Balthazar's advice keeps Antipholus of Ephesus from breaking into his own house; in a rage, however, he invites his guests to eat with him at the house of a courtezan, and sends Angelo to get a gold chain which he had intended to give to Adriana, but which he now declares he will present to the girl. At his home, in the meantime, his twin brother is making love to Luciana, and poor Dromio of Syracuse is trying to escape from a fat and greasy kitchen wench who claims him as husband. Convinced that "none but witches do inhabit here," the Syracusian sends his Dromio to inquire about ships leaving port. Angelo meets him and, mistaking him for his brother, presses upon the puzzled man the gold chain which his twin ordered. Antipholus is even more eager to flee the city.

Act IV

Angelo, needing money to save himself from being arrested for debt, later demands from Antipholus of Ephesus payment for the chain; but that twin naturally denies that he ever received it, and the goldsmith has him arrested. When Dromio of Syracuse appears with news that a bark is about to leave the port, the Ephesian sends his brother's slave to his wife for money to bail him out. Returning with the ducats Dromio meets his own master, and is surprised to find him at liberty. While the Syracusian gentleman is wondering about the money, the courtezan with whom his brother dined appears and, seeing the gold chain about his neck, demands it in exchange for a ring which she declares that she gave him. Upon his refusal she goes off to tell Adriana that Antipholus is insane. Meanwhile Dromio of Ephesus meets his own master, still in custody, but when the Ephesian demands from his slave the money for his ransom, poor Dromio gives him a piece of rope which he declares he was sent to buy, and in spite of the officers, Antipholus beats him with it. Adriana, Luciana, and the courtezan rush in with a Doctor Pinch, a "doting wizard," who is brought to drive Satan out of the mad man. The enraged Ephesian beats the conjurer but is finally subdued, and after Adriana has paid the officer his fee, master and man are led off in bonds to be locked in their own house. While Adriana and the officers are still talking, Antipholus of Syracuse and his Dromio enter with drawn sword, and thinking that the prisoners have escaped, the group rush pell-mell away.

Act V

Before the thoroughly distracted Syracusians can get to their ship, however, they are met by Angelo, who charges Antipholus with just having denied his possession of the chain which now hangs about his neck. The quarrel into which he is drawn is interrupted by the appearance of Adriana, Luciana, and others, and to escape, the two Syracusians take sanctuary in a neighboring priory. When the Lady Abbess not only refuses to surrender Antipholus to his supposed wife but also rebukes her for having caused his madness with her jealousy, Adriana appeals to the Duke, who is passing at that moment to the place of execution with the condemned Aegeon. Before the abbess can be summoned, however, Antipholus of Ephesus and his Dromio, having escaped from their prison, enter and likewise appeal to the Duke for justice. Antipholus does not, of course, recognize his father and denies having dined with his wife or having received the chain from Angelo, and there is much confusion until the Lady Abbess reënters with Antipholus of Syracuse and his Dromio. Then, with many exclamations of astonishment and some added confusion, the ERRORS are solved. The aged Aegeon, pardoned by the Duke, discovers in the abbess his long-lost wife Aemilia; the two Antipholuses and the twin Dromios embrace and Antipholus of Ephesus is reconciled to his wife and sees his brother happily courting the fair sister. Thus the Comedy of Errors ends in happy reunions.

The Two Gentlemen of Verona

Dramatis Personæ

VALENTINE, "a gentleman and well derived," a true friend and a constant lover.

PROTEUS, his changeable foil, a traitor to both love and friendship, yet "complete in feature and in mind with all good grace to grace a gentleman." "Were man but constant, he were perfect. That one error fills him with faults."

} the two gentlemen of Verona.

SILVIA, "a virtuous gentlewoman, mild and beautiful," daughter of the Duke of Milan, and beloved of Valentine.

JULIA, the constant love of Proteus, who disguises as a page, Sebastian.

THURIO, suitor of Silvia and Valentine's homely, foolish rival whom Silvia's father "likes only for his possessions are huge."

SIR EGLAMOUR, a true courtly votary to Love, "a knight well-spoken, neat, and fine," who aids Silvia in making her escape.

ANTONIO, father of Proteus, "a gentleman of worth and worthy estimation."

THE DUKE OF MILAN, father of Silvia.

SPEED, clownish servant of Valentine, an "illiterate loiterer" whose sluggish nature belies his name.

LAUNCE, the like of Proteus, "a slave, that still an end turns [him] to shame."

CRAB, Launce's dog, "one that [he] brought up of a puppy . . . [and] sav'd from drowning," for whom he has "sat in the stocks for the puddings he hath stolen . . . [and] in the pillory for geese he hath kill'd," and yet "the sourest-natured dog that lives."

LUCETTA, sharp-tongued waiting-woman of Julia.

PANTHINO, trusted servant of Antonio.

The Host of the Inn where Proteus lodges.

Outlaws in the Forest near Mantua, some of them gentlemen, "such as the fury of ungovern'd youth thrust from the company of awful men."

Servants, Musicians, and Attendants.

Scene of the Action: Verona, Milan, and a Forest near Mantua.

Act I

Proteus and Valentine, two gentlemen of Verona who are devoted friends, are to separate. Valentine, convinced that "homekeeping youth have ever homely wits," seeks honor at the Emperor's court in Milan, while Proteus remains at home to seek success in love, his affections having settled upon the "heavenly"

47

Julia, who has many suitors. But no sooner has Proteus' love begun to thrive, than his father, Antonio, who knows nothing of his son's love-affair and believes that it "would be great impeachment to his age, in having known no travel in his youth," determines to send him after Valentine to Milan.

Act II

In Milan, Valentine has fallen in love with an exquisite beauty named Silvia, the daughter of the Duke. Although he has not as yet presumed to speak of his love, she makes clear her inclination toward him by commissioning him to write love letters which she says she wishes for her friend and then returning them to him again to be "writ more movingly." Silvia's father, however, wishes her to marry Thurio, a foolish fellow who has money. Meanwhile, in Verona, Proteus, having exchanged rings with Julia, sworn constancy, and sealed the bargain with a holy kiss, in tears sets out for Milan to join his friend. Valentine receives the unexpected visit of his Proteus with great joy, introduces him to Silvia, and, revealing to him his plans of eloping with her at night, asks his aid. Proteus, however, has also fallen in love with Silvia at first sight, and unmindful of his vows to Julia or his friendship for Valentine, determines to have her for himself. Meanwhile, back in Verona, the doting Julia disguises as a page and sets out for Milan to join her lover.

Act III

A traitor to both love and friendship, Proteus reveals to the Duke of Milan Valentine's plans of elopement with his daughter. The old gentleman thereupon seeks out Valentine, interrupts him as he is hastening away with a rope ladder under his cloak, and finding upon the young lover confirmatory evidence of the use he plans to put it to, banishes him from his dukedom. With his more formidable rival out of the way, Proteus pretends to aid the suit of the bumpkin Thurio, who has also confidently enlisted his help because he is sure that Proteus is "already Love's firm votary and cannot soon revolt and change [his] mind."

Act IV

In the forest near Mantua, Valentine is captured by a band of outlaws who, like him, have been banished for venial offences, and they are so pleased with his manly bearing that they elect him their chief. Back in Milan, under color of commending Thurio, Proteus pays his attentions to Silvia, but finds her "too fair, too true, too holy, to be corrupted by [his] worthless gifts." The disguised Julia arrives just in time to hear him assisting Thurio in a serenade to Silvia and to overhear Silvia reproach him as a "subtle, perjur'd, false, disloyal man." On the next day, Julia presents herself to Proteus under the name of Sebastian and is taken into his service as a page. The page's first commission is to carry to Silvia, as a love-token, the very ring which Julia had given Proteus on his departure from Verona. Silvia, of course, refuses the ring, but learning that the page is acquainted with the lady Julia, rewards him for his fidelity to her.

Act V

With the aid of Sir Eglamour, a chivalrous votary to Love, Silvia escapes from Milan and sets out to join Valentine. In the forest she is captured by the outlaw band, but is rescued from them by Proteus and his page, who have come in pursuit of the runaways. Taking advantage of the situation, Proteus woos Silvia ardently and is about to force his attentions upon her, when Valentine, who has heard everything, emerges from his cave. Thus found out, the perfidious friend becomes ashamed of his unfaithful acts and is readily forgiven by Valentine, the true friend, who proves the sincerity of his forgiveness by turning to Proteus with the generous words: "All that was mine in Silvia I give thee." At this offer the page Sebastian faints, and by the ring which he wears on his finger is recognized as the deserted Julia. As she forgives her lover's infidelity the Duke and Thurio, who have also been seeking Silvia, are brought before Valentine by the outlaws. The craven Thurio refuses to fight Valentine for Silvia, and the Duke thereupon bestows her upon her true lover, pardons all the outlaws, and with the happy couples returns to Milan.

A Midsummer Night's Dream

Dramatis Personæ

THESEUS, Duke of Athens.

HIPPOLYTA, fair Queen of the Amazons, betrothed to Theseus, who won her with his sword.

EGEUS, Hermia's stubborn father.

LYSANDER,
DEMETRIUS, } Athenian youths.

HERMIA, daughter of Egeus, in love with Lysander; a vivacious little brunette with a mind of her own. "When she's angry, she is keen and shrewd. She was a vixen when she went to school, and though she be but little, she is fierce."

HELENA, in love with Demetrius, a tall blonde with "no gift at all in shrewishness," and a "right maid for her cowardice."

PHILOSTRATE, Theseus' master of the revels.

QUINCE, a carpenter, author and nominal director of the "lamentable comedy" presented before the Duke.

BOTTOM, a weaver, who plays Pyramus and virtually manages the show.

FLUTE, a bellows-mender, who does not want to play the part of Thisby because he has a beard coming.

SNUG, a joiner, who is "slow of study" but "roars well" as Lion.

STARVELING, a tailor, who essays the Moon in the play but "wanes" early.

SNOUT, a tinker, who presenteth Wall.

"Hard-handed men," who "never labored in their minds till now . . . and now have toil'd with this same play."

OBERON, jealous King of the Fairies.

TITANIA, proud Queen of the Fairies, tiny enough to wrap herself in the enamelled skin of the snake.

ROBIN GOODFELLOW, the PUCK, a knavish hobgoblin, who "jests to Oberon and makes him smile," and who plays pranks in the village and thinks all mortals fools; link between the fairies and the various groups of mortals.

PEASEBLOSSOM,
COBWEB,
MOTH,
MUSTARDSEED, } Queen Titania's fairies who serve as personal attendants upon Nick Bottom.

Other Fairy Attendants upon Oberon and Titania; Attendants upon Theseus and Hippolyta.

Scene of the Action: Athens and a wood nearby.

A Midsummer Night's Dream

Act I

Theseus, Duke of Athens, is to wed Hippolyta, Queen of the Amazons, at the next new moon and has ordered Philostrate, his master of the revels, to "stir up the Athenian youths to merriments." Among those who are preparing to entertain the royal couple is a group of Athenian craftsmen, who select parts in a home-spun tragedy entitled "The most lamentable comedy, and most cruel death of Pyramus and Thisby" and disband after having agreed to meet for rehearsal at the Duke's oak. But not all Athenian youths are happy. Lysander and Demetrius both love Hermia; she favors Lysander, but Egeus her father insists in the Duke's presence that she must marry Demetrius or suffer the alternative of death or life in a nunnery. To escape the Athenian law, Lysander and Hermia arrange to meet in the same wood, "a league without the town," in which the craftsmen are to rehearse their play, and to escape thence to a place of safety. The lovers err, however, in revealing their plot to Hermia's friend Helena, who still loves Demetrius although he has jilted her; this jealous girl in turn tattles to her erstwhile suitor, thinking to win his favor by her duplicity.

Act II

The wood in which the lovers and the craftsmen have planned to meet is haunted by fairies who have come from India to bless the wedding of Theseus and Hippolyta. But even with the fairies not all is harmonious; Oberon, the king, is quarreling with Titania, the queen, over the possession of "a little changeling boy," and all nature is disturbed by their bickerings. To punish the Queen for keeping the child, Oberon sends the knavish Puck, his hobgoblin jester, to get a flower, the juice of which squeezed into sleeping eyelids will make the victim dote on the first live creature that he sees; the fairy king plans to embarrass Titania by causing her to fall in love with some monster. While Puck is on the errand, Oberon is disturbed by two quarreling mortals; Demetrius, warned by Helena of Hermia's flight, is trying to find the runaways in the wood and is chiding the foolish Helena for following him. When Puck returns, therefore, Oberon commands him to anoint

51

the eyes of "the disdainful youth," whom the hobgoblin will know "by the Athenian garments he hath on;" he himself seeks Titania, asleep on a flowery bank, and squeezes the juice of the flower into her eyes. Puck's mission is not, however, so well carried out; for he finds not Demetrius but Lysander asleep on the ground with Hermia near him, and anoints this true lover's eyes. Thus when Helena, still pursuing Demetrius, finds and awakens Lysander, he makes violent love to her and pursues her into the wood. Hermia, awakening and finding herself alone, wanders off in search of Lysander.

Act III

The craftsmen meet near the bower of the fairy queen to rehearse their crude play. But Puck, who has been spying on them, takes a part by slipping an ass's head upon the shoulders of Nick Bottom, the most foolish of the yokels. The others flee in terror, but Bottom, singing to keep up his courage, awakens the fairy queen, who falls violently in love with him and assigns fairy servitors to wait upon him. While Puck is reporting this prank to Oberon, Hermia and Demetrius, who has encountered her, come quarreling through the wood. Hermia accuses him of having murdered Lysander and runs from him; and he, exhausted, lies down to sleep. Having sent Puck to bring in Helena, Oberon anoints the eyes of Demetrius with the flower-juice. Helena comes in with Lysander following; their squabbling awakens Demetrius, who falls in love with her, and the men begin competing for her favor as they did before for that of Hermia. Hearing the noise, Hermia returns, and believing that Helena has stolen her lover's devotion, she berates her savagely. The youths seek a level place to fight, and Helena, fearing to be left alone with the unhappy Hermia, runs off with her rival after her. At Oberon's command, Puck amends his mistake by causing the four lovers to sleep near each other, and by removing the enchantment from Lysander's eyes with the juice of another flower.

Act IV

While the lovers sleep on the ground, Queen Titania carries on her absurd courtship of the ass-headed Bottom. Finally, the ill-assorted pair go to sleep in each other's arms. Oberon, having previously secured possession of the changeling child, removes the spell from the Queen's eyes, awakens her in her right mind, and orders Puck to pluck the ass's head from Bottom's shoulders. The sun rises, and Theseus, Hippolyta, and their train come into the wood to hunt. There they discover the sleeping lovers, and awaken them with the hunting horns. Again Egeus demands that his daughter marry Demetrius, but that youth, now in love with Helena, gives up to Lysander all claim to Hermia, a solution of the disagreement which so pleases the Duke that he invites the lovers to be wed in one festivity with him and his fair bride. Nick Bottom, the last of the sleepers, stretches and awakes, certain that he has had "a most rare vision." He returns to his fellows, who have given him up for lost, and the craftsmen prepare to put on their play for the Duke's wedding.

Act V

The "most lamentable comedy" of Pyramus and Thisby is chosen by the Duke as an "abridgment" for the evening, and Bottom as Pyramus, Flute as Thisby, and the others as Wall, Moonshine, and Lion, put time to flight with the "tragical mirth" of the heroic interlude. The craftsmen end the play with a "Bergomask dance" and leave well pleased with themselves. "The iron tongue of midnight" tolls twelve, and the lovers retire. Into the palace come Oberon and Titania with their train; dancing and singing, they bless the sleepers and trip away, leaving only Puck as Epilogue to present the apologies of "the shadows" and to beg the plaudits of the audience.

The Merchant of Venice

Dramatis Personæ

ANTONIO, the Merchant of Venice, a wealthy gentleman of a generous but melancholy disposition, "reputed wise for saying nothing;" "the best condition'd and unwearied spirit in doing courtesies;" of a princely nature, he "lends out money gratis" and hates usurers.

SHYLOCK, a rich Jew, a usurer controlled by strong emotions of love and hate, shrewd in his business dealings, loving in his family relations, bitter in his hatred of the enemies of his race; foil to the Christian Antonio.

THE DUKE OF VENICE, presiding officer at the trial of Shylock against Antonio.

BASSANIO, Antonio's friend, an irresponsible but attractive young man, "a scholar and a soldier," clever, quick-witted, and gay but perpetually impecunious and thoughtlessly selfish in his willingness to sponge on his rich friends.

PORTIA, of Belmont, a "lady richly left" who marries Bassanio; "fair and . . . of wondrous virtues," merry-hearted but noble-minded, of high intelligence and boldness of execution; in judgment "a second Daniel;" "the poor rude world hath not her fellow."

NERISSA, Portia's waiting-maid and confidante, who marries Gratiano; a sprightly wench who plays a merry second fiddle in her mistress' pranks; in male garb she makes "a little scrubbed boy."

GRATIANO, "too wild, too rude, and bold of voice," the talkative and mercurial friend of Bassanio, who "speaks an infinite deal of nothing . . . [and whose] reasons are as two grains of wheat hid in two bushels of chaff, you shall seek all day ere you find them: and when you have them, they are not worth the search."

LORENZO, an artistic, music-loving friend of Bassanio, too dreamy to be practical but so essentially honest as to be trusted completely by Portia.

JESSICA, Shylock's daughter, who marries Lorenzo; "wise, fair, and true," too much a lover of life not to find her father's strictly managed house a tedious hell.

SALANIO,
SALARINO, } friends of Antonio and Bassanio.
SALERIO,

TUBAL, a rich Jew, friend of Shylock.

THE PRINCE OF MOROCCO, } two of Portia's foreign suitors.
THE PRINCE OF ARRAGON,

LAUNCELOT GOBBO, a clownish, chop-logic servant, first of Shylock and then of Bassanio, a "wit-snapper" who "hath planted in his memory an army of good words," a "merry devil," "kind enough but a huge feeder, snail-slow in profit," and a sleeper by day.

OLD GOBBO, Launcelot's "sand-blind, high-gravel blind" old father, with whom the youth tries "confusions."

LEONARDO, Bassanio's servant.

STEPHANO,
BALTHASAR, } two of Portia's servants.

Magnificoes of Venice, Officers of the Court of Justice, a Jailer, Portia's servants, and Attendants.

Scene of the Action· Venice, and Portia's seat at Belmont.

54

Act I

Among the many suitors who flock to court the rich, fair, and virtuous lady, Portia of Belmont, is Bassanio, an impecunious young Venetian gentleman. Feeling that he cannot succeed in his courtship without adequate revenue, he turns for help to Antonio, an older friend from whom he has often borrowed money, and asks that generous merchant for a loan of three thousand ducats for three months. To this request Antonio readily accedes; however, not having the full amount on hand, he breaks his usual custom of never borrowing on interest and asks for the money from Shylock, a rich Jewish money-lender. In Antonio's need Shylock sees an opportunity to "catch [his hated rival] once upon the hip . . . [and] feed fat the ancient grudge [he] bear[s] him." He therefore agrees to lend the money to Antonio without interest, if the merchant will sign "in a merry sport" a bond stipulating that "the forfeit be nominated for an equal pound of [his] fair flesh to be cut off and taken in what part of [his] body pleaseth [Shylock]." Although Bassanio protests that he likes "not fair terms and a villain's mind," Antonio is confident that many of his merchandise-laden ships will "come home a month before the day," and he willingly signs the bond, feeling even that "the Hebrew will turn Christian: he grows kind."

Act II

Fully equipped with the money obtained under this blood-bond, the light-hearted Bassanio goes to Belmont to court the heiress. With him he takes a mercurial friend, Gratiano, after that young man has promised "to allay with some cold drops of modesty [his] skipping spirit, . . . put on a sober habit . . . talk with respect and swear but now and then." With him also goes Shylock's former servant the clown Launcelot Gobbo, who is delighted by the "rare new liveries" the extravagant Bassanio has been bestowing on his retinue. Bassanio's departure and the banquet and masque which celebrate it give opportunity for young Lorenzo to elope with Shylock's daughter Jessica, who disguises herself as a page and appropriates her father's treasure while he is feasting with the "prodigal Christian." In Belmont, Portia is following the terms of her father's will by putting her many suitors to the test of the three caskets. Choosing the golden casket, the Prince of Morocco finds in it "a carrion Death;" in the silver casket the Prince of Arragon sees "the portrait of a blinking idiot;" and both suitors are dismissed. Then comes the news that Bassanio has arrived to make his trial.

Act III

At his trial, aided by a hint embedded in a song which Portia orders sung while he comments to himself on the caskets, the happy Bassanio finds in the leaden casket "fair Portia's counterfeit;" and when he turns to claim his bride, he receives from her a ring which she pledges him to keep. His friend Gratiano has in the meantime successfully courted Portia's waiting-maid Nerissa; and to complete the trio of lovers, Lorenzo, an artistic young friend of Bassanio, enters with the fair Jessica, the nimble-spirited daughter of Shylock with whom he has eloped. But the happiness of all is short-lived; from Venice comes "the unpleasant'st words that ever blotted paper"—Antonio's ventures from all ports of the world are lost, the bloody bond is forfeited, and Shylock demands his pound of flesh. After hurrying Bassanio through a marriage, Portia dispatches her husband to Venice to "deface the bond," announcing that she and Nerissa will remain in Belmont as maids and widows. Meantime, in Venice, Antonio's only wish is that "Bassanio comes to see [him] pay his debt." Left behind in Belmont, Portia refuses to remain inactive; she turns her house over to Lorenzo and Jessica, disguises herself as a young doctor of laws and Nerissa as her clerk, and sets out for Venice to save Antonio.

Act IV

Portia arrives at the court of justice in Venice just as the trial of Shylock against Antonio is beginning and presents to the Duke, who is presiding, a letter from her kinsman Bellario, a famous lawyer, in which she is introduced as "a young doctor of Rome . . . Balthasar." Acting as judge in the case, the disguised lady first attempts to soften Shylock's heart by convincing him that "the quality of mercy is not strained;" then she begs him to accept "thrice the sum." But Shylock declares that he has "an oath in heaven" to demand the forfeiture, and he charges Portia "by the law . . . [to] proceed to judgment." The "most righteous judge" then awards the pound of flesh to the Jew, but immediately checks his elation by further decreeing that if, in cutting the flesh, he "shed one drop of Christian blood [his] lands and goods are, by the laws of Venice confiscate. . . ." Forced by this decision to forego his revenge, Shylock offers to take three times the bond, but the "second Daniel" then decrees that since he has refused his money in open court, he may have "nothing but the forfeiture." Finally, when the defeated Jew would depart with empty hands, Portia tells him that because he has plotted against the life of a Venetian citizen, half of his goods are forfeit to Antonio and half to the state. Demanding nothing for himself, Antonio nevertheless asks that Shylock make a deed of gift "of all he dies possessed unto his son and his daughter" and "presently become a Christian." After the broken old man has left the court, Portia refuses from Antonio and Bassanio any fee for her services, but she and Nerissa contrive to beg from their husbands the rings which Bassanio and Gratiano have vowed always to wear; then the "learned judge" and her "clerk" hasten back to Belmont.

Act V

The merry jest of the rings brings about the revelation to the astonished Bassanio and Gratiano that the noble Portia and her maid have played the rôles of judge and clerk; for the women demand the rings from their husbands, and then pretend to think that other women are wearing them. After teasing their protesting husbands to the full, the ladies return the rings, declaring that they received them from the doctor of laws and his clerk; and the amazed men realize that "Portia was the doctor, Nerissa there her clerk." Lorenzo and Jessica are given the "special deed of gift" forced from Shylock; word comes that three of Antonio's argosies have come richly to harbor; and thus what might have been general tragedy turns for all but Shylock to happiness and merriment.

The Taming of The Shrew

Dramatis Personæ

In the Induction:

CHRISTOPHER SLY, a drunken tinker.

A Lord, a Hostess, a Page, Players, Huntsmen, and Servants.

In the Play:

BAPTISTA MINOLA, a rich gentleman of Padua.

KATHERINA, his beautiful elder daughter, "as brown in hue as hazel nuts," whose "only fault, and that is faults enough, is that she is intolerable curst and shrewd and froward."

BIANCA, her younger sister, as modest and gentle as Katherina is wild and unruly.

PETRUCHIO, "a mad-brain rudesby" and a "swearing Jack," yet a gentleman of Verona, resolved to tame Katherina.

VINCENTIO, an old gentleman of Pisa.

LUCENTIO, his son, "a proper stripling and an amorous," in love with Bianca.

HORTENSIO,
GREMIO, } other suitors of Bianca.

TRANIO,
BIONDELLO, } servants of Lucentio.

GRUMIO, a "three-inch fool"
CURTIS, } servants of Petruchio.

A Pedant, a Widow, a Tailor, a Haberdasher, and Servants.

Scene of the Action: Padua and Petruchio's country house.

Induction

Christopher Sly, a tinker, is found dead drunk by a nobleman, who, for amusement, has him carried to his fairest chamber, and dressed up in rich clothes. When he awakes, Sly finds himself surrounded by attendants, including a boy disguised as a "wife," who congratulate him upon his recovery from a fit of insanity which has lasted for fifteen years. To induce merriment and so to prevent a return of the malady, a company of itinerant players perform before him this comedy of THE TAMING OF THE SHREW.

58

Act I

Baptista Minola, a rich merchant of Padua, has two daughters. The elder, Katherina, is notorious far and wide as a "hilding of a devilish spirit" while the younger, Bianca, is famed for sweetness and gentility. Naturally, Bianca has suitors, but her father refuses to admit a bid for the hand of his younger daughter until he has a husband for the elder. Lucentio, a young student from Pisa, falls in love with Bianca and, overhearing Baptista request her suitors to send him schoolmasters for his daughter, resolves to change clothes with his servant, Tranio, and offer himself as a tutor. Meanwhile, Gremio and Hortensio, disappointed rivals for the hand of Bianca, join forces in the rather hopeless task of finding a husband for her elder sister. In good time, Hortensio meets his old friend Petruchio, come from Verona to seek his fortune, who, when he hears of Katherina's dowry, vows to woo this "wild-cat" were she "as curst and shrewd as Socrates' Xanthippe." Gremio also welcomes Petruchio and in a moment they are joined by Tranio, who is masquerading as his master, and who to assist Lucentio is resolved to woo Bianca, too; and the three rival suitors agree to defray Petruchio's expense in wooing Katherina for the opportunity it may give them of wooing the younger sister.

Act II

Together Petruchio, Gremio, and Tranio present themselves at Baptista's house. The first brings his friend Hortensio, disguised as a music teacher that he may have access to Bianca; the second has hired the true Lucentio as a tutor in languages that he may read love books to her in his behalf; and the third presents a lute and some Greek and Latin books. Petruchio is impatient to begin his wooing, and his introduction to Katherina comes just after she has broken the lute across Hortensio's head. She gives him a violent tongue lashing, but, undaunted, he praises her gentleness, protests that he finds her "pleasant, gamesome, passing courteous, but slow of speech," and concludes by setting their wedding date for the following Sunday. Gremio and Tranio, meanwhile, have ceased to be friendly rivals, and Baptista, to keep peace, at last agrees to bestow Bianca upon the one who can assure her of the greater dowry. Each tries to outboast the other, and Baptista at length agrees on the Sunday following Katherina's wedding to accept the supposed Lucentio if he can present his father to vouch for the agreement; if not, to accept Gremio. Tranio, therefore, begins to look for some one to impersonate Vincentio in order that his master may marry Bianca with her parent's consent.

Act III

The second pair of rivals for Bianca's hand, the "schoolmasters," are getting along no more peaceably. Under the pretext of a Latin lesson, however, the real Lucentio reveals his identity to Bianca and receives the admonition, "presume not, despair not," while Hortensio, pleading his cause over his lute, receives only discouragement. On the appointed day when Katherina and Petruchio are to be married, that "mad-cap" humiliates his lady by being very late for the ceremony. When he does appear, it is in disreputable apparel and on a sway-backed, broken-down horse. In the church he behaves like a very fury, making his responses with an oath, frightening the vicar, and at last kissing the bride with such "a clamorous smack that all the church did echo." As a climax he refuses to stay for the wedding feast, and in spite of Katherina's vigorous protests, carries her away to his country house.

Act IV

On the way home Petruchio manages to make the horses run away and to have Katherina fall into the mire and beats the servant so unmercifully because the horse stumbled that his wife wades through the mud to stay his arm. Once home, under the pretext that it is out of loving consideration for her, he curses the servants, throws out the food because it is badly cooked, scornfully rejects some fine dresses he has ordered for her, and keeps her awake all night by finding fault with the bed and flinging the covers about. As a result, poor Katherina is completely worn out and ready to do anything to keep her husband quiet. With the cure almost complete, the newlyweds return to

Padua, on the road meeting old Vincentio, Lucentio's father, on his way to visit his son. Meanwhile, in Padua, Tranio bullies an aged pedant into impersonating his master's parent so that the wooing of Bianca may thrive.

Act V

When the true Vincentio arrives, he is confronted by the imposters. Fearing for the life of his son, he is about to have them all arrested; the knaves try to turn the law upon him and throw him into jail. But the real Lucentio appears with Bianca, with whom he has eloped, and receives his father's blessing. Hortensio, having long ago lost heart, has meanwhile consoled himself with a widow, and at the triple-wedding feast, Petruchio demonstrates to the assembly that his Kate is the most gentle and obedient of the three brides, by having her lecture the ladies on the duty they owe their husbands.

The Merry Wives of Windsor

Dramatis Personæ

SIR JOHN FALSTAFF, an old lecher, "well nigh worn to pieces with age," who nevertheless fancies himself a lady-killer.

MASTER FORD,
MASTER PAGE, } gentlemen of Windsor.

MISTRESS FORD,
MISTRESS PAGE, } who prove that "wives may be merry and yet honest, too."

"SWEET ANNE PAGE," daughter of the Pages "with seven hundred pounds and possibilities."

FENTON, a gentleman who has kept company with wild Prince Hal; "he capers, he dances, he has the eyes of youth, he writes verses, he speaks holiday, he smells April and May," ("Have not your worship a wart above your eye?")

DR. CAIUS, a cantankerous French physician, usually "abusing God's patience and the King's English,"

SLENDER, "though well-landed, . . . an idiot," with a "little whey-face" and a little yellow beard, a "Cain-colored beard." ("Does he not hold up his head as it were, and strut in his gait?")

suitors of Anne Page.

MISTRESS QUICKLY, hostess to Dr. Caius, and professional go-between.

SHALLOW, "four score years and upward," a country justice, cousin of Slender.

SIR HUGH EVANS, a Welsh parson, who speaks "flannel" and "makes fritters of English."

ROBIN, roguish page to Falstaff.

BARDOLPH, "he in the red face,"

PISTOL, a braggart,

NYM, another "fellow frights English out of his wits,"

"coney-catching rascals," followers of Falstaff.

SIMPLE, servant to Slender.

RUGBY, servant to Dr. Caius.

MINE HOST of the Garter Inn.

WILLIAM PAGE, young son of the Pages.

Scene of the Action: Windsor and the parts adjacent.

Act I

Shallow, a country justice, and his cousin, Slender, are loud in their complaints against the wrongs done them by Sir John Falstaff and his coney-catching rascals, Bardolph, Nym, and Pistol, but Master Page invites them in to "drink down all unkindness." There Falstaff meets Mrs. Ford and Mrs. Page, who both have the rule of their husbands' purses, and imagining that they have both given him the leer of invitation, he sets about "translating them out of honesty into English." Accordingly, he hands Pistol and Nym duplicate love-letters to be delivered to the two ladies; but when these rogues righteously refuse to be his panders, he cashiers them and sends the letters by his little page, Robin. In revenge, Pistol and Nym resolve to inform the husbands. Meanwhile, Anne, the daughter of Mistress Page has three suitors. Slender, supported by his Uncle Shallow and Sir Hugh Evans, a Welsh parson, is the selection of Master Page; Dr. Caius, a French physician, has the support of Mistress Page; and Fenton, an honest gentleman and friend of Prince Hal, woos for himself. Each seeks the support of Mrs. Quickly, at whose house Dr. Caius is lodging, and, professing to "know Anne's mind," she finds it profitable to give no one undue encouragement. Dr. Caius, however, discovers that Sir Hugh Evans has sent a letter in Slender's behalf, and challenges the parson to a duel.

Act II

The merry wives compare Falstaff's letters to them and with a good laugh at how they might be "knighted," determine to be revenged upon him at all costs. Accordingly, with the aid of Hostess Quickly, an expert in the art, each sends the fat knight tokens of encouragement. Mistress Ford makes an appointment with him in her husband's absence, and Mistress Page requests that he send his little page. Meanwhile, the husbands have been warned by the cast-off rogues. Page has no jealous doubts of his wife, but Ford resolves to go to Falstaff disguised as Master Brook and sound him out. Pretending also to be in love with Mrs. Ford, Brook solicits Falstaff's aid as a go-between, and is assured that before night he shall know Ford for a knave and a cuckold.

Act III

In the meantime, Mine Host of the Garter has made fools of both Dr. Caius and Sir Hugh by sending them to different places to await the duel, but the cowards at length meet and are reconciled. When Falstaff arrives for his assignation, Mrs. Ford is just sorting the soiled linen to send it to wash, and the wooing is almost immediately interrupted by the hurried entry of Mrs. Page with word that Ford, with all the officers in Windsor, is on his way home. In his desire to escape, Falstaff, who has ensconced himself behind the arras at the coming of Mrs. Page, throws his pride to the winds, and with the aid of Robin, the women pile him into the buck-basket, cover him with foul linen, and send him to be dumped into a muddy ditch in Datchet-mead. Ford's jealousy, of course, is laughed to scorn. Bedraggled by his drenching, Falstaff is visited a second time by Dame Quickly, with profuse apologies for the accident and the promise of another tryst with Mrs. Ford. He also tells his friend Brook of his adventure, but bids him keep up hope.

Act IV

At the second rendezvous, Ford again surprises them, and though the buck-basket is again ready, Falstaff prefers to flee in a woman's dress, disguised as Mother Prat, the fat woman of Brainford, whom Ford detests. And although he escapes again, he is thoroughly beaten by the irate husband; and Ford's jealousy is again laughed at. The merry wives then tell their husbands of their sport with Falstaff, and all join in a scheme for his final humiliation by having him disguise as Herne the hunter and meet the ladies at night in Windsor Park. At the same time, each of the three persons concerned plans to bring the wooing of Anne Page to a successful conclusion by arranging an elopement.

Act V

In Windsor Park, Falstaff, wearing a buck's head, is met by the merry wives, who flee at a noise and leave the old fool to be ignominiously pinched and burned with tapers by Sir Hugh, disguised as a satyr, Pistol as a hobgoblin, Hostess Quickly as Queen of the Fairies, and boys "like urchins, ouphes, and fairies, green and white." During the sport, Dr. Caius steals away with a fairy in green, Slender takes another in white, and Fenton runs off with a third. Ford, Page, and their wives reveal themselves to Falstaff, and while their fun at his expense is at its height, it is revealed that Dr. Caius and Slender has each eloped with a great lubberly boy, and that Fenton has married Anne Page.

Much Ado About Nothing

Dramatis Personæ

Don Pedro, the genial Prince of Arragon.

Don John, his silent, saturnine, bastard brother.

Leonato, "the white-bearded fellow," Governor of Messina.

Claudio, "a proper squire" of Florence, "Monsieur Love," possessed of the "May of youth and bloom of lustihood."

Hero, "Leonato's short daughter," the somewhat colorless foil to Beatrice.

Benedick, a mirthful young lord of Padua, "of a noble strain, of approved valor, and confirmed honesty," but an unsentimental woman-hater; foil to Claudio. "He hath twice or thrice cut Cupid's bowstring, and the little hangman dare not shoot at him."

Beatrice, niece of Leonato, "a pleasant-spirited" "Lady Tongue," but one who on occasion "speaks poniards and every word stabs."

Borachio,
Conrade, } villainous followers of Don John.

Margaret,
Ursula, } gentlewomen attending Hero.

Dogberry, a pompous Jack-in-office, constable of Messina, "one that hath two gowns and everything handsome about him."

Verges, the headborough, "a good old man, sir; he will be talking."

Antonio, brother of Leonato.

Balthazar, a singing squire in Don Pedro's train.

Friar Francis, who suggests the plan for reestablishing Hero's wounded reputation.

Watchmen, Messengers, a Sexton, and Attendants.

Scene of the Action: Messina.

Act I

Don Pedro of Arragon returns to Messina to visit Leonato, the governor, after an almost bloodless victory over his base-born brother Don John, with whom he has been reconciled and by whom he is accompanied. In his train are two young lords, Benedick and Claudio, who have distinguished themselves in the campaign and who are already well acquainted at the court of Messina. Benedick and Beatrice, his "dear Lady Disdain," renew at once their "merry war" of saucy wit skirmishes and scornful repartee, while Claudio, having completed the rough tasks of war, looks with the eyes of love upon Hero, the mild cousin of Beatrice. Learning of Claudio's love, the genial Don Pedro offers to aid him by impersonating him at a masquerade and wooing for him. An eavesdropping servant mishears their plan and reports to Hero's uncle that the Prince rather than Claudio is in love with Hero, and another eavesdropper carries the correct news to Don John. Don John, as malicious as his brother is kindly, hates Claudio because the "young start-up hath all the glory of [his] overthrow," and sees in the intended marriage an opportunity for mischief and for evening scores with both the favorite and the Prince.

Act II

That evening at a masked ball Don John plants in Claudio's mind the suspicion that Don Pedro is wooing for himself (an idea further encouraged by a mistake of Benedick's), but this hasty suspicion is quickly dispelled when Don Pedro appears with Hero and Leonato, who, even if they expected a proposal from another, joyfully consent to Claudio's suit. Because arrangements for the wedding cannot be completed short of a week, Don Pedro proposes that they pass the interim by undertaking "one of Hercules' labors," that of making Benedick and Beatrice fall in love with each other. Accordingly, they set afoot a conspiracy of "honest slander" by letting Benedick overhear some plain truths about his "contemptible spirit," and many expressions of pity for poor Beatrice, who, they say is desperately in love with him, in spite of her contrary actions, but fearful of his scorn should she reveal her affections. At the same time Don John lays a plot of villainous slander to break up the match between Claudio and Hero by having both Don Pedro and his friend present at a secret meeting between Borachio and a waiting-maid, and making them suppose it an assignation between Hero and a lover.

Act III

Perceiving outward signs of their success with Benedick, the honest conspirators try a similar method upon Beatrice, and are soon rewarded by hearing that proud lady sigh. Meanwhile, Don

John's scheme has also succeeded in deceiving Claudio and Don Pedro. Some stupid night-watchmen, however, overhear Borachio drunkenly describe to his crony Conrade the success of Don John's villainy. The watchmen, instructed to "comprehend all vagrom men," bring them to their superiors, Dogberry and Verges, who, in turn, produce them before the Governor, just at the moment when he is hastening to his daughter's wedding. Dogberry's involved story tries the patience of Leonato, who hurries out, telling the constable to examine the prisoners himself.

Act IV

In the church Claudio and Don Pedro shame Hero before the whole congregation by telling what they had witnessed the night before at her window. The innocent Hero falls in a swoon, and the gentlemen turn on their heels and leave the church. Friar Francis, however, is certain that there has been some mistake and suggests that her father give out the report that Hero is indeed dead and await developments. Only Beatrice really trusts her cousin, and looking about helplessly for someone to right this wrong, she finds Benedick at her side. Under the stress of the moment, he declares his love for her, offering to do anything to prove it. Beatrice's command is, "Kill Claudio." In the meantime, Dogberry is pompously and fussily examining his prisoners for "as flat burglary as ever was committed." Were it not for a sexton who was present at Hero's shame, the truth might never have been known.

Act V

Old Leonato, repenting his lack of faith in his daughter, exchanges sharp words with Claudio and Don Pedro, even pathetically challenging the young warrior to a duel. In search of someone to cheer them up, the two gentlemen find Benedick, only to have him ignore their teasing about Beatrice and hiss a challenge into Claudio's ear. Dogberry and Verges appear with their prisoners, and a full confession of the villainy convinces Claudio and Don Pedro that what their wisdoms could not discover, these shallow fools had brought to light. Accordingly, in great grief, the young men beg of old Leonato forgiveness for their credulity, and he readily grants it on condition that Claudio make public demonstration of his belief in Hero's innocence by hanging an epitaph on her tomb and marrying his niece, who, he says, is almost a copy of the dead Hero. Meanwhile, Benedick, has reported his challenge to Beatrice, and though they revert to their wit-combats, the spirit is not the same. Next day, at church, Claudio is married to a masked bride and rejoices to find his lost Hero again. The conspiracy against Benedick and Beatrice almost comes to nothing, but when each is confronted by a "halting sonnet of his own pure brain" the couple take each other "out of pity," as they say, and in defiance of a "whole college of wit-crackers." As the play closes, word is brought that Don John has been captured and is being brought to Messina for punishment.

As You Like It

Dramatis Personæ

DUKE SENIOR, living in exile in the Forest of Arden.

FREDERICK, his younger brother and usurper of his dominions, "of rough and envious disposition."

ORLANDO, youngest son of Sir Roland de Boys, "never school'd, and yet learn'd; full of noble device; of all sorts enchantingly beloved."

OLIVER, his wicked elder brother.

ROSALIND, the beautiful witty daughter of the banished Duke. "There is a pretty redness in [her] lip, a little riper and more lusty red than that mix'd in [her] cheek."

CELIA, daughter of Duke Frederick, but the devoted friend of Rosalind.

TOUCHSTONE, a "motley-minded," "roynish" court jester, who directs his realistic professional wit against courtiers' oaths, the pastoral life, sentimental love, and the etiquette of duelling, and who "sometimes speaks wiser than he is ware of."

JAQUES, a cynical, sentimental malcontent, who "can suck melancholy out of a song as a weasel sucks eggs," and who "most invectively, . . . pierceth through the body of the country, city, court, yea, and this our life." Though attached to the banished Duke's court, he is no more at home in Arden than is Touchstone.

AMIENS, a singer attending the banished Duke.

LE BEAU, an affected courtier attending Duke Frederick.

CHARLES, the Duke's wrestling champion.

ADAM, "almost four-score," a faithful old servant and friend of Orlando.

DENNIS, a servant of Oliver.

CORIN, a pastoral philosopher,

SILVIUS, a love-sick shepherd,

PHEBE, a dainty, disdainful little shepherdess, beloved of Silvius,
} Arcadian rustics, natives of Arden.

AUDREY, an unpoetical, sluttish goat-girl, "a poor virgin, . . . an ill-favor'd thing," . . . but Touchstone's own, and the foil to Phebe,

WILLIAM, a country bumpkin, in love with Audrey,

SIR OLIVER MARTEXT, a hedge-priest; "a most wicked Sir Oliver, . . . a most vile martext,"
} realistic natives of Arden.

JAQUES DE BOYS, brother of Oliver and Orlando, who has been away to school and returns as messenger.

A person representing Hymen, god of marriage.

Attendants, Pages, Messengers, and Foresters.

Scene of the Action: Oliver's house, the Usurper's Court, and the Forest of Arden.

As You Like It

Act I

A French Duke has been deprived of his throne by his younger brother Frederick, and is now living like old Robin Hood of England in the Forest of Arden with many merry men about him. Similarly, another pair of brothers, the sons of Sir Roland de Boys, are at odds. Oliver, the elder, though charged with his younger brother's education, keeps him "rustically at home," and the younger, Orlando, begins to rebel against this unnatural treatment. Hearing that Orlando is planning to try his strength against Charles, the Duke's wrestling champion, Oliver incites Charles to foil his brother. Orlando, however, despite the fears of Celia and Rosalind, Frederick's daughter and niece, wins the match. When he learns that Orlando is the son of an old friend of the banished Duke's, Frederick snubs the lad instead of rewarding him; but Rosalind, having already conceived an interest in Orlando, presents the tongue-tied victor with a chain from her neck. Meanwhile, because of this reminder of his brother, Frederick grows more and more angry, and banishes Rosalind, the old Duke's daughter, whom he has tolerated at court as a companion for Celia. Celia, however, insists upon accompanying her cousin, and together they plan to seek the old Duke in Arden. For safety, Rosalind, the taller, disguises as a boy, and Touchstone, her uncle's jester, goes along as a companion.

Act II

In the meantime, Oliver's anger is so aroused against Orlando that he, too, must flee, accompanied by Adam, a faithful old servant. Worn out from travel, first the girls and then Orlando arrive in Arden. Rosalind and Celia purchase a flock of sheep and a pasture and adopt the life and garb of shepherds, under the names of Ganymede and Aliena. Orlando, who is destitute, rushes with drawn sword upon the followers of the banished Duke and demands food of them, but is welcomed to their table and invited to join the band of foresters, who spend their time in hunting and singing. So completely has the Duke Senior translated the stubbornness of fortune into a quiet and sweet existence, that all of his followers, except Jaques, a cynical melancholy railer, profess

71

they feel "no enemy but winter and rough weather." In addition to the make-believe shepherds and the make-believe foresters, Arden is inhabited by some Arcadian beings—Corin, a feeder of flocks, Silvius, a shepherd, and Phebe, a disdainful little shepherdess with whom Silvius is desperately in love.

Act III

Back at the court, in the belief that Orlando and the girls have run away together, Duke Frederick sends for Oliver and orders him to produce his younger brother on pain of losing his lands. Thus the fates of the two brothers are linked. In Arden, love turns Orlando into a versifier, and he hangs his compositions on the trees and carves the name of Rosalind on their bark. There his tokens are found by the disguised lady, who is impressed by them until Touchstone parodies them and offers to rhyme her so "eight years together, dinners and suppers and sleeping hours excepted." As Ganymede, she meets Orlando in the forest, twits him about disfiguring the trees, and protesting that he hardly looks like a lover being so point device in his attire offers to cure the love-sick swain if he will but woo her as if she were Rosalind. Amused by the saucy youth, but hardly wishing to be cured, Orlando agrees. Still in her rôle as a railer on love, Ganymede speaks sharply to Phebe about her indifference to Silvius, and so charms that little shepherdess by her chiding that on the pretext of writing a bitter rejoinder to her raillery Phebe sends a declaration of love by the unsuspecting Silvius. Meanwhile, Touchstone, who still wears his motley in the forest and allows his wit to play amusingly over all this Arcadian make-believe, is paying his court to Audrey, a sluttish country wench whom he has found in the forest.

Act IV

As they have agreed, Orlando carries on his wooing of Ganymede, who stands for his Rosalind, and who banters him saucily as long as he is present, but is overwhelmed with love for him when he is out of sight. On one occasion, while on his way to meet Ganymede, Orlando comes upon his brother Oliver asleep under

an oak with a "green and gilded snake" about his neck and a
hungry lioness crouching in the bushes waiting for him to stir.
Orlando saves his brother's life, but being wounded in the encounter, sends his converted brother to explain to Ganymede why
he is late for his tryst. When she sees a bloody handkerchief
Oliver has brought as proof, Ganymede faints.

Act V

One result of the reunion of the brothers is still another love
affair in the forest of Arden. Oliver and Celia have no sooner met
than they fall in love and plan matrimony. The wedding is to take
place the next day, and to Orlando's complaint that "it is a bitter
thing to look into happiness through another man's eyes," Ganymede promises to do wonders. By means of magic, she says that
she can produce Rosalind on the morrow. Meanwhile Phebe comes
to rebuke Ganymede for so ungraciously showing Silvius her love-
letter and to renew her ardent declaration by word of mouth, and
Ganymede promises on the morrow also to unravel to every one's
satisfaction the love-tangle in which the three find themselves, on
condition that Phebe marry the faithful Silvius should she change
her mind about marrying Ganymede. On the morrow, with the
banished Duke and his followers as guests, Rosalind appears in
feminine attire, and with great rejoicing a quadruple ceremony is
performed—Orlando is united to Rosalind, Oliver to Celia, Silvius
to Phebe, and Touchstone to Audrey. Moreover, the joy of the
occasion is immeasurably increased by word that the evil Duke
Frederick, on his way into Arden with an expedition to kill his
elder brother, has also been converted and "put on a religious
life," restoring all their lands to those who were in exile.

Twelfth Night: Or, What You Will

Dramatis Personæ

ORSINO, sentimental Duke of Illyria, "in dimension and the shape of nature a gracious person."

OLIVIA, his neighbor, a rich countess, "of beauty truly blent," . . . "a virtuous maid," . . . who "hath abjured the company and sight of men."

VIOLA, Orsino's "page" Cesario, who "never told her love, but let concealment, like a worm i' the bud, feed on her damask cheek."

SEBASTIAN, Viola's twin brother.

SIR TOBY BELCH, Olivia's riotous uncle, harbored at her house.

MARIA, Olivia's gentlewoman, a lively-witted little "wren," a "beagle, true-bred."

SIR ANDREW AGUECHEEK, a foolish knight upon whom Sir Toby is sponging, "dubb'd with unhatch'd rapier and on carpet consideration."

MALVOLIO, Olivia's ambitious steward, "sick of self-love; . . . a timepleaser; an affectioned ass."

FABIAN, a servant of Olivia.

FESTE, Olivia's "allowed fool," who has "an excellent breast" to sing.

ANTONIO, a sea captain, friend of Sebastian.

ANOTHER SEA CAPTAIN, friend of Viola.

VALENTINE,
CURIO, } gentlemen attending Orsino.

Lords, a Priest, Officers, Sailors, Musicians, and Attendants.

Scene of Action: A city in Illyria, and the sea-coast near it.

Act I

Orsino, Duke of Illyria, is ecstatically stimulating his own sentimentalism by playing the rôle of languishing lover and courting the rich Countess Olivia by deputy. To present his suit, he sends to her Cesario, a favorite page who has just come into his employ; but he does not know that the page is really Viola, a shipwrecked gentlewoman in disguise, who has fallen in love with him. Olivia is like the Duke in being a sentimentalist; she is indulging in a season of grief and mourning for a dead brother and is refusing to entertain the advances of any man. Although she admires her royal suitor, she cannot love him. Her sorrow over the loss of her brother is not so profound, however, as to keep her from falling passionately in love with the Duke's envoy, the disguised Viola, and from determining to see more of the youth. Of Olivia's household only her steward, the melancholy Malvolio, finds a morbid pleasure in the atmosphere of mourning which she has decreed. Her irresponsible uncle, Sir Toby Belch, a riotous gentleman who sponges on her, does not believe in excessive grief; he employs his time chiefly in drinking with Olivia's clown Feste and with his dupe, Sir Andrew Aguecheek, a wealthy but foolish and faint-hearted knight, who keeps Sir Toby in funds while the latter pretends to advance his courtship of the Countess.

Act II

Sebastian, Viola's twin brother, whom she supposes to have been drowned in the shipwreck, arrives in Illyria with a sea captain, Antonio. Olivia sends a ring to Cesario by the peevish and haughty Malvolio. This conceited fellow has been so arrogant toward Sir Toby and Olivia's servants that her chamberwoman, Maria, plots with Sir Toby to get him into trouble with the Countess. This they succeed in doing by placing where he will find it a forged letter which seems to be in Olivia's handwriting and in which she professes love for someone, begging that lover, if he responds, to "be opposite with a kinsman, surly with servants," to wear yellow stockings cross-gartered, and to smile perpetually in her presence. Meanwhile, Orsino once more sends his messenger to the Lady Olivia.

Act III

When Cesario returns to Olivia, the Countess can no longer conceal her passion but makes love to him openly. Fearing that Sir Andrew will leave Illyria in disgust, Sir Toby prods the cowardly knight into challenging the supposed page to a duel. In another part of the city, Antonio parts from Sebastian after having lent his purse to the youth. The revenge plot against Malvolio comes to a successful climax; his unaccountable antics lead Olivia to think him mad, and Sir Toby and Maria have little difficulty in having him committed to a dark room. With Malvolio disposed of, Sir Toby presses the fearful Sir Andrew and Cesario into a duel, but as they draw unwilling swords against each other, Antonio rushes in to rescue—as he supposes—his friend Sebastian. Recognizing the sea captain as an old enemy of the state, officers arrest him, and to his astonishment his appeal to the supposed Sebastian for money is met with a denial from Cesario that he ever saw him.

Act IV

Seeing Cesario so timid, Sir Andrew rushes after him to complete the duel but encounters Viola's twin brother Sebastian, who draws sword readily and wounds the astonished knight and also Sir Toby, who has come to the rescue. Olivia interferes and, mistaking Sebastian for Cesario, leads him into her house, sends for a priest, and marries the astonished young man. At Maria's suggestion the clown completes the plot against Malvolio by going to the dark room in the guise of the curate and badgering the steward unmercifully.

Act V

The Duke Orsino with the disguised Viola and other attendants appears before Olivia's house just as the Duke's officers enter with Antonio. Orsino supports Cesario's claim that he does not have the sea captain's purse, but turns upon him savagely when the Countess addresses the supposed youth as her husband and calls the priest to testify to the marriage. There is still more confusion when Sir Toby and Sir Andrew enter bleeding and accuse Cesario of having wounded them. The appearance of the twin brother astounds all, but clears up the mystery; and the Duke gladly yields the Countess to the newcomer when he learns that his "boy" is a lovely maiden who will marry him. Sir Toby weds Maria for her wit, and only Malvolio, released from his captivity, seems characteristically dissatisfied with the happiness of the others.

All's Well That Ends Well

Dramatis Personæ

COUNTESS OF ROUSILLON, mother of Bertram.

BERTRAM, Count of Rousillon, a youth of great charm and promise.

HELENA, "his sweet disaster," "the most virtuous gentlewoman that ever Nature had praise for creating," daughter of a famous physician, and ward of the Countess of Rousillon.

AN OLD WIDOW OF FLORENCE.

DIANA, her daughter, wooed by the Count of Rousillon.

VIOLENTA, }
MARIANA, } neighbors and friends of the widow.

THE KING OF FRANCE.

THE DUKE OF FLORENCE.

LAFEU, an old lord, friend of the Countess.

PAROLLES, "a snipt-taffeta fellow," "a red tail'd bumble-bee," "a damnable both-sides rogue," follower of Bertram. "The soul of this man is his clothes."

TWO FRENCH LORDS, serving with Bertram in the Florentine war.

STEWARD, }
LAVACHE, a clown, } Servants of the Countess of Rousillon.
A PAGE, }

Lords, Officers, and Soldiers.

Scene of the Action: Rousillon, Paris, Florence, and Marseilles.

Act I

Bertram, the young Count of Rousillon, accompanied by his worthless companion, Parolles, leaves his home for service at the court of France. Behind him he leaves his mother and her ward, the beautiful and accomplished Helena, daughter of a famous physician, Gerard de Narbon. While living in the Countess' household, Helena has fallen in love with Bertram, but believing that their difference in rank made her affection hopeless, she has disclosed her love to no one. As soon as Bertram is away, however, the girl's melancholy reveals her secret to the Countess, who overcomes her fears, treats her as a daughter, and tenderly encourages her love. She even encourages her plan of following Bertram to

Paris and of attempting the cure of the King, who has been pro-
nounced incurable of a fistula which Helena is certain can be healed
by a rare prescription bequeathed her by her father.

Act II

Arriving at court Helena persuades the King to try her
remedy, offering her life as a pledge for its efficacy and requesting
that if she is successful, she be permitted to choose a husband from
among the bachelors of his court. Within two days the King is
completely well, and, confirming his promise, permits his physician
to select her husband as her fee. Naturally, Helena chooses Bertram, but the young Count ungraciously reminds his sovereign
of her low rank and refuses. Although Helena offers to withdraw
her request, the King insists upon the marriage, and Bertram is
obliged to submit. Immediately after, however, he pretends that
urgent business calls him away, orders his unkissed wife to return
to his mother, bearing a letter, and with Parolles, hurries off to
the wars under the Duke of Florence.

Act III

Once home, Helena too receives a letter which confirms the
news contained in that to the Countess: "When thou canst get the
ring upon my finger which shall never come off, and show me a
child begotten of thy body that I am father to, then call me
husband; but in such a 'then,' I write a 'never.' Till I have no
wife, I have nothing in France." Longing for death, and especially
grieved that because of her, Bertram has left his native land, she
steals out of the house at night on a pilgrimage to St. Jaques le
Grand and sometime later permits word to reach the Countess that
she is dead. Meanwhile, Bertram has distinguished himself in the
wars, and is returning to Florence with his troops just as Helena,
dressed as a pilgrim, arrives in the city. From a widow with
whom she secures lodging, Helena learns that Bertram has been
trying to seduce her daughter Diana. Perceiving an opportunity
of fulfilling Bertram's conditions, Helena tells the woman who
she is, and promises the daughter a handsome dowry if she will

get the Count's ring and arrange a midnight assignation with him in which, unknown to Bertram, she may take the girl's place.

Act IV

Helena's plan succeeds admirably. Not only does Diana obtain the ring from her ardent lover, but she also extracts from Bertram a lightly given promise that when his wife is dead, he will marry her. Helena takes the girl's place at night and puts on Bertram's finger a ring which the King of France had given her. Soon afterwards Bertram receives a letter from his mother informing him that his wife is dead and urging him not to continue the King's displeasure any longer by his absence. Accordingly, he returns home, but not before he has learned what a liar and a coward his crony Parolles really is.

Act V

The King visits Rousillon, and the aged Countess, still mourning her daughter-in-law, begs the King to restore her son to favor. The King is about to bestow upon him the hand of the daughter of Lafeu, an old lord and friend of the Countess, when he spies on Bertram's finger the ring he had given Helena and accuses him of being implicated in Helena's death. While the Count is trying to explain, with no more truth than necessary, how he obtained it, Diana and her mother appear to demand that Bertram keep his promise of marrying her. Diana so exasperates the King, however, by answering his questions in riddles, that he orders her to prison, when the widow reappears leading Helena, who explains that both of the conditions imposed upon her by Bertram are fulfilled. Struck by his wife's devotion, and being thus doubly won, Bertram declares his willingness to "love her ever, ever dearly."

Measure for Measure

Dramatis Personæ

VINCENTIO, kindly, philosophical Duke of Vienna, a "gentleman of all temperance," who has been too easy in his enforcement of the laws, yet, "let him be but testimonied in his own bringings-forth, and he shall appear [even] to the envious a scholar, a statesman, and a soldier." He "love[s] the people, but do[es] not like to stage [him] to their eyes" and does "not relish well their loud applause and Aves vehement."

ANGELO, the "outward-sainted" Lord Deputy in the Duke's absence and the foil of Vincentio, "a man of stricture and firm abstinence," "whose blood is very snow-broth . . . one who never feels the wanton stings and motions of the sense . . . but doth rebate and blunt his natural edge with profits of the mind, study, and fast." "A due sincerity governed his deeds till he did look on" Isabella.

ISABELLA, a sister of Claudio about to enter a nunnery, the saint with which the cunning enemy baited the hook for Angelo.

MARIANA, of "the moated grange," the pathetic, jilted fiancée of Angelo, cast off when her dowry was lost.

CLAUDIO, a young Viennese gentleman, made an example by Angelo for a venial offence.

JULIET, betrothed of Claudio, one "who, falling in the flaws of her own youth, hath blister'd her report."

ESCALUS, a wise old counsellor, joined with Angelo in the deputation.

VARRIUS, a gentleman attending the Duke.

THE PROVOST OF THE PRISON.

ELBOW, an ignorant, blundering constable.

MISTRESS OVERDONE, "a bawd of eleven years' continuance" and of nine husbands, —"Overdone by the last."

POMPEY, her servant, "a tapster, sir, parcel bawd; one that serves a bad woman." "Truly, sir, . . . a poor fellow that would live."

LUCIO, a graceless, slanderous, talkative "fellow of much license."

FROTH, a foolish man-about-town.

THOMAS, }
PETER, } friars.

FRANCISCA, a nun.

ABHORSON, an executioner.

BARNARDINE, a dissolute, stubborn prisoner.

Lords, Gentlemen, a Justice, Guards, Officers, and Attendants.

Scene of the Action: Vienna.

MEASURE FOR MEASURE

Act I

Because of lax law enforcement "liberty plucks justice by the nose" in Vienna, and the too kindly Duke, Vincentio, determines to retire from the city for a time and to leave the cares of state in the hands of Angelo, a man of "unsoil'd name" and austere life, and of Escalus, a wise counsellor, so that certain moral reforms may be introduced. The Deputy's first act is to revive an old statute which imposes a death penalty for fornication, and the first victim of whom he makes an example is Claudio, a young noble, who "upon a true contract" has got his beloved, Juliet, with child. The severity of the new executive arouses much comment among the lechers and bawds of Vienna, for Claudio and Juliet are sincerely in love and would have been married but for some formal difficulties about dowry. As he is paraded in disgrace through the streets on his way to prison, Claudio begs his friend Lucio to go to his sister, Isabella, who that day is entering a convent, and enlist her aid in obtaining from the new governor a pardon for his offence. Meanwhile, instead of visiting Poland as he had announced, the Duke disguises himself as Friar Lodowick in order that he may observe the rule of his deputies.

Act II

Both Escalus and a Justice intercede with Angelo for Claudio's life, but to no avail; and when Isabella, whose purity is emphasized by the corruption of the city in which she lives, appears before the Deputy, she, too, at first pleads in vain. The beautiful novice, however, arouses in the breast of Angelo a passion which hitherto had always seemed foreign to his austere nature, and in a second interview, he plainly intimates to her that she may purchase her brother's life with her own honor. Isabella, of course, refuses, and in despair, she helplessly determines to tell her brother the shameful price proposed for his freedom and to prepare him for his fate, saying: "More than our brother is our chastity." Meanwhile, Friar Lodowick, posing as a confessor, has visited Claudio's prison, met Juliet, and learned from the unhappy lady the story of their true love.

81

Act III

In hiding, the disguised friar overhears the interview between the erring brother and his sister. At first Claudio commends Isabella for her virtuous decision, but, overwhelmed by the thought that "death is a fearful thing," he pleads pitifully with her that she commit what is, after all, a venial sin to save him. As she scornfully reproaches him for the suggestion, Friar Lodowick interrupts the interview, and drawing the novice apart, shows her a way of saving her brother without sacrificing herself. Five years before, he reveals, Angelo and a noble lady, Mariana, had entered into a solemn betrothal, which, like that of Claudio and Juliet, had virtually amounted to marriage, but before the formalities could be solemnized, Mariana's brother Frederick had been lost at sea with the girl's dowry, and Angelo had cruelly refused to go through with the wedding. The friar's proposal is that Isabella pretend to yield to Angelo and make a midnight assignation with him, then substitute in her place the wronged Mariana, and so right the twofold offence which Angelo had committed to the jilted girl and to Claudio.

Act IV

Mariana readily consents to the plan, and with the aid of the friar and Isabella it is carried out successfully. Angelo, however, does not keep his part of the agreement. As soon as he has had his will with the supposed Isabella, fearing that his villainy will be disclosed, he orders the head of Claudio sent to him immediately. Persuaded by Friar Lodowick, the Provost of the prison keeps Claudio in hiding and substitutes for his head the head of another prisoner who has just died a natural death. The friar, however, allows Isabella to believe that her brother is dead, counsels her to seek justice from the Duke, and sends letters to the Deputy announcing his immediate return to Vienna.

Act V

On the morrow, Angelo, accompanied by Escalus and the other officials, meets the Duke at the city gates, where Isabella openly accuses Angelo as a murderer, a hypocrite, and a virgin-violator, and demands redress of her wrongs. With mock anger, the Duke refuses to believe her, orders her arrest, and leaves Angelo to conduct her trial and to satisfy the claims of Mariana, who also demands recognition as the Deputy's wife. In a little while, he returns in his disguise as Friar Lodowick to act as witness for the two ladies. Attacked as a false witness, the friar loses his cowl, and the truth is revealed. Angelo is ordered to wed Mariana, and after the ceremony has been performed, the Duke proceeds to the just demands of "an Angelo for Claudio, death for death." Mercy, however, tempers Justice. The severe penalty against the Deputy is revoked by the pleading of both Mariana and Isabella, Claudio is produced and married to Juliet, and the Duke himself sues for the hand of Isabella.

Pericles, Prince of Tyre

Dramatis Personæ

GOWER, Chorus and Presenter of the Drama; an English poet of the Middle Ages who had told this tale before Shakespeare.

ANTIOCHUS, wicked, incestuous King of Antioch.

HIS DAUGHTER, "so buxom, blithe, and full of face."

PERICLES, Prince of Tyre, "a better prince and benign lord."

THAISA, "a most virtuous princess," fair daughter of Simonides, King of Pentapolis, and wife of Pericles.

MARINA, "a piece of virtue," beautiful daughter of Pericles and Thaisa.

LYCHORIDA, nurse of Marina.

HELICANES, "a figure of truth, of faith, of loyalty," a lord of Tyre.

ESCANES, another lord of Tyre.

CLEON, Governor of Tarsus.

DIONYZA, his evil wife.

SIMONIDES, King of Pentapolis, father of Thaisa.

LYSIMACHUS, Governor of Mytilene.

CERIMON, a skillful physician of Ephesus.

DIANA, goddess of the Ephesians.

THALIARD, gentleman of the chamber to Antiochus and a murderer in his employ.

PHILEMON, servant of Cerimon.

LEONINE, murderous servant of Dionyza.

A PANDER.

BOULT, his servant.

A BAWD.

A MARSHALL.

Lords, Ladies, Knights, Pirates, Sailors, Fishermen, and Messengers.

Scene of the Action: Antioch, Tyre, Tarsus, Pentapolis, Ephesus, and Mytilene.

Act I

Gower, serving as chorus and presenter of the drama, first reveals Pericles, Prince of Tyre, in Antioch, searching for adventure, as a suitor for the hand of the beautiful daughter of King Antiochus. Those who aspire to her under penalty of death, must solve a riddle in which the King has concealed the horrible secret of their incest, and guessing the meaning, Pericles contrives an answer that only the King and his daughter understand. Fearing for his life if he remains, Pericles returns home, but still fearful that Antiochus' wrath will follow him, he leaves his kingdom in the hands of the faithful Helicanus, and embarks on a voyage to Tarsus, just before Thaliard, an assassin from Antioch, arrives to kill him. The people of Tarsus are suffering from famine, and when Pericles brings them a shipload of provisions, he is welcomed and invited to tarry there until his luck shall change.

Act II

In the meantime, as Gower explains, word from Tyre warns Pericles that he is not safe in Tarsus; and when he next appears, he has been cast destitute upon the coast of Pentapolis, the only survivor of a shipwreck. Almost in despair, he is heartened by the recovery of his suit of armor, which some fishermen draw up in their nets. Again equipped as a knight, he enters a tournament celebrating the birthday of Thaisa, beautiful daughter of King Simonides, and so distinguishes himself by his chivalric accomplishments, that Thaisa falls in love with him, and Simonides shows him marked favor. When Thaisa announces that she will wed no one else, her father approves, and the marriage with Pericles is arranged.

Act III

Meanwhile Gower explains that news from Tyre reports that Antiochus and his daughter are dead, that the nobles, believing that Pericles has perished, wish to make Helicanus king, and that as a result, Pericles has at last revealed his full identity to his wife and father-in-law, and set out with Thaisa for Tyre. When he next appears, therefore, Pericles is on shipboard. During a terrific storm, a nurse reports that Thaisa has died giving birth to a daughter, and to satisfy the superstitions of the sailors, Pericles agrees to her burial at sea. The chest in which her body has been placed, however, is washed ashore at Ephesus, where she is revived by Cerimon, a skillful physician, who to assuage her grief, helps her to become a priestess of Diana. Pericles, meanwhile, fearing for his little daughter, has bent his course for Tarsus, where he leaves the infant, whom he names Marina, in the care of his friends Cleon and Dionyza.

Act IV

Gower again serves as a bridge over the years. Pericles has returned to Tyre; his woeful Queen, thinking him lost, remains in Ephesus, and Marina, their little daughter, has grown so beautiful and gifted that she has become a general wonder. Unfortunately, Marina's accomplishments have aroused the jealousy of Dionyza because her own daughter Philoten is completely eclipsed, and Dionyza bribes a villain to murder her. The girl, however, is saved by pirates, who take her to Mytilene and sell her to the keeper of a brothel. Even in these sordid surroundings, Marina not only preserves her innocence, but actually reforms those who frequent the resort, including Lysimachus, Governor of Mytilene. As a result, the keeper gladly permits her to take up an honest calling. Meanwhile, Pericles has gone to Tarsus to fetch his daughter home and is bowed down with grief at the false report of her death.

Act V

Returning to Tyre, Pericles' ship is driven to Mytilene, where Marina has now become famous as an embroiderer, a singer, and a dancer. In the hope that she can ease his guest's sorrow, Lysimachus has Marina perform before him. Reminded of his dead wife, Pericles speaks with the girl, and is overjoyed to find that she is his lost daughter. As he falls asleep to supernatural music, he sees the goddess Diana in a vision and is commanded to make a sacrifice at her temple in Ephesus. There he tells his story to a priestess and rejoices to recognize in her his lost wife. Marina and Lysimachus are married and made rulers of Tyre, while Pericles and Thaisa return to rule in Pentapolis, word having come of the death of Simonides. Gower speaks the epilogue, and summarizes for his hearers the wonders they have seen:

> "In Antiochus and his daughter you have heard
> Of monstrous lust the due and just reward.
> In Pericles, his queen and daughter seen . . .
> Virtue preserved from full destruction's blast,
> Led on by heaven, and crown'd with joy at last."

Cymbeline

Dramatis Personæ

IMOGEN, daughter of Cymbeline, King of Britain, and the tender, constant wife of Posthumus, "more goddess-like than wife-like," and "a lady so tender of rebukes that words are strokes and strokes death to her."

POSTHUMUS LEONATUS, husband of Imogen, a "poor but worthy gentleman," brought up at court where he is "a sample to the youngest, to the more mature a glass that feated them." "A nobler sir ne'er lived 'twixt sky and ground."

CLOTEN, son of Cymbeline's queen by a former marriage, an arrogant fool "too bad for bad report," whose love-suit to Imogen has been "as fearful as a siege." Foil to Posthumus and "too base to be his groom."

IACHIMO, "yellow Iachimo," a "slight thing of Italy," and a crafty villain.

CYMBELINE, King of Britain, dominated by his wicked wife.

QUEEN OF CYMBELINE, "a crafty devil," "hourly coining plots," and a "woman that bears all down with her brain."

BELARIUS, a banished British nobleman disguised under the name of Morgan.

GUIDERIUS, ARVIRAGUS, sons of Cymbeline, kidnapped by Belarius and reared as his sons under the names of Polydore and Cadwal: "as gentle as zephyrs blowing below the violet . . . and yet as rough, their royal blood enchaf'd, as the rud'st wind, . . . 'tis wonder that an invisible instinct should frame them to royalty unlearn'd, honor untaught, civility not seen from other valor that wildly grows in them, but yields a crop as if it had been sow'd."

PHILARIO, an Italian friend of Posthumus.

CAIUS LUCIUS, ambassador and general of the Roman forces.

PISANIO, faithful servant of Posthumus.

CORNELIUS, an honest physician.

HELEN, maid to Imogen.

A SOOTHSAYER.

Lords, Ladies, Senators, Tribunes, Musicians, Officers, Soldiers, Jailers, Messengers, Attendants, Jupiter, and Apparitions.

Scene of the Action: Britain and Rome.

Act I

Angered because his only daughter, Imogen, has secretly married Posthumus, "a poor but worthy gentleman" who has been brought up with her at court, instead of Cloten, his step-son, Cymbeline, King of Britain, cruelly banishes the bridegroom.

87

Posthumus takes a sorrowful leave of his wife and exchanges gifts with her at parting, giving Imogen a bracelet of unique design, and receiving in turn a handsome diamond ring which he promises to wear for her sake. In Rome, at the house of Philario, the noble Posthumus meets the crafty Iachimo, who scoffs at all feminine virtue, and soon involves the banished husband in a wager of ten thousand ducats against his diamond that his British wife is more fair, virtuous, constant, and less attemptable than any other lady whatever. With a letter of introduction from the husband, Iachimo hastens to Britain to make a test of Imogen's virtue. Soon perceiving that the Princess can never be won by fair means, Iachimo resorts to trickery. First, he describes Posthumus as a loose reveller in Rome and offers himself to Imogen as a means of avenging herself upon her husband. The lady, however, refuses to believe his lies and repulses his advances with scorn. Then he tries to make amends by pretending to have used slander merely as a test to determine whether Imogen is as true to her husband as Posthumus is to her. The Princess accepts his apologies, and also agrees to keep safely over night in her chamber a chest which Iachimo professes is filled with treasure entrusted to his care. Meanwhile, the malicious step-mother of Imogen has been experimenting with drugs and has engaged her physician, Cornelius, to supply her with a deadly poison. The box containing it she gives to Pisanio, Posthumus' trusted messenger, whom she wishes out of the way, telling him it contains a sovereign restorative. Cornelius, however, has distrusted the Queen and prepared, not a poison, but a drug which but stupefies and dulls the senses for a time.

Act II

Having hidden himself in the chest which has been carried to Imogen's room, Iachimo creeps out after she is asleep, makes detailed notes of the decorations of her bedchamber and of her person, and steals from her arm the bracelet which Posthumus had given her as a parting gift. With these "proofs" he hastens back to Italy and easily convinces Posthumus of his wife's infidelity. Meanwhile, at the British court, the foolish Cloten continues to force his attentions upon Imogen, who at last expresses her utter contempt for him by saying that the meanest garment that ever Posthumus wore is more dear to her than Cloten.

Act III

Soon after, Lucius, the Roman ambassador, comes to Britain to demand the tribute which is justly due to Augustus. Dominated by Cloten and the wicked Queen, Cymbeline is defiant, and Lucius declares war. About the same time, Posthumus in despair sends a letter to Pisanio ordering him to kill Imogen because of her adultery, and, to provide him with an opportunity, another letter to his wife with false news that he is at Milford Haven and wishes her to join him. Pisanio, however, is convinced that Posthumus is the victim of some villain, helps Imogen to escape from the court, and persuades her to disguise as a page and seek service in the train of Lucius so that she can go to Rome and observe her husband. As a parting gift he presents her with the Queen's "sovereign restorative." Lost in the Welsh hills, Imogen at last finds refuge in a cave which is the home of Belarius, a banished British nobleman who twenty years before has kidnapped the two infant sons of Cymbeline. These young men, Guiderius and Arviragus, feel an unaccountable affection for the lonely little page, Fidele (who is really their sister) and invite him to live with them. At the court, when Imogen's absence is discovered, the faithful Pisanio sends Cloten upon a false pursuit by showing him Posthumus' letter bidding Imogen meet him at Milford Haven. Recalling Imogen's taunt, he secures some of Posthumus' clothes and sets out to pursue the runaway, intending to ravish her and kill her husband.

Act IV

While seeking the fugitive couple, Cloten encounters Belarius, who recognizes him and fears an ambush. He and Arviragus reconnoitre, but Guiderius, insulted by Cloten, fights with him, and cuts off his head. In consternation at possible revenge for this deed, Belarius hides the princes in their cave. Meanwhile, sick at heart, Imogen has taken some of the Queen's restorative, and the brothers are horrified to find the page apparently dead. Sadly they carry the body to the forest, place it beside the headless trunk of Cloten, and cover both with fresh flowers. When Imogen awakes from the effects of her drug, she recognizes the garments which had belonged to her husband, and falls into a faint. As she recovers, the Roman Lucius passes with his attendants, and accepts the masterless page as a servant. Meanwhile, from Gaul, a Roman army under the command of Iachimo is making ready to invade Britain, the wicked Queen has gone mad over the disappearance of her son, and the two mountain princes chafe at the caution of Belarius and wish to join in the defense of their country.

Act V

Having returned to Britain with the Roman armies, the remorseful Posthumus disguises as a British peasant and seeks death fighting against the invaders. Together with Belarius and the two princes, he performs such valiant deeds in battle that the British soldiers believe the unknown warriors angels. Cheated of death in battle, Posthumus seeks it by professing to be a Roman. In prison, however, he has a vision in which he hears a riddling prophecy that his miseries shall end when "a lion's whelp shall . . . be embraced by a piece of tender air, and when from a stately cedar shall be lopp'd branches, which, being dead many years, shall after revive, be jointed to the old stock and freshly grow." Meanwhile, the wicked Queen dies confessing her misdeeds, and Iachimo, Lucius, and the page, Fidele, are all captured and brought to Cymbeline's tent. At Lucius' request, Fidele is pardoned by the King and, granted a boon, disappoints his master by begging, not the life of Lucius but an explanation from Iachimo as to how he obtained the diamond he wears on his finger. Iachimo, thereupon, makes a remorseful confession, Posthumus reveals himself, and in a paroxysm of grief and revenge, strikes the little page who tries to comfort him. Pisanio, then, discloses the truth, Belarius confesses that his supposed sons are really the

King's heirs and a soothsayer interprets the prophecy: Posthumus *Leo-natus* is the lion's whelp; the "piece of tender air" (*mollis aer*) is *mulier,* the King's daughter; Cymbeline is the stately cedar; and his sons, the lopped branches. Husband and wife, father and sons, sister and brothers, are thus reunited. Finally, though victorious in battle, the King joyfully makes peace with Rome, acknowledges his submission to Caesar, releases all his prisoners, and gives orders that "a Roman and a British ensign wave friendly together."

The Winter's Tale

Dramatis Personæ

LEONTES, King of Sicilia, boyhood friend of Polixenes.

HERMIONE, his good Queen, "a precious creature," patient in adversity.

POLIXENES, King of Bohemia and guest at the court of Sicilia.

CAMILLO, an honest, trusted counsellor of Leontes, and cup-bearer of Polixenes.

PAULINA, an honest, outspoken lady of the court, attendant on Hermione, and female counterpart of Camillo.

ANTIGONUS, husband of Paulina.

MAMILLIUS, "a gallant child," son of Leontes and Hermione.

CLEOMENES, } Sicilian lords, messengers to the oracle of Delphi.
DION,

EMILIA and other ladies attending the Queen.

ARCHIDAMUS, a Bohemian lord.

TIME, as Chorus.

FLORIZEL, Prince of Bohemia, son of Polixenes.

PERDITA, lost daughter of Leontes and Hermione, brought up as a shepherdess, "the queen of curds and cream."

OLD SHEPHERD, foster-father of Perdita.

CLOWN, his son.

MOPSA, } realistic shepherdesses, contrasts to Perdita.
DORCAS,

AUTOLYCUS, a ballad-monger and "snapper-up of unconsidered trifles," who, "having flown over many knavish professioi., . . . settled only on rogue."

Lords, Ladies, Attendants, Jailers, Officers of the Court of Justice, Satyrs for a dance, Shepherds, Shepherdesses, Guards, etc.

Scene of the Action: Sicilia and Bohemia

Act I

Leontes, King of Sicilia, has been entertaining his boyhood friend, Polixenes, King of Bohemia, at his court, and being unable to persuade him to remain longer, begs his wife, Hermione, to see what she can do. When she succeeds, Leontes quite unreasonably misconstrues their innocent courtesy to one another as a guilty intimacy. His jealousy immediately becomes an obsession, and he orders Camillo, his faithful counsellor and Polixenes' cup-bearer, to poison his friend. Instead, Camillo, knowing that Polixenes and the Queen are guiltless, warns him of the King's insane jealousy, and escapes with him by night to Bohemia.

Act II

Believing his suspicions confirmed by the flight of Polixenes and Camillo, Leontes wreaks his anger upon Hermione alone. Publicly, he proclaims her an adulteress, deprives her of her young son, and throws her into prison in spite of the fact that she is about to become a mother. Throughout, Hermione bears her adversity with patient dignity, but her avowals of innocence and the protests of the court are of no avail. Convinced himself of her guilt, Leontes nevertheless sends messengers to the oracle at Delphi so that the minds of others may be set at rest. When a daughter is born to the Queen, her waiting-woman, Paulina, hoping that the sight of the innocent babe will soften the King's heart, takes the Princess to him. He violently disowns the child, and when Paulina tells him plainly what a jealous tyrant he is, he seeks first for some one to kill the infant, and then orders Antigonus, the husband of Paulina, to take it to some desert place and abandon it.

Act III

Brought to public trial, Hermione with quiet dignity declares her fidelity to her husband and the honesty of both Polixenes and Camillo, and appeals for judgment to the oracle of Apollo. Leontes' ambassadors return with the sealed oracle: "Hermione is chaste; Polixenes blameless; Camillo a true subject; Leontes a jealous tyrant; his innocent babe truly begotten; and the King shall live without an heir, if that which is lost be not found." Still unconvinced, Leontes orders the sessions to proceed, and is brought to his senses only by news that his only son Mamillius has died of grief for his mother's sufferings, and by the deathlike swoon of his Queen. Hermione is carried out and soon reported dead, while Leontes bitterly repents his blindness and goes into mourning. Meanwhile, Antigonus, instructed in a vision to name the babe Perdita, leaves her on the desolate coast of Bohemia, where she is found by a shepherd. Immediately after, he is devoured by a bear, and the ship which brought him is wrecked, and hence no news of the fate of the little Princess reaches Sicilia. Thus, his groundless obsession has cost the King his friend, his counsellor, an honest courtier, his daughter, his son, and his wife.

Act IV

Sixteen years elapse, and Florizel, Prince of Bohemia, is spending much of his time at the cottage of a shepherd who has a beautiful daughter. To verify the rumors about the Prince, Polixenes and old Camillo in disguise attend a sheep-shearing and are deeply impressed by the charm of Perdita, the "prettiest low-born lass that ever ran on the green-sward," and indeed "the queen of curds and cream." There, too, Autolycus, a merry rogue, is peddling all sorts of holiday trumpery, including ballads, and there is much Arcadian merry-making. When Florizel is about to enter into a formal betrothal with the shepherdess, however, the King reveals himself, and threatens all implicated with dire punishments. Perdita, who has always known that no happiness could come of being in love with a prince, meets her trial heroically, but Florizel really loves her and determines to elope with her. Their ally is the faithful old Camillo, who offers to help them escape to Sicilia and sees in this escapade a possibility of visiting his old home again. Meanwhile, to save himself from the King's wrath, the old shepherd determines to tell Polixenes that Perdita is not his own child, but a foundling, and to show him the garments and jewels that were found with her. On the way to the palace he meets Autolycus, who is also conniving with the Prince, and with his son is taken aboard the ship which bears the lovers to Sicilia.

Act V

Pretending to come with greetings from Bohemia, Florizel and Perdita are welcomed to Leontes' court, but are immediately followed thither by Polixenes and Camillo. The old friends are reconciled, Camillo is welcomed back by his old master, and the shepherd's evidence establishes beyond doubt the identity of Perdita as Leontes' lost daughter. Only the remembrance of his dead wife mars Leontes' joy that the old wound caused by his jealousy is now to be healed by the betrothal of the son of his friend and his new-found daughter. Paulina, then, offers to show the company a perfect statue of the Queen which stands in her chapel. As they gaze upon it in wonder, music gives it animation, and it turns into the real Hermione, who has lived in seclusion all these years hoping for the return of her daughter. Thus, Leontes has restored to him once more, his friend, his counsellor, his daughter, his wife, and for the son who died another son in Florizel. Only Paulina is left without her loss restored, though in recognition of their loyalty, Leontes suggests that she and Camillo be married.

The Tempest

Dramatis Personæ

PROSPERO, the rightful Duke of Milan, wise and virtuous philosopher and most mighty magician.

MIRANDA, his daughter, who has seen no man save her father; "the top of admiration . . . . so perfect and so peerless . . . . created of every creature's best."

FERDINAND, son of the King of Naples, so gallant a spirit that Miranda has "no ambition to see a goodlier man."

ARIEL, a "tricksy," "delicate," "dainty," bird-like spirit, servant of Prospero and symbolical of the magician's control of the upper elements of air and fire.

CALIBAN, the earthy spawn of devil and witch, "a freckled whelp . . . . not honor'd with a human shape," Prospero's "poisonous slave," a foil to the delicate Ariel, and symbolical of the magician's control of the lower elements of earth and water.

ALONSO, King of Naples, weak-willed ruler, who is not, however, incapable of sincere remorse and true penitence.

SEBASTIAN, traitorous brother of Alonso.

ANTONIO, Prospero's wicked and unnatural brother, led by evil ambition to usurp the dukedom of Milan and to "expel remorse and nature."

GONZALO, the "good old lord" and philosopher, who acted as Prospero's "true preserver and a loyal sir."

TRINCULO, Alonso's jester, "reeling ripe" and dull with drink. A "jesting monkey," "a pied ninny," a "scurvy patch."

STEPHANO, the King's "drunken butler," made loquacious and courageous by the "celestial liquor" which has pickled him.

ADRIAN, } lords attending the King of Naples.
FRANCISCO, }

MASTER OF THE SHIP, BOATSWAIN, and numerous Mariners.

IRIS, }
CERES, }
JUNO, } rôles assumed by spirits in Prospero's pageant.
NYMPHS AND REAPERS, }

Scene of the Action: A ship at sea, and an enchanted island.

Act I

On an enchanted tropical island dwell the magician Prospero and his lovely daughter Miranda. Twelve years before, Prospero was Duke of Milan. Absorbed in his necromantic studies, he had allowed the affairs of the state to drift into the hands of his brother Antonio, a treacherous and unnatural man, who usurped the dukedom with the assistance of Alonso, King of Naples, and set Prospero and Miranda adrift in a boat. The two would have perished had not Gonzalo, an honest and loyal counsellor, provisioned and equipped the bark and supplied Prospero with his wand, his conjuring robes, and his books on magic. Ultimately the banished Duke and his infant daughter drifted to an island occupied only by Caliban, the motherless cub of the wicked witch Sycorax. Prospero's attempts to civilize this monster were unavailing, for the creature was inherently evil and fitted only to become a hewer of wood and a drawer of water. Besides this crude slave Prospero is served on the island by a dainty spirit of the winds, Ariel, an airy contrast to the earthy, "fish-like" Caliban, and by numerous other spirits of the air and water. Knowing through his magic that his ancient enemies are sailing to the island after the wedding of the Princess of Naples in Africa, Prospero batters their ship with the aid of Ariel, but brings the voyagers safely ashore, scattered in groups about the island. Ferdinand, the gallant son of the King of Naples, is led by Ariel's magic singing to the cave of Prospero. Miranda, who does not remember ever having seen any other man than her father, falls in love with the handsome Prince, but Prospero, not to have the young man's conquest too easy, pretends to frown upon him and subdues him with his magic arts.

Act II

In another part of the island Alonso, Sebastian, Antonio, Gonzalo, and others wander disconsolately, convinced that the young Prince is dead. All but Sebastian and Antonio are lulled asleep by Ariel's magic music, but these two remain awake to plot the death of the sleeping King and the aged counsellor, as, years before, Antonio has—as he supposes—destroyed his own brother. They might have succeeded in their wicked plot had not the watchful air-spirit awakened the intended victims just in time to save them. Meanwhile, not far away, Trinculo, the King's jester, reeling drunk, encounters Caliban; they are joined by Stephano, a drunken butler, who so delights the moon-calf with his "celestial liquor" that Caliban swears to follow him forever.

Act III

The plot of Sebastian and Antonio to kill the King of Naples has a grotesque parallel in that of Caliban, Stephano, and Trinculo to kill Prospero and seize the island. Stephano is to be king, and Miranda his queen-consort. But the alert Ariel reports this plot also to his master. Quite unaware of the vile scheme of the drunken butler, Miranda has meanwhile exchanged vows with Prince Ferdinand, whose love for this goddess of the isle has eased the labor of log-bearing which her father has forced upon him as a trial of his sincerity. While the two lovers are conversing, Prospero and Ariel mock the King's party with a banquet which vanishes as they try to eat, and the spirit in the guise of a harpy rebukes them for their crime against "good Prospero . . . . and his innocent child" until Alonso, saddened by the supposed death of his son, is mellowed into repentance.

Act IV

Before Prospero's cell the magician presents to Prince Ferdinand, whom he has released from enchantment, and the lovely Miranda, a prenuptial pageant, enacted by spirits in the guise of Iris, Ceres, Juno, and nymphs and reapers who dance. Remembering Caliban's plot, the magician stops the masque abruptly and orders Ariel to punish the foul conspirators. This the spirit does by tempting them with glittering raiment displayed on a line, and then setting upon them with his fellow spirits in the form of hunting dogs and driving them howling about the island.

Act V

The major conspirators are then brought, spell-bound by Ariel's music, into the charmed circle before Prospero's cell. Attired as the wronged Duke of Milan Prospero discloses himself to them, tells Antonio to restore his dukedom, and warns Sebastian against further plots against the King. To the repentant

Alonso he reveals within the cave Prince Ferdinand and the fair
Miranda playing at chess. Ariel brings in the Master and the
Boatswain, who report that the ship "is tight and yare and bravely
rigg'd" with all the mariners safe below hatches. The magician's
airy messenger finally drives in the three grotesque conspirators,
still drunk and sore with the pinching which the spirits have given
them. Prospero abjures his magic, invites the King of Naples
and his train to share the cave that night, and as a last order to
the dainty Ariel before freeing him, commands "calm seas and
auspicious gales" for the morrow's voyage back to Naples and
Milan.

Histories

England and Northern France in **SHAKESPEARE'S PLAYS**

Shakespeare's History Plays

PLAY	DATES OF REIGN	PERIOD COVERED BY THE PLAY	HISTORICAL EVENTS TREATED IN THE PLAY
KING JOHN	1199-1216	1199-1216	Claim of Arthur to the English throne: John's compromise first with Philip of France (1200), and then with the Pope (1213); death of Arthur (1203); defection of the barons (1215); invasion of England by Louis of France (1216); and death of John (1216).
RICHARD II	1377-1399	1398-1400	The Lancastrian Revolution of 1399: quarrel of Bolingbroke and Mowbray (1398); death of John of Gaunt (1399); war in Ireland (1399); deposition of Richard by Henry, Duke of Lancaster (1399); and death of Richard (1400).
1 HENRY IV	1399-1413	1402-1403	Civil War: The Percy Rebellion: Battle of Holmedon (1402); Battle of Shrewsbury (1403); death of Henry "Hotspur."
2 HENRY IV	1399-1413	1403-1413	Civil War: Complete suppression of faction: Meeting of the opposing forces on Shipton Moor (1405); death of Henry IV and coronation of Henry V (1413).
HENRY V	1413-1422	1414-1420	Conquest of France: Siege of Harfleur (1415); Battle of Agincourt (1415); Treaty of Troyes and betrothal of Henry V and Katharine of France (1420).
1 HENRY VI	1422-1471	1422-1453	England's loss of France and growth of civil factions: funeral of Henry V (1422); Siege of Orleans (1428-9); Siege of Rouen (fictitious); coronation of Henry VI at Paris (1431); death of Talbot (1453); capture and execution of Joan of Arc (1430-1); marriage of Henry VI and Margaret of Anjou (1445).

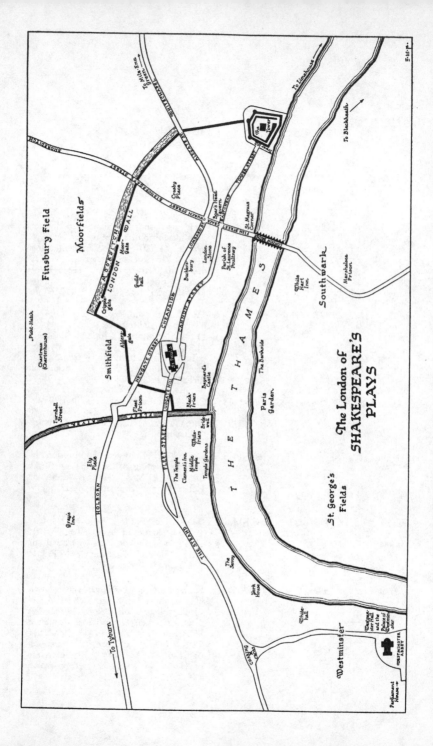

The London of SHAKESPEARE'S PLAYS

PLAY	DATES OF REIGN	PERIOD COVERED BY THE PLAY	HISTORICAL EVENTS TREATED IN THE PLAY
2 HENRY VI	1422-1471	1445-1455	The Wars of the Roses: Murder of Humphrey, Duke of Gloucester (1447); Jack Cade's Rebellion (1450); Yorkist victory at St. Albans (1455).
3 HENRY VI	1422-1471	1455-71	The Wars of the Roses: declaration of York as heir to the throne (1460); Lancastrian victory at Wakefield, death of York (1460); Yorkist victory at Mortimer's Cross (1461); Lancastrian victory at St. Albans (1461); proclamation of Edward IV as king (1461); Yorkist victory at Towton (1461); marriage of Edward IV and Elizabeth Woodville (1464); Yorkist victory at Hexham (1464); imprisonment of Henry VI (1465); restoration of Henry VI (1470); return of Edward IV (1471); death of Warwick the Kingmaker at Barnet (1471); defeat of Queen Margaret at Tewkesbury and death of Prince Edward (1471); murder of Henry VI in the Tower (1471).
	Edward IV, 1461-70; 1471-83		
RICHARD III	1483-1485	1471-1485	Union of the Red Rose and the White: funeral of Henry VI (1471); marriage of Richard and Anne (1472); execution of Clarence (1478); death of Edward IV (1483); Richard first Protector and then King (1483); murder of the Princes in the Tower (1483); death of Anne (1485): defeat and death of Richard at Bosworth Field (1485); proclamation of Henry Richmond as Henry VII, and his marriage with Elizabeth of York, daughter of Edward IV (1485).
	Edward IV, 1471-83		
	Edward V, 1483		
HENRY VIII	1509-1547	1520-1533	Intrigue at the Tudor Court: Field of the Cloth of Gold (1520); arraignment of Buckingham (1521); meeting of Henry and Anne Bullen (1527); creation of Anne Bullen Marchioness of Pembroke (1532); commencement of divorce proceedings against Queen Katharine of Arragon (1527); trial of the Queen (1529); fall of Wolsey (1529); death of Wolsey (1530); death of Queen Katharine (1536); marriage of Henry and Anne (1533); birth of the Princess Elizabeth (1533).

King John

Dramatis Personæ

JOHN, King of England, without grandeur, strength, or any other regal quality, so weak that he is cowardly and mean rather than cruel, evasive rather than frank, disgusting rather than dignified.

PHILIP FAULCONBRIDGE, (the Bastard), illegitimate son of King Richard the Lion-hearted, a "good blunt fellow," a "madcap" who is "perfect Richard" with even a "trick of Cœur-de-Lion's face;" the honest, bluff foil to King John, a thorough Englishman.

LADY FAULCONBRIDGE, seduced by the late King Richard, and mother by him of the Bastard Faulconbridge.

ROBERT FAULCONBRIDGE, legitimate son of Sir Robert and Lady Faulconbridge, so thin that his legs are "riding-rods" and arms "eel-skins stuff'd."

QUEEN ELINOR, the mean-spirited, dishonest, masculine, and blustering widow of Henry II and mother of King John.

CONSTANCE, widow of Geoffrey, John's older brother, and mother of Arthur; ambitious for her son and furious in her defense of his claims against Elinor and John; she becomes "as fond of grief as of her child."

ARTHUR, Duke of Bretagne, son of Constance and nephew of John, an innocent and pretty boy who believes that he is "not worth this coil that's made for [him]." "This little abstract doth contain that large which died in Geoffrey."

PHILIP, fickle King of France, who worships "tickling Commodity" and perjures himself.

LEWIS, the Dauphin, "a beardless boy, a cocker'd silken wanton," forsworn, like his father Philip.

BLANCH OF SPAIN, niece of King John, who becomes bride of the Dauphin, and who "in beauty, education, blood, holds hand with any princess of the world."

LYMOGES, Archduke of Austria, a "slave," a "wretch," a "coward," a "ramping fool," "ever strong upon the stronger side," advised by the Lady Constance to doff his lion's hide and "hang a calf's-skin on those recreant limbs."

CARDINAL PANDULPH, the Pope's legate, whose "breath first kindled the dead coal of wars," but who could not always blow the fire out.

HUBERT DE BURGH, King John's chamberlain and Prince Arthur's keeper, whose "form, . . . howsoever rude exteriorly is yet the cover of a fairer mind than to be butcher of an innocent child."

THE EARL OF PEMBROKE,
THE EARL OF SALISBURY, } English noblemen who revolted from John.
THE LORD BIGOT,

106

KING JOHN

THE EARL OF ESSEX, and other English lords.

MELUN, a French count whose "grandsire was an Englishman."

CHATILLON, ambassador from King Philip of France to King John.

PRINCE HENRY, son of King John, who succeeds him.

PETER OF POMFRET, an English prophet.

JAMES GURNEY, Lady Faulconbridge's servant.

Citizens of Angiers, Heralds, Officers, Soldiers, a Sheriff, Messengers, and Attendants.

Scene of the Action: England and France.

Act I

King Philip of France sends an ambassador to King John of England to demand the surrender of his crown to his nephew, young Arthur, Duke of Bretagne, the fatherless son of John's elder brother Geoffrey. John returns an indignant refusal and prepares promptly to invade France. The King appoints as one of the leaders of the expedition the bluff Philip Faulconbridge, an illegitimate son of his brother, the late King Richard Coeur-de-lion, upon whom he has whimsically conferred the title and name of "Sir Richard Plantagenet," but who becomes known popularly as "The Bastard Faulconbridge."

Act II

The English and the French armies meet before Angiers, and when the citizens refuse to acknowledge either John or Arthur as their ruler, they fight an indecisive skirmish for the control of the city. At the suggestion of the Bastard the two kings plan to unite their forces against the stubborn town but are induced by the burghers to settle their differences by agreeing to a marriage between Lewis the Dauphin and the Lady Blanch, daughter of John's sister Eleanor, Queen of Castile. As her dowry, John offers the provinces in France which Philip has been claiming for Arthur. This shameful peace, whispered into the king's ears by "that smooth-faced gentleman, tickling Commodity," is abhorrent to the Bastard and the Lady Constance, Arthur's mother.

Act III

The peace created by "false blood to false blood join'd" does not last long, for Pandulph, the "holy legate of the Pope" curses and excommunicates John for his refusal to seat Stephen Langton in the archbishopric of Canterbury and orders Philip and Lewis to break the new compact and war against the English. In a battle near Angiers the French are defeated, the Duke of Austria, allied with Philip, is killed by the Bastard, and Arthur falls into the hands of his uncle, who orders his chamberlain, Hubert de Burgh, to kill the young Prince. Meanwhile, on the ground that King John is certain to order Arthur's death, and that the English are disaffected because of their King's quarrel with the Church, Pandulph persuades the Dauphin to claim the crown of England in the right of Lady Blanch, his wife, and to invade that country.

Act IV

In an English prison Hubert de Burgh, ordered by King John to burn out Arthur's eyes, yields to the pitiful pleadings of the boy and spares him. But in an attempt to escape from the castle in which he is imprisoned the Prince leaps from the walls and is killed on the stones below. Finding his broken body, Pembroke, Salisbury, and Bigot, English noblemen who have suspected the King's evil purposes, are convinced that Hubert has murdered the child at the King's orders, and in spite of the Bastard's loyal advice they break their allegiance to John and go off to join the Dauphin, who has meanwhile landed in England with a large army.

Act V

To secure Pandulph's aid against the French, John submits to the Pope by surrendering his crown to the papal legate on Ascension-day and receiving it back again in fief, thus fulfilling a prophecy that on that day he would deliver up his crown. Pandulph's attempts, however, to persuade the Dauphin to return immediately to France are in vain, and the French, assisted by the English traitors who have joined them, fight an indecisive engagement with the English under the Bastard. In this battle Melun, a French count who is dying from his wounds, warns the revolting noblemen that it is the Dauphin's purpose to have them executed as soon as he has obtained his objectives with their aid; thereupon, they return to their allegiance to the English king just in season to find him dying miserably—apparently from poison—in an orchard at Swinstead Abbey. After John's death Pandulph succeeds in bringing about an honorable peace between French and English, and the crown of England passes to John's son Henry, with the Bastard Faulconbridge declaring:

> "This England never did, nor never shall,
> Lie at the proud foot of a conqueror,
> But when it first did help to wound itself.
> Now these her princes are come home again,
> Come the three corners of the world in arms,
> And we shall shock them. Nought shall make us rue,
> If England to itself do rest but true."

Richard II

Dramatis Personæ

RICHARD II, King of England, at once weak, pitiful and tragic, a wasteful mixture of intelligence and incapacity to meet realities; his selfish prodigality moves him into a "rash, fierce blaze of riot" and makes his "reputation sick," while his aesthetic sentimentalism and his rich imagination lead him to think of himself as "woe's slave" and a king only in his griefs.

HENRY, surnamed BOLINGBROKE, Duke of Hereford, and afterwards King Henry IV, son of John of Gaunt, cousin and foil of Richard II; crafty and cold, subtle and icy-hearted, a "silent king," who rules while he seems to serve and controls by indirection until the power for which he thirsts seems to come unsought into his hands.

THOMAS MOWBRAY, Duke of Norfolk, accused by his enemies as "fell" and "false."

JOHN OF GAUNT, Duke of Lancaster, "old John of Gaunt, time-honored Lancaster," the stern, sturdy, and outspoken father of Henry Bolingbroke and uncle of Richard II.

EDMUND OF LANGLEY, Duke of York, uncle of Richard II and of Henry Bolingbroke, "weak with age," a "prisoner to the palsy," essentially honest and loyal but almost senile in his hand-wringing lack of decision.

THE DUKE OF AUMERLE, son of the Duke of York, who "digressed" into treachery.

THE DUCHESS OF YORK, "fond" mother of Aumerle, who becomes a "shrill-voiced suppliant" for her "transgressing boy."

THE EARL OF NORTHUMBERLAND, cold and impassive follower of Henry Bolingbroke, a "haught, insulting man."

HENRY PERCY, nicknamed HOTSPUR, Northumberland's son, as yet "tender, raw, and young," but of good service to Bolingbroke.

QUEEN OF RICHARD II, sad and "weeping," who joined "woe to woe, sorrow to sorrow."

THE DUCHESS OF GLOUCESTER, aunt by marriage of King Richard and Henry Bolingbroke.

THE EARL OF SALISBURY, SIR STEPHEN SCROOP, THE BISHOP OF CARLISLE, THE ABBOT OF WESTMINISTER, of the party of Richard II.

BUSHY, BAGOT, GREEN, followers and favorites of King Richard.

LORD FITZWATER, opponent and accuser of Aumerle.

THE DUKE OF SURREY, friend and supporter of Aumerle.

LORD BERKELEY, messenger of the Duke of York.

LORD WILLOUGHBY,
LORD ROSS, } of the party of Henry Bolingbroke.

SIR PIERCE OF EXTON, the "friend" of Henry IV who rids him "of this living fear" by murdering King Richard.

Lord Marshall, a Welsh Captain, a Lady attending upon the Queen, Lords, Heralds, Officers, Soldiers, two Gardeners, a Keeper, a Messenger, a Groom, and Attendants.

Scene of the Action: England and Wales.

RICHARD II

Act I

King Richard II summons into his presence his cousin Henry Bolingbroke and Thomas Mowbray, Duke of Norfolk, to hear Bolingbroke's charges against the Duke of having misappropriated military funds and plotted the death of the King's uncle, the Duke of Gloucester. The King permits the adversaries to appear in the lists at Coventry for trial by combat, but before their lances have crossed, the fickle monarch forbids the contest and banishes Norfolk for life and Bolingbroke for six years, requiring both to swear that they will never plot against him. Bolingbroke's banishment is followed shortly after by the fatal illness of his father, John of Gaunt.

Act II

From the tongue of the dying Duke of Lancaster Richard hears charges of his profligacy and misrule and prophecies that the unhappy kingdom will suffer for his sins. No sooner has that tongue become "a stringless instrument," however, than the King seizes "the plate, coin, revenues, and movables" of the dead nobleman, overriding the protests of the Duke of York in behalf of the banished heir, Henry Bolingbroke, and justifying his high-handed act by urging the need of money for his Irish wars. The King's seizure of his property gives Bolingbroke an excuse for returning from exile to claim his rights, and on his arrival he is joined immediately by Northumberland, Henry Percy, Ross, Willoughby, and other disaffected noblemen. Meanwhile, the King has gone to Ireland leaving the kingdom in the hands of the feeble old Duke of York.

Act III

Richard returns from Ireland to Wales only to learn that a Welsh army upon which he has depended has dispersed upon hearing rumors of his death, and that Bolingbroke has executed his favorites Bushy and Green. The deserted, "plume-plucked" King takes refuge in Flint Castle, where he is soon found by Bolingbroke. Although protesting that he has returned from exile only to claim his title and rights as Duke of Lancaster, the subtle nobleman takes Richard to London as a virtual prisoner.

Act IV

At a meeting of the Parliament in Westminster Hall the sentimental, vacillating Richard and the cold, politic Henry come face to face. Richard is formally charged with his high crimes against the state, but though his enemies have prepared for signature a full confession of his guilt and a complete abdication, Richard temperamentally refuses even to read the papers. But with these documents to support him and despite the Bishop of Carlisle's dire prophecy that "the blood of English shall manure the ground, and future ages groan for this foul act," Bolingbroke sends Richard to the Tower and announces "on Wednesday next . . . [his] coronation." But Aumerle, the Abbot of Westminster, and the Bishop are moved by the "woeful pageant" to counterplot against the new monarch.

Act V

The new ruler changes his mind about the place of Richard's imprisonment and orders him conveyed to Pomfret Castle, whither he is taken after a sad parting from his Queen. Aumerle's plot against Henry IV is discovered by the young nobleman's father; but in spite of York's loyal demand that his traitorous son be executed, Henry pardons his cousin on the stubborn insistence of the Duchess of York that her "transgressing boy" be forgiven. At Pomfret Castle the deposed Richard is murdered by Sir Pierce of Exton on the new ruler's hint, "Have I no friend will rid me of this living fear?" But on learning of this foul act, Henry banishes the regicide, protesting:—"My soul is full of woe, that blood should sprinkle me to make me grow," and announcing that he will do penance by making "a voyage to the Holy Land, to wash this blood off from [his] guilty hand."

Henry IV: Part I

Dramatis Personæ

KING HENRY IV, who met his crown by "by-paths and indirect crook'd ways," so that to the former supporters who became his enemies he was a "subtle king," . . . "a king of smiles," . . . "a fawning greyhound," so filled with mistrust himself that he saw its reflection in his son Prince Hal.

HENRY, PRINCE OF WALES, popularly known as Prince Hal, son of the King, a noble, high-spirited, and chivalrous youth, the incarnation of the most gracious and generous elements in English manhood, whose love of fun is misconstrued by his sober father as indicating a corrupt and riotous nature which is in no sense an essential part of his character.

JOHN OF LANCASTER, younger brother of Prince Hal, courageous in battle but much like his father and possessed of but few of the manly virtues of the brother to whom he serves as foil.

HENRY PERCY, nicknamed HOTSPUR, a hot-headed but chivalrous "infant warrior," "altogether governed by humors," so high-spirited that he thinks "it were an easy leap, to pluck bright honor from the pale-faced moon," and despises idleness, riot, and sentimentalism. "The theme of Honor's tongue," he is "no more in debt to years" than Prince Hal, to whom he is the foil. "He kills me some six or seven dozen Scots at a breakfast, washes his hands, and says to his wife, 'Fie upon this quiet life! I want work.'"

HENRY PERCY, EARL OF NORTHUMBERLAND, Hotspur's father, haughty, crafty, cold, and politic, in sharp contrast to his son.

THOMAS PERCY, EARL OF WORCESTER, the turbulent, suspicious, and ungenerous uncle of Hotspur.

LADY PERCY, Hotspur's gay, sprightly, and affectionate wife.

EDMUND MORTIMER, EARL OF MARCH, brother of Lady Percy and claimant of the throne of England.

OWEN GLENDOWER, Welsh warrior, ally of the Percys, an imaginative and poetic dreamer, reputed to be a great magician who could "call spirits from the vasty deep."

LADY MORTIMER, daughter of Glendower and wife of Mortimer, a sentimental lady who could speak no English to a husband who could speak no Welsh.

ARCHIBALD, EARL OF DOUGLAS, leader of the Scottish forces and ally of his former enemies, the Percys, in their rebellion against Henry IV, a "hot, termagant Scot" who knows, however, when to fight and when also to allow discretion to be the better part of valor.

RICHARD SCROOP, ARCHBISHOP OF YORK, ally of the Percys in their rebellion against the King.

SIR MICHAEL, a follower of the Archbishop of York.

SIR RICHARD VERNON, a rebel nobleman of generous nature.

THE EARL OF WESTMORELAND, } noblemen who lead the King's army.
SIR WALTER BLUNT,

Sir John Falstaff, the irresponsible and merry companion of Prince Hal, "some fifty, or by'r Lady, inclining to three score," "wither'd like an old apple-john," an amazing bundle of contrasts, a liar without malice, a lover of wine, women, and song, and the most irrepressible of mortals—"this sanguine coward, this bed-presser, this horseback-breaker, this huge hill of flesh," "that trunk of humors, that bolting hutch of beastliness, that swollen parcel of dropsies, that huge bombard of sack . . . that reverend Vice, that grey Iniquity, that Father Ruffian, that Vanity in years," "that villainous abominable misleader of youth," "that white-bearded Satan." He is not only witty himself, "but the cause that wit is in other men."

Poins, Prince Hal's companion at the Boar's-Head Tavern in Eastcheap—"straight enough in the shoulders."

Gadshill, Peto, Bardolph, Falstaff's riotous and rascally companions at the Boar's-Head Tavern.

Mistress Quickly, the stupid but kindly hostess of the Boar's-head Tavern.

Lords, Officers, a Sheriff, a Vintner, a Chamberlain, Drawers, two Carriers, Travellers, and Attendants.

Scene of the Action: England and Wales.

Act I

Henry IV's plan to do penance for the death of Richard II by leading an expedition to the Holy Land is interrupted by the disaffection of the northern barons who had helped to plant him on the throne. Hotspur refuses to surrender to the King the Scottish prisoners whom he has captured at the battle of Holmedon unless Henry will ransom Lady Percy's brother, Edmund Mortimer, Earl of March, who has been captured by Owen Glendower while leading an English force against that Welsh warrior. Because Mortimer is the rightful heir to the English throne after Richard II, Henry refuses flatly to "redeem a traitor home," but repeats his own demands for the Scottish prisoners. Hotspur, with his father, the Earl of Northumberland, and his uncle, the Earl of Worcester, returns home in great anger, planning to raise a rebellion against "this vile politician, Bolingbroke" by combining their forces with those of Richard Scroop, the Archbishop of York, Owen Glendower, Edmund Mortimer, and Douglas, a valiant leader of the Scots, whose help they will purchase by releasing the Scottish prisoners. While this plot of the ambitious Hotspur and his kinsmen is threatening to fulfil the prophecy of the Bishop of Carlisle at the deposition of Richard II that "future ages [shall] groan for this foul act," another young nobleman, Henry IV's son, the madcap Prince of Wales, is wildly plotting

with his favorite companion Sir John Falstaff and other rioters
to rob a group of travellers at Gadshill, near London.

Act II

After Sir John Falstaff and some of his low companions have
set upon and robbed the travellers at Gadshill, they are themselves
attacked and put to ridiculous flight by Prince Hal and Ned Poins,
masked, and disguised in buckram. In Prince Hal's favorite haunt,
the Boar's-Head Tavern in Eastcheap, Falstaff later tells a fabu-
lous tale of his valiant exploits against *eleven* men in buckram,
and the Prince's disclosure of the practical joke upon the fat
knight fails to put Falstaff out of countenance but adds to the
general merriment. Their riotous fun-making is interrupted by
the arrival of a nobleman from the King to summon the Prince to
court, for "there's villainous news abroad" of the rising in the
North of "that fiend Douglas, that spirit Percy, and that devil
Glendower."

Act III

In conference in the north of Wales the rebels—not without
some dissension among themselves—plan the campaign against the
royal forces and the subsequent "tripartite" division of the country
which they have not yet won. In London, in the meantime, the
King has rebuked Prince Hal for his wild ways, comparing his
son unfavorably with "this Hotspur, Mars in swathling clothes,
this infant warrior." On the Crown Prince's pledging to redeem
his wounded reputation "on Percy's head," the King not only forgives him and puts him in command of a part of the royal forces,
but even allows Sir John Falstaff to go to the wars in charge of
a company of foot soldiers.

Act IV

In the rebel camp near Shrewsbury the fiery Hotspur and the
noble Douglas find themselves deserted by Northumberland, who
pleads that he is sick, and by Glendower, who, "o'er-ruled by
prophecies," "cannot draw his power this fourteen days;" despite
these losses they determine to meet the royal forces, which are

marching against the rebels under the command of the Earl of Westmoreland, Prince John of Lancaster, and "the nimble-footed madcap Prince of Wales." The Percys' ally, Richard Scroop, Archbishop of York, already reads in the news the failure of the rebellion and takes steps to meet the King when the armies are turned to the North.

Act V

By the Earl of Worcester and Sir Richard Vernon, generals in the rebel camp, King Henry offers complete pardon to the rebels if they will disband, but Worcester's suspicions of the King are so great that instead of delivering the gracious terms of the monarch he delivers to his associates a challenge to immediate battle. In the hot engagement which follows, Prince Hal rescues his father from the sword of Douglas and then encounters and kills his spirited rival Hotspur. Worcester and Vernon are captured and executed, Douglas is taken prisoner but released by the generous Crown Prince, and the rebel forces are utterly defeated and scattered. The King follows up his victory by dispatching Prince John of Lancaster against "Northumberland and the prelate Scroop," and departing himself with Prince Hal toward Wales "to fight with Glendower and the Earl of March."

Henry IV: Part II

Dramatis Personæ

RUMOR, "painted full of tongues," an allegorical figure who appears first to give the audience the link between this play and *Henry IV, Part I*.

KING HENRY IV, who continues to suffer from a guilty conscience.

HENRY, Prince of Wales, afterward King Henry V, the madcap son of Henry IV; in this play "consideration, like an angel, came and whipp'd the offending Adam out of him."

PRINCE JOHN OF LANCASTER, son of Henry IV and general of his father's forces, who breaks faith with the rebels in a most unjust and dishonorable manner; foil to Prince Hal.

PRINCE HUMPHREY OF GLOUCESTER,
THOMAS, Duke of Clarence,
} other sons of Henry IV.

THE EARL OF WARWICK,
THE EARL OF SURREY,
} counsellors of the King.

THE EARL OF WESTMORELAND, leader of the royal forces against the rebels.

GOWER,
HARCOURT,
BLUNT,
} officers in the royal army.

THE EARL OF NORTHUMBERLAND,
SCROOP, Archbishop of York,
LORD MOWBRAY,
LORD HASTINGS,
LORD BARDOLPH,
SIR JOHN COLVILLE,
} leaders of the rebellion in the North.

TRAVERS and MORTON, retainers of Northumberland.

LADY NORTHUMBERLAND, wife of the Earl and mother of the dead Hotspur.

LADY PERCY, widow of Hotspur.

THE LORD CHIEF-JUSTICE OF THE KING'S BENCH, the learned and intrepid judge who was appointed by Henry V to continue to bear his "unstained sword" of righteousness. "Though not clean past [his] youth, [he] hath yet some smack of age in [him], some relish of the saltness of time."

A SERVANT of the Lord Chief-Justice.

SIR JOHN FALSTAFF, "a fool and a jester," who requires "two and twenty yards of satin" for a suit. To Prince Hal he is the nimble-witted and irresponsible companion, who follows "the young Prince up and down like his ill angel;" to King Henry V the "tutor and feeder of [the] riots of [his] youth"—foil to the Lord Chief-Justice. "Have you not a moist eye, a dry hand, a yellow cheek, a white beard, a decreasing leg, an increasing belly? Is not your voice broken, your wind short, your chin double, your wit single, and every part about you blasted with antiquity? And will you yet call yourself young?"

FALSTAFF'S PAGE, "a little tiny thief," "fitter to be worn in [his] cap than to wait at [his] heels."

BARDOLPH, Falstaff's drinking companion and corporal, an "arrant malmsey-nose knave."

117

PETO, another of Falstaff's companions.

PISTOL, Falstaff's "ancient" or ensign, a ranting "swaggerer," a "mouldy rogue," and a "cut-purse rascal" whose bombastic words, quoted at large from scraps of blood-curdling plays, conceal a cowardly heart.

POINS, Prince Hal's companion at the Boar's-Head Tavern. "He swears with a good grace, and wears his boots very smooth . . . and breeds no bate with telling of discreet stories."

MISTRESS QUICKLY, hostess of the Boar's-Head Tavern in Eastcheap, whose reputation for respectability constantly threatens to break down.

DOLL TEARSHEET, a prostitute at the Boar's-Head Tavern with an extensive and vitriolic vocabulary.

FANG and SNARE, sheriff's officers who prove no match for Falstaff.

ROBERT SHALLOW, "a poor esquire . . . and one of the King's justices of the peace," conceited victim of Falstaff's capacity for borrowing; he is "like a man made after supper of a cheese-paring . . . like a forked radish, with a head fantastically carved upon it with a knife, . . . the very genius of famine." " 'A came ever in the rearward of the fashion."

SILENCE, another country justice, friend and admirer of Shallow.

DAVY, Shallow's servant.

RALPH MOULDY, "a good limb'd fellow, young, strong, and of good friends,"

SIMON SHADOW, a "half-faced fellow," "he presents no mark to the enemy; the foeman may with as great aim level at the edge of a penknife."

THOMAS WART, "a very ragged wart,"

FRANCIS FEEBLE, a woman's tailor, "as valiant as the wrathful dove or most magnanimous mouse,"

PETER BULL-CALF, "a diseased man,"—"a whoreson cold, sir, a cough,"

} Falstaff's unpromising recruits for the royal army.

FIRST BEADLE, a "damn'd tripe-visag'd rascal," a "blue-bottle rogue," a "filthy famish'd correctioner."

Lords and Attendants, a Porter, Beadles, Grooms, etc.; a Dancer who speaks the Epilogue.

Scene of the Action: England.

Act I

Despite early rumors that Hotspur has defeated the royalist forces and slain the Crown Prince, the true report of the defeat of the insurgents and the death of their impetuous young leader is finally brought to the Earl of Northumberland together with the news that Prince John of Lancaster and the Earl of Westmoreland are leading an army against him. The enraged earl plans to join forces with the Archbishop of York in meeting the royal army. In London, Sir John Falstaff is finding it difficult to bid farewell to his associates of the Boar's-Head Tavern and to start north with the King's commission to enlist en route soldiers for the army that is advancing against the rebels.

Act II

Falstaff's "hasty employment in the King's affairs" helps to save him from being arrested for debt at the suit of Mistress Quickly, the hostess of the Tavern, and the clever rascal concludes the whole matter by borrowing still more money from her and rioting and jesting with Prince Hal and other companions until messengers from the King summon both merry-makers to their army duties against the rebels. In the North, the Earl of Northumberland's wife and daughter-in-law, Hotspur's widow, prevail upon the cold-blooded nobleman to desert the Archbishop of York and take refuge in Scotland until "time and vantage crave [his] company."

Act III

In Westminster Palace the King, enfeebled by anxieties and ill-health, discusses the rebellion with his counsellors, the Earl of Warwick and the Earl of Surrey. As the monarch beholds the truth of Richard II's prophecy regarding Northumberland, he realizes that "uneasy lies the head that wears a crown" and wishes that "these inward wars [were] once out of hand" so that he might make his long-deferred expedition to Jerusalem. While the sick King courts sleep to "steep [his] senses in forgetfulness," the irresponsible Falstaff is in Gloucestershire at the house of Justice Shallow, where he misuses "the King's press damnably" by allowing likely recruits for the northern army to buy themselves off while he enlists only a crew of ragged scare-crows.

Act IV

In the insurgent camp in Yorkshire, the rebel Archbishop of York with Mowbray (son of Bolingbroke's old enemy), Hastings, and others are chilled by the news of the Earl of Northumberland's defection. Through the agency of the Earl of Westmoreland the rebel leaders are prevailed upon to present a schedule of their various grievances to John of Lancaster and these the Prince swears "by the honor of [his] blood" to redress with speed. Upon this "princely word" the rebel armies are dispersed; but no sooner have the insurgents disbanded than the perjured Prince orders the rebel noblemen to be executed, and their miserable followers to be pursued and slaughtered. The report of this treacherous act reaches the King in Westminster together with the news that Northumberland and Lord Bardolph have been defeated by the Sheriff of Yorkshire. But the King is too sick to hear even good tidings; putting his crown upon his pillow, he falls into a stuporous slumber, and the Crown Prince, summoned to the palace and alone in the chamber with his father, thinks the King dead and sorrowfully removes from the room the golden circlet of his father's cares. Awakening alone and misunderstanding his son's action, the King accuses him of desiring his death, but the genuine grief of the young Prince then becomes apparent, and the two are reconciled. The dying monarch advises his son to "busy giddy minds with foreign quarrels" so that rebellion at home may slumber. He is then carried off to die in the "Jerusalem Chamber," thus fulfilling a prophecy that he "should not die but in Jerusalem."

Act V

Upon the death of his father, Prince Hal becomes ruler as Henry V. The news of these events speeds to Gloucestershire, and Falstaff hurries to London to reap the benefits of his long companionship with the Prince. But he finds that the young King is not the riotous boon companion; the monarch rebukes him publicly with

> "I know thee not, old man: fall to thy prayers;
> How ill white hairs become a fool and jester,"

and banishes from his presence all the misleaders of his youth, charging the Lord Chief-Justice to see the order carried out, but providing for them competence of life lest lack of means force upon the rogues a life of crime. To make sure, the Justice sends Falstaff and all his companions to the Fleet. Thus, having made a public demonstration of his purposes, Henry V plans to assemble Parliament to discuss an invasion of France.

Henry V

Dramatis Personæ

KING HENRY V, Prince Hal ripened into noble manhood, courageous, energetic, generous, just, modest, warm-hearted, wise, and practical, "with a stubborn outside, with an aspect of iron."

THE DUKE OF GLOUCESTER,
THE DUKE OF BEDFORD, } the King's brothers.

THE DUKE OF EXETER, the King's uncle.

THE DUKE OF YORK, the King's cousin.

THE ARCHBISHOP OF CANTERBURY, } the King's learned counsellors on the jus-
THE BISHOP OF ELY, } tice of his claims to the French crown.

THE EARL OF SALISBURY,
THE EARL OF WARWICK, } leaders of the English forces in France.
THE EARL OF WESTMORELAND,

SIR THOMAS ERPINGHAM, } English officers in the King's army.
GOWER,

FLUELLEN, an honest Welsh captain in the English army, a man of "much care and valor" but "out of fashion" and absurdly pedantic in his claim to know the "discipline of war."

JAMY, a Scots captain in the English army.

MACMORRIS, an Irish captain in the English army.

BATES, COURT, WILLIAMS, common soldiers in the King's army in France.

THE EARL OF CAMBRIDGE, } English traitors who conspire with the French against
LORD SCROOP, } the life of Henry V.
SIR THOMAS GREY,

PISTOL, } of the old Boar's-Head Tavern group, now become camp-followers,
NYM, } cheaters, and thieves in the English army in France.
BARDOLPH,

A BOY attending the three rogues in France.

An ENGLISH HERALD.

HOSTESS of the Boar's-Head Tavern, formerly Nell Quickly but now the wife of Pistol.

CHARLES VI, King of France.

ISABEL, his Queen.

LEWIS, the DAUPHIN, a conceited coxcomb full of hollow and ostentatious valor, who overestimates himself and underestimates Henry V and the English army.

KATHARINE, charming, coy, and feminine daughter of King Charles and Queen Isabel, betrothed to King Henry, who believes that she has "witchcraft in [her] lips" and is like an angel.

121

ALICE, a waiting-lady attending the Princess, who, because she has been in England and speaks the language—after a manner—serves as Katharine's instructor and interpreter.

THE DUKE OF BURGUNDY, active as peace-maker between France and England.

THE CONSTABLE OF FRANCE,
THE DUKE OF ORLEANS,   } leaders of the French army at the Battle of Agin-
THE DUKE OF BOURBON,   court.

RAMBURES,   } noblemen in the French army.
GRANDPRE,

THE GOVERNOR OF HARFLEUR.

MONTJOY, a French herald.

Ambassadors from the Dauphin to Henry V.

Lords, Ladies, Officers, Soldiers, Citizens, Messengers and Attendants.

Scene of the Action: England and France.

Act I

One of the first public acts of the young King Henry V is to carry out his dying father's advice that he "busy giddy minds with foreign quarrels" and so quiet rebellion at home. That he may claim the throne of France "with right and conscience," he secures from the learned and politic Archbishop of Canterbury a declaration that the "Salic law" barring women and their descendants could not be urged legally against his claims to titles "usurp'd from [him] and [his] progenitors." The King resolves, therefore, "by God's help . . . to bend [France] to [his] awe, or break it all to pieces." His purpose is strengthened by the arrival of French ambassadors who bring from the Dauphin in reply to Henry's demand for "certain dukedoms [in France] in the right of [his] great predecessor, King Edward the Third," an insolent message that he "cannot revel into dukedoms there," and, in lieu of these territories, an insulting gift of tennis-balls. The angry King retorts that he will turn the Dauphin's tennis-balls to gun-stones; and he hurries his preparations for the invasion.

Act II

In London, the hostess of the Boar's-Head Tavern reports to Falstaff's old cronies that "the King hath killed his heart" and that he has died of a "burning quotidian tertian" and gone "to Arthur's bosom." Pistol, Nym, and Bardolph resolve to follow the King to Southampton and thence to France. In Southampton, on the point of sailing, Henry orders to execution three English noblemen who have taken French gold to assassinate him. At the French royal palace the King and the Dauphin receive from the English ambassadors the demand that the "crown and kingdom" be resigned to the English ruler.

Act III

The evidence of King Henry's ability to unite all factions under his banner appears in the bravery displayed in the siege of the French city of Harfleur by Captain Fluellen, a Welshman, Captain Jamy, a Scot, and Captain Macmorris, an Irishman. Failing to receive help from the Dauphin, the Governor of the town yields to the English, who occupy and defend it against the French. Later, Henry, his men sick, underfed, and war-worn, marches toward Calais and crosses the Somme. At Agincourt he finds himself face to face with a much larger French army under the Dauphin and the Constable of France.

Act IV

To test the temper of his common soldiers the young King goes in disguise about the camp conversing with many and gathering a solemn sense of his royal responsibilities; but even in such an hour the spirit of the fun-loving Prince Hal breaks out in a prank which he plays on one of his men. In the opposite camp, the overconfident French leaders jest at the "beggar'd host" of their enemies, and the Constable of France derisively sends a herald to King Henry to "mind [his] followers of repentance." But in the battle which follows on the morrow the badly generalled French forces, though vastly superior to the English in numbers and equipment, are overwhelmingly defeated, and the field of Agincourt is strewn with the corpses of French princes and nobles.

Act V

For insulting the Welsh the swaggering Pistol is thoroughly cudgelled by Captain Fluellen and forced to eat the Welsh leek which he has derided. To save himself from a possible worse fate—for both his cronies Nym and Bardolph have been hanged for theft—this knight of the "killing tongue and quiet sword" resolves to return to England. Through the friendly services of the Duke of Burgundy the French King yields to the demands of King Henry, granting him the hand of the fair Katharine, his daughter, and acknowledging him heir to the French crown. And from the union of the bluff English King and the French Princess is born—the Epilogue Chorus announces—a son "Henry the Sixth, in infant bands crown'd king, of France and England."

Henry VI: Part I

Dramatis Personæ

HENRY VI, young King of England, son of King Henry V.

HUMPHREY, Duke of Gloucester, uncle of the King, and Protector of the Realm during his infancy, a foe to citizens, one that still motions war and never peace."

THE DUKE OF BEDFORD, of "crazy age," uncle of the King and Regent of France.

HENRY BEAUFORT, Bishop of Winchester, and afterwards Cardinal, a "hollow-hearted," arrogant great-uncle of the King, and rival of Gloucester "that regards nor God nor King."

THOMAS BEAUFORT, Duke of Exeter, great-uncle of the King, and his personal guardian.

EDMUND MORTIMER, Earl of March.

RICHARD PLANTAGENET, son of Richard, late Earl of Cambridge, afterwards Duke of York, heir of Richard II, and hence, head of the House of York.

RICHARD NEVILLE, Earl of Warwick, later called "the king-maker,"

VERNON,

} of the White Rose, or York, faction.

JOHN BEAUFORT, Earl, and afterwards, Duke of Somerset, of the House of Lancaster.

WILLIAM DE LA POLE, Earl of Suffolk,

BASSET,

} of the Red Rose, or Lancaster, faction.

LORD TALBOT, afterwards Earl of Shrewsbury, leader of the English armies, an "ominous and fearful owl of death," and "the terror of the French;" "a stouter champion never handled sword." To his foes, "alas, this is a child, a silly dwarf! It cannot be this weak and writhled shrimp should strike such terror to his enemies."

JOHN TALBOT, his valiant son.

THE EARL OF SALISBURY, "mirror of all martial men," English general in France.

SIR WILLIAM LUCY,

SIR WILLIAM GLANSDALE,

SIR THOMAS GARGRAVE,

} English leaders.

SIR JOHN FASTOLFE, an English captain, and a coward.

THE DUKE OF BURGUNDY, maternal kinsman of Henry VI, fighting on the English side, but a traitor.

CHARLES, Dauphin, and afterwards King, of France, "a proper man."

REIGNIER, Duc d'Anjou, and titular King of Naples,

THE DUC D'ALENCON,

THE BASTARD OF ORLEANS,

} his generals.

JOAN LA PUCELLE, commonly called Joan of Arc, "the English scourge;" to the French, a maid inspired by heaven and fighting "with the sword of Deborah," but to the English, a "railing Hecate," and a "damned sorceress," "a vile fiend and a shameless courtezan."

125

AN OLD SHEPHERD, father of Joan la Pucelle.

THE COUNTESS OF AUVERGNE, a French noblewoman who lays a trap for Talbot.

MARGARET, a "gorgeous beauty," daughter of Reignier, afterwards married to King Henry VI.

WOODVILLE, Lieutenant of the Tower.

THE MAYOR OF LONDON.

THE GOVERNOR OF PARIS.

GENERAL of the French forces in Bordeaux.

Lords, Warders of the Tower, Heralds, Officers, Soldiers, Gunners, Porters, Messengers, and Attendants, both French and English, Fiends.

Scene of the Action: England and France.

Act I

Mourning in England for "death's dishonorable victory" over "the mirror of all Christian kings," Henry V, is immeasurably increased by the arrival of successive messengers at Westminister Abbey with news of the loss of all of the French possessions gained by Henry's sword, the coronation of Charles the Dauphin at Rheims, and the imprisonment of Talbot, commander of the English forces. In England, the child king, Henry of Windsor, is surrounded by his uncles, who take advantage of their regency to advance their own interests to the neglect of the affairs of the nation, while the London streets are in tumult because of the riots of the blue-coat servants of Humphrey of Gloucester, Lord Protector, and the tawny-coats of Henry Beaufort, Bishop of Winchester. In France, the English commanders, Salisbury and Talbot (who has been exchanged for a French prisoner) without supplies and support, nevertheless fight bravely against the French, who take advantage of these dissensions in England. Unexpected aid comes to the French in the person of Joan la Pucelle, the shepherd maid who proclaims herself inspired by visions from heaven, wins the love and respect of the Dauphin, and raises the siege of Orleans. Unfortunately for the English, Lord Salisbury and Sir Thomas Gargrave are killed by a sniping French gunner.

Act II

Taking advantage of the celebration going on within Orleans, the English show their contempt for the power of Joan by scaling the walls, retaking the city, and putting the French to flight clad only in their shirts. The Countess of Auvergne, planning an exploit that will make her as famous as Tomyris of Scythia, sends an invitation to Talbot to visit her. Suspecting treachery, he plants his troops outside, and when she taunts him with being a "weak and writhled shrimp," and but a shadow, he winds his horn, as the English forces batter down the doors, assures her "that Talbot is but a shadow of himself, these are his substance, sinews, arms, and strength." Meanwhile, in England, in the Temple Gardens, Richard Plantagenet, the heir of the House of York, quarrels with John Beaufort, Earl of Somerset, and heir of Lancaster, and bids all who side with him to pluck white roses, while Somerset and his followers pluck red. Thus, with bitter taunts, the civil Wars of the Roses have their beginning, fulfilling the prediction of the Bishop of Carlisle at the deposition of Richard II. Soon after, at the death-bed of Edmund Mortimer, Earl of March, in the Tower, Richard Plantagenet learns that his father, the late Earl of Cambridge, executed by command of Henry V, has not died a traitor, as his enemies have insisted, and that he himself is the true heir of King Richard II.

Act III

Hurrying to Parliament to demand his titles and estates, Plantagenet finds Gloucester and Winchester quarreling defiantly before the young King, who helplessly warns them that "civil dissension is a viperous worm that gnaws the bowels of the commonwealth." Even their factions, forbidden to carry weapons, have renewed their riots in the streets by fighting with stones. At the King's order a peace is patched up between the rivals, and at Warwick's petition, Plantagenet is restored to his titles and created Duke of York. The court then sets out for France that Henry of Windsor may be crowned in Paris. In France, the French army, led by Joan, takes Rouen by strategy, only to lose it almost immediately to the English under Talbot. While in retreat, the French meet the brave Duke of Burgundy, who has been fighting on the English side, and Joan wins him back to France by "fair persuasion mix'd with sug'red words" and arguments that the English are using him merely as a tool. Meanwhile, Henry creates Talbot Earl of Shrewsbury for his valiant service.

Act IV

Even at the coronation, in spite of the efforts of the young King, the quarrel between the white rose and the red flares up with renewed vigor. A pretended reconciliation results; York, appointed Regent of France, is made general of infantry, and Somerset, general of the horse; and both are sent into the field against the French. Meanwhile, Talbot is trying to take Bordeaux from the Duke of Burgundy. Without reinforcements because of a lack of coöperation between the factions, Talbot and his valiant son go down in defeat, fighting against the Dauphin's superior force; and Talbot, broken-hearted, dies with his dead son in his arms.

Act V

Overtures of peace are made to the English by the Emperor and the Pope, the truce to be sealed by marriage between young King Henry and the daughter of the Earl of Armagnac, who offers a large and sumptuous dowry. The Bishop of Winchester, now made Cardinal through bribery, is appointed the ambassador to conclude the peace and bring the bride to England. Meanwhile, in a battle at Angiers, Joan of Arc is taken prisoner by York. Forsaken by the fiends who have in the past supported and assisted her, pretending that she is with child to save her life, and raving and cursing, she is burned at the stake for witchcraft. At the same time, the Earl of Suffolk takes captive Margaret of Anjou, daughter of Reignier, titular King of Naples, and falls in love with her; but since he is already married, he resolves to marry her to King Henry. Peace is declared between England and France, to the disgust of York, with Charles as viceroy of France under Henry. Suffolk's description of Margaret so pleases the young King that he breaks his contract to the daughter of Armagnac, and against the wishes of Gloucester and Exeter, dispatches Suffolk to bring Margaret to England. The play closes with the prophecy of Suffolk:

> "Margaret shall now be Queen, and rule the King;
> But I will rule both her, the King, and realm."

Henry VI: Part II

Dramatis Personæ

HENRY VI, King of England, "being of age [now] to govern of himself," a pathetic, wholly negative monarch, "too full of foolish pity" to be a good king, but a pure and saintly man, "whose church-like humors fits not for a crown;" "his champions are the prophets and apostles, his weapons holy saws of sacred writ, his study is his tiltyard, and his loves are brazen images of canonized saints."

HUMPHREY, Duke of Gloucester, uncle of the King, and "haught" Protector of the Realm, "the good Duke Humphrey," in whose face is "the map of honor, truth, and loyalty"—the one unselfish character in a cruel and ambitious court.

CARDINAL BEAUFORT, Bishop of Winchester, "the imperious churchman," great uncle of the King, and haughty, treacherous leader of the opposition against Gloucester, one whose "red sparkling eyes blab his heart's malice."

THE DUKE OF SUFFOLK, favorite of the King, who changed "two dukedoms for a fair duke's daughter" whom he made Queen, and one "whose filth and dirt troubles the silver spring where England drinks."

THE DUKE OF SOMERSET,

THE DUKE OF BUCKINGHAM,

LORD CLIFFORD, his son,

LORD SAY,

} members of the King's party and of the Lancaster faction.

RICHARD PLANTAGENET, "grumbling," "dogged York, that reaches for the moon," head of the White Rose, or York faction.

EDWARD,

RICHARD, a "heap of wrath, a foul indigested lump, as crooked in [his] manners as [his] shape,"

} his sons.

THE EARL OF SALISBURY,

THE EARL OF WARWICK,

} members of the York faction.

JACK CADE, alias Lord Mortimer, a loud-voiced demagogue.

MATTHEW GOFFE, GEORGE BEVIS, JOHN HOLLAND, DICK the BUTCHER, SMITH the WEAVER, MICHAEL, etc., belonging to the rabble following Cade.

SIR HUMPHREY STAFFORD,

WILLIAM STAFFORD, his brother,

} warriors fighting against Jack Cade.

ALEXANDER IDEN, a Kentish gentleman who kills Jack Cade.

MARGARET OF ANJOU, Queen of King Henry, "the fairest queen that ever king receiv'd," but a hard, cruel, strong-minded, imperious woman.

ELEANOR COBHAM, Duchess of Gloucester, "a woman of invincible spirit" a "proud dame," not "slack to play her part in Fortune's pageant."

HUME,

SOUTHWELL,

} wicked priests.

MARGERY JORDAN, a witch.

129

ROGER BOLINGBROKE, a conjurer.

ASMATH, a spirit.

SIR JOHN STANLEY, the Duchess of Gloucester's escort into exile.

LORD SCALES, Governor of the Tower.

VAUX, a messenger.

A SEA CAPTAIN, MASTER, and MASTER'S MATE.

WALTER WHITMORE, murderer of the Duke of Suffolk.

THOMAS HORNER, an armorer, and PETER, his man.

THE MAYOR OF ST. ALBANS.

THE CLERK OF CHATHAM.

SIMPCOX, an imposter, and his WIFE.

Lords, Ladies, Gentlemen, Attendants, Petitioners, Aldermen, Officers, Soldiers, Guards, Heralds, Falconers, Messengers, Citizens, Apprentices, Murderers.

Scene of the Action: Various parts of England.

Act I

The arrival in England of Margaret of Anjou discloses immediately the disgraceful terms of the marriage treaty signed by the Earl of Suffolk, namely the surrender of the duchies of Anjou and Maine and the omission of dowry with the bride. Gloucester reads the conditions with dismay, but the young King is delighted with his wife, accepts them, creates the Earl the first Duke of Suffolk, and relieves York of his regency in France. Since the treaty is the work of the Beauforts, the Lancastrian faction takes the Queen's part and bends its efforts toward ousting the faithful Gloucester from his responsible post as Protector on the ground that the King is old enough to govern by himself, while York lies patiently in wait for an opportunity to seize the crown. Contemptuous of the weak, monk-like King, and eager to get complete control over him, Margaret is extremely jealous of Eleanor Cobham, Duchess of Gloucester, and, willing to assist the cabal against the Protector by undermining him through the aspirations of his wife. Knowing Eleanor's desire to be queen, the plotters involve her with witches and conjurers. While the Duchess and her associates are at their sorceries, York and Buckingham break into the garden, and according to the law, arrest them all as traitors. The Duchess, however, has received a cryptic message from the spirits that the Duke yet lives that shall depose King Henry, that the Duke of Suffolk shall die by water, and that the Duke of Somerset should avoid castles.

HENRY VI: PART II

Act II

While the hatred between Gloucester and Cardinal Beaufort continues to smolder, the devout young King is easily duped by any so-called "miracle." York, reciting his long lineage to Salisbury and Warwick, convinces them that he is the rightful heir and gains their support in his attempt to seize the throne. Meanwhile, the Duchess of Gloucester is tried for her sorcery and banished to the Isle of Man, while her husband, unable to justify her before the law, and overcome by grief and shame, begs leave to retire. Henry thereupon relieves him of his staff of office, and the Queen and her allies have the satisfaction of seeing both of their objects attained. As he takes leave of his repentant Duchess, Humphrey is surprised by a summons to a meeting of Parliament in Bury St. Edmunds.

Act III

While Gloucester is on his way to Parliament, the Queen and Suffolk, assisted by the Cardinal and York, do all in their power to poison the mind of the King against him, and when the Duke appears, they accuse him of high treason and send him to prison. Knowing Gloucester's popularity with the Commons and the favor of the King, the conspirators plot to murder him; Suffolk is to censure well the deed, and the Cardinal is to provide the executioners to strangle him. Meanwhile, the old feud between the two houses is revived. A rebellion has broken out in Ireland, and the Cardinal and Suffolk, assuming royal authority, try to get rid of their rival by sending York to suppress it. York is delighted at the opportunity of raising an army, and before leaving on his expedition, encourages Jack Cade of Ashford, a common laborer, to stir up trouble in England in order that he may return to usurp the throne. When their leader, Gloucester, is dead, the Commons revolt and, selecting Salisbury and Warwick as spokesmen, accuse Suffolk and demand his banishment. The King agrees, and Suffolk bids farewell to the Queen, who confesses her love for him and vows either to have him recalled or to contrive to follow him. Meanwhile, a sudden illness has

131

seized Cardinal Beaufort, who dies blaspheming God and cursing men on earth.

Act IV

Suffolk, taken prisoner by pirates off the coast of Kent, is killed by a seaman named Walter Whitmore, who thus fulfills the prophecy to the Duchess of Gloucester that he should die by water. His head is sent to the Queen, who mourns him grievously. At Blackheath, Jack Cade, followed by a rabble of citizens, is in rebellion, claiming that he is John Mortimer and heir to the crown. He seizes London Bridge, and sitting on London Stone, lays claim to the city; but Lord Clifford, by skilful allusions to Henry V and hatred of the French, has little difficulty in turning the fickle mob against their leader. Meanwhile, word reaches the King that York is in arms to second Cade, and the conciliatory Henry sends Buckingham to make peace with promises that Somerset shall be confined in the Tower. Cade flees, and after hiding for several days, is killed by Alexander Iden, who is knighted by the King.

Act V

York, backed by his army, is at first conciliatory, professing only to desire the removal of Somerset; but finding Somerset at liberty, he becomes openly defiant, declaring that the King's hand is more fit to grasp a palmer's staff than to wield a princely sceptre, and is proclaimed a traitor. Clifford and his son bring their forces to support the King, Warwick and Salisbury support York, and the two armies withdraw to prepare for battle. At St. Albans the houses of York and Lancaster meet in conflict; York is victorious, and his son, crook-back Richard, distinguishes himself by killing Somerset near the Castle Inn, thus fulfilling the third prophecy to the Duchess of Gloucester. Hearing that the King and Queen have fled, York hastens to reach London before the monarch can call Parliament together.

Henry VI: Part III

Dramatis Personæ

HENRY VI, King of England, the same "bashful," "timorous," "shamefac'd Henry," "whose hand is made to grasp a palmer's staff, and not to grace an awful princely sceptre."

EDWARD, Prince of Wales, his manly son, every inch a prince, "framed in the prodigality of nature," "young, valiant, wise, and, no doubt right royal," and hence, a foil to his father.

MARGARET, Queen of King Henry, "Captain Margaret," the "stern, obdurate, flinty, rough, remorseless," "she-wolf of France" who does not know when she is beaten.

THE DUKE OF SOMERSET,
THE EARL OF OXFORD,
THE EARL OF WESTMORELAND,
THE EARL OF NORTHUMBERLAND } of the Red Rose, or Lancaster, faction.
THE MARQUIS OF MONTAGUE,
THE DUKE OF EXETER,
LORD CLIFFORD,

HENRY, Earl of Richmond, "England's hope," "a pretty lad;" "his looks are full of peaceful majesty, his head by nature fram'd to wear a crown."

RICHARD PLANTAGENET, Duke of York, the ambitious pretender to the throne.

EDWARD, Earl of March, "the lustful Edward," a "proud insulting boy," afterwards King Edward IV,
EDMUND, Earl of Rutland, a lad still in the hands of his tutor.
GEORGE, afterwards Duke of Clarence, a "quick-sand of deceit," } his sons.
RICHARD, afterwards Duke of Gloucester, "hard-favor'd Richard," "a ragged fatal rock," and "an undigested and deformed lump,"

RICHARD NEVILLE, Earl of Warwick, "long-tongu'd," "wind-changing Warwick," "proud setter-up and puller down of kings,"
THE DUKE OF NORFOLK,
THE EARL OF PEMBROKE,
LORD HASTINGS, } of the White Rose,
LORD STAFFORD, or York, faction.
SIR JOHN MORTIMER, } uncles of the Duke of Suffolk,
SIR HUGH MORTIMER,
SIR JOHN MONTGOMERY,
SIR WILLIAM STANLEY,
SIR JOHN SOMERVILLE,

ELIZABETH WOODVILLE, widow of Sir Richard Grey (slain at St. Albans), and afterwards Queen of Edward IV.

LORD RIVERS, brother of Lady Grey.
LOUIS XI, King of France.
BONA, sister of the French Queen, betrothed to Edward IV.
THE MAYOR OF YORK, a "good old man."
THE LIEUTENANT OF THE TOWER.
TUTOR to Rutland.
A SON that has killed his father, and A FATHER that has killed his son.
Noblemen, Soldiers, Keepers, Huntsmen, Messengers, Watchmen, and Attendants.

Scene of the Action: Various parts of England, and France.

Act I

When Henry arrives in London, Richard of York, backed by Warwick, is already seated on the throne in the House of Parliament. Arguing that Henry VI holds a crown inherited from a usurper (Henry IV), York moves only when Henry weakly begs to be allowed to wear the crown during his lifetime and confirms the succession to York on his death. When she hears of his disgrace, Margaret denounces her timorous husband and vows to raise an army against the usurpers. Meanwhile, yielding to the ambition of his heirs, Edward and Richard, York agrees to usurp the throne at once. Word is brought that Margaret is advancing with her army, and in a battle near Wakefield, she is victorious; York's young son, Edmund, Earl of Rutland, is tortured and slain; York himself is cruelly stabbed by Clifford and the Queen after being crowned with a paper crown; and his head is set up over the gates of York.

Act II

Edward and Richard, sons of the dead York, hear the news of their father's defeat, and joined by Warwick, who has suffered defeat in a second encounter with the Queen at St. Albans, resolve to carry on the fight. For the sake of the young Prince, Clifford and the Queen meanwhile do their best to instill some manhood into the King, whose conscience is troubling him about the ill-gotten crown he wears. After a parley of mutual defiance, the forces meet between Towton and Saxton, in Yorkshire. While the King, chid from the battle by his Queen, sits on a hill wishing he were dead or permitted to live the quiet life of a homely

swain, father's hand is raised against son's and son's against
father's in civil war, and the Queen's forces are defeated. Clifford
is captured and beheaded, Edward of York is declared King
Edward IV, and Warwick hastens to France to obtain for the
new King the hand of Bona, sister-in-law of Louis XI. His
brother George is made Duke of Clarence and Richard, Duke of
Gloucester.

Act III

Henry, the deposed King, stealing from Scotland, where he
has been hiding, for a sight of his own dear land, is recognized
in a forest by two gamekeepers, sent to London, and imprisoned
in the Tower. Edward, the King, visited by the widowed Lady
Elizabeth Grey, who begs for the restoration of her husband's
estates, falls in love with her, and finding her averse to dishonorable proposals, offers to make her his Queen. Meanwhile, crook-
back Richard plans to get the crown. At the French court, Warwick meets Margaret, the deposed Queen, and her son Edward,
seeking aid to recover the crown. Knowing that if the proposed
marriage is consummated, Henry's claims will come to naught,
Margaret denounces Warwick, who, nevertheless, obtains the
consent of Bona and Louis to the alliance. Just as the negotiations
are being completed, word arrives that Edward has married Lady
Grey, and incensed at this breach of honor and the insult to himself, Warwick denounces Edward and is reconciled with Margaret, while France joins forces with them to restore Henry to
the throne. As a pledge for his good faith, Warwick offers his
eldest daughter to the young Prince Edward in marriage, and
Edward accepts.

Act IV

Meanwhile, in England, the brothers have fallen into dissension, which is interrupted by the news from France. Gloucester, for love of the crown, not of his brother, supports Edward,
while Clarence joins Warwick and is betrothed to his second
daughter. Near the town of Warwick the invading forces succeed in wresting the crown from Edward's head, release Henry
from the Tower, and replace him on the throne. The passive

King, however, resigns his government to Warwick and Clarence and plans to lead a simple life in retirement. Meanwhile, Edward escapes from his careless captor, the Archbishop of York, makes his way to Burgundy, returns with an army, recovers his estates in York, and marches upon London. Henry is again thrown into the Tower, Edward resumes the crown, and sets out for Coventry to meet Warwick.

Act V

In the battle, Clarence, that "quick-sand of deceit" removes the red rose from his helmet and refuses to be so unnatural as to fight his brothers, and Warwick, "the bug that fear'd [them] all," after fighting valiantly, is slain. Margaret, bringing reinforcements from France, is met near Tewkesbury, defeated, and taken prisoner. Prince Edward, nobly defying the three brothers, is treacherously stabbed to death, while Richard, Duke of Gloucester, hastens to London. Finding the King reading in the Tower, he stabs him to death. Edward and Elizabeth with their infant son reclaim the throne which has cost so many noble lives, Queen Margaret is ransomed by her father, and Richard of Gloucester bides his time.

Richard III

Dramatis Personæ

RICHARD, Duke of Gloucester, afterwards King Richard III, brother of the King, Edward IV, "hell's black intelligencer," "that foul defacer of God's handiwork," and "that bottl'd spider, that foul bunch-back'd toad."

THE DUKE OF BUCKINGHAM, his "second self," his "counsel's consistory," his "oracle," and his "prophet."

HENRY TUDOR, Earl of Richmond, afterwards King Henry VII, "God's captain" and "minister of chastisement," the agent of justice against Richard.

EDWARD IV, King of England, "sickly, weak, and melancholy," on his death-bed.

ELIZABETH, his Queen, "a care-craz'd mother to a many sons, a beauty-waning and distressed widow, even in the afternoon of her best days."

EDWARD, Prince of Wales, afterwards King Edward V; "so wise so young, they say, do never live long."

RICHARD, Duke of York, "bold, quick, ingenious, forward, capable, he is all the mother's from top to toe."

> young sons of Edward IV.

GEORGE, Duke of Clarence, the unhappy "false, fleeting, perjur'd Clarence," brother of the King and of Richard of Gloucester, a well-spoken, guileless dreamer, afflicted by premonitions and a bad conscience.

THE DUCHESS OF YORK, mother of Edward IV, Clarence, and Gloucester.

LADY ANNE, widow of Edward, Prince of Wales, son of King Henry VI; afterwards married to Richard of Gloucester.

MARGARET, widow of King Henry VI, once a proud, beautiful queen, now a pitiful shrunken hag and the speaker of horrible prophecies.

SIR WILLIAM CATESBY,
SIR RICHARD RATCLIFF,
LORD LOVEL,
THE DUKE OF NORFOLK,
THE EARL OF SURREY, his son,
SIR JAMES TYRREL,

> supporters of King Richard.

EARL RIVERS, brother of Queen Elizabeth.
THE MARQUIS OF DORSET, sons of Queen Elizabeth
LORD GREY, by a former marriage,
LORD HASTINGS,
LORD STANLEY, the Earl of Derby,
SIR THOMAS VAUGHAN,

> supporters of the Queen.

THE EARL OF OXFORD,
JOHN MORTON, Bishop of Ely,
SIR JAMES BLUNT,
SIR WALTER HERBERT,
SIR WILLIAM BRANDON, Keeper of the Tower,

> followers of the Earl of Richmond.

137

Cardinal Bourchier, Archbishop of Canterbury.

Thomas Rotherham, Archbishop of York.

Sir Robert Brakenbury, Lieutenant of the Towers.

Tressel and Berkeley, gentlemen attending the Lady Anne.

The Lord Mayor of London.

Christopher Urswick, a priest.

Another Priest.

The Sheriff of Wiltshire.

A Young Son and Daughter of Clarence.

A Scrivener.

Several Murderers.

Lords, Gentlemen, Citizens, Messengers, Soldiers, Ghosts, and Attendants.

Scene of the Action: England.

Act I

Now that the wars are over, deformed Richard, who is unsuited to the dalliance of peace and feels keenly the fact that he was "cheated of feature by dissembling nature," determines to play the villain and seize the throne. He begins by reviving an old prophecy "that G of Edward's heirs the murderer shall be," and arouses the hatred of King Edward against his brother George, Duke of Clarence. When Clarence is arrested, Richard lays the blame upon Lady Grey, the King's wife, promises to secure his brother's release as soon as possible, and gives orders that he be murdered. Next, he interrupts the funeral procession of King Henry VI. In the very presence of the corpse of one of his victims, Richard listens to the curses of the Lady Anne, widow of Prince Edward, and in spite of his murder of her father, her husband, and her king, succeeds in convincing her that all was done for love of her and in getting her to accept an engagement ring. Again seeming a saint when most he plays the devil, Richard visits the court where Edward lies ill, braves the curses of Queen Margaret, and by complaining of his wrongs, succeeds in convincing Derby, Hastings, and Buckingham, that it is Queen Elizabeth and her allies who have poisoned the mind of the King against Clarence. Meanwhile, Clarence, repenting the sins he had committed for Edward, is cruelly stabbed in the Tower, and his body drowned in a butt of malmsey wine.

RICHARD III

Act II

On his death-bed, Edward gathers the members of the hostile factions of his wife and Richard and succeeds in achieving at least the semblance of peace. Gloucester brings word of Clarence's death, and Edward, believing himself responsible for it, repents his suspicions of him and dies. In her grief, Elizabeth joins the Duchess of York, who now has two sons to mourn, and together they lament the loss of all their comfort. The young Prince Edward is sent for from Ludlow to be crowned, and Buckingham, Richard's "other self," promises his cousin to separate the Prince from the Queen's proud kindred. Hence, word soon reaches Elizabeth that her staunchest supporters, Lord Rivers, Lord Grey, and Sir Thomas Vaughan, have been imprisoned by Richard in Pomfret Castle, and fearful of her safety, the Queen seeks sanctuary with her younger son.

Act III

Arriving in London with the young Prince of Wales, Richard contrives to get the boy's brother, the Duke of York, away from his mother, and with the greatest show of affection and courtesy has them lodged in the Tower, as if in preparation for the coronation. Through his henchman, Catesby, he sounds out Hastings as to his possible support in a claim for the crown, but finds him a loyal adherent to the young Prince. Richard then summons Hastings to a council called to make plans for the approaching coronation, and though apparently in the very best of humors, in the merest petulance accuses him of treason and orders his immediate execution before dinner. About the same time, the other supporters of the Prince, Rivers, Grey, and Vaughan, prisoners at Pomfret Castle, are executed. Then, in company with Buckingham and dressed in rusty, battered armor, Richard pretends that great danger threatens, and by his hypocritical tears, he craftily convinces the Lord Mayor of the justice and necessity of Hastings' hurried execution. At the same time, Buckingham is sent to the Guildhall to emphasize again the immorality of the dead King Edward, to imply that his children are all illegitimate, and even to hint that Edward

139

himself was basely born. As a result, the citizens of London, headed by the Lord Mayor, wait upon Richard to offer him the crown. Pretending to be deeply occupied with his devotions, Richard seems loath to permit even serious affairs of state to interrupt his meditations, but at length he appears on a balcony attended by two bishops and absorbed in a prayer book. His obvious piety, duly emphasized by Buckingham, so impresses the citizens that they at length overcome his hypocritical reluctance and persuade him to accept the crown. Arrangements are made for an immediate coronation.

Act IV

News of Richard's usurpation reaches the Queen Mother first when, in company with the Duchess of York and Lady Anne, she attempts to gain admission to the Tower to visit her sons. The despair of all three is unbounded, and when an order comes to Anne to hasten to Westminster to be crowned, she does so woefully. When Richard, having attained the crown through Buckingham's assistance, suggests to him the murder of the little princes to secure his position there, Buckingham falters and begs for a little time to consider. Meanwhile, news that the Marquis of Dorset had fled to Brittany to join Henry Richmond sets Richard planning further villainies. He orders Catesby to give out rumors that his wife Anne is mortally ill, arranges a lowly match for Margaret, daughter of the Duke of Clarence, imprisons Clarence's son, and engages Tyrrel to undertake the murder of the princes. When Buckingham returns to tell Richard of his decision, the King treats him coolly and ignores utterly his request for the earldom of Hereford, which he had previously promised him. Buckingham, knowing well what he may expect from the villainous King, resolves to join Richmond. Tyrrel reports the murder of the princes, Anne dies as Richard had arranged, and accompanied by the curses of the Queen Elizabeth, Richard offers himself as a husband for his niece, his brother Edward's daughter, the Princess Elizabeth, already betrothed to Richmond. Meanwhile, Richmond with a mighty army has landed at Milford, and joined by many English nobles, is marching inland to claim the crown. While Richard is gathering his forces to meet him, word is brought of the capture of Buckingham, who is subsequently executed at Salisbury.

Act V

The two armies meet on Bosworth Field, and on the night before the battle, while the two leaders are encamped side by side, the ghosts of all of Richard's victims parade before them, appearing as terrifying visions to Richard and prophesying his defeat, but seeming the "fairest boding dreams" to Richmond in their assurances that "God and good angels" will fight upon his side. Completely unnerved, Richard sets out to spy upon his troops to determine their loyalty, while Richmond, in jocund mind, confidently prepares for battle. Both harangue their armies, Richmond appealing to his men to rid the land of a bloody tyrant, who "hath ever been God's enemy," and Richard urging his forces to drive out the foreign invaders, "a scum of Bretons, and base lackey peasants" led by a "milk-sop." Though he fights desperately, Richard is overcome and slain in personal combat with Richmond. Accepting the crown as Henry VII, Richmond proposes to marry Elizabeth of York, thus uniting the white rose and the red, and bringing to an end this civil strife:

> "England hath long been mad, and scarr'd herself . . .
> O, now, let Richmond and Elizabeth, . . .
> And let their heirs, God, if thy will be so,
> Enrich the time to come with smooth fac'd Peace,
> With smiling Plenty and fair prosperous days!"

Henry VIII

Dramatis Personæ

HENRY VIII, King of England, a proud, selfish monarch.

THOMAS WOLSEY, Cardinal of York, Lord Chancellor of England, an arrogant, over-bearing churchman, "by Fortune and his Highness' favor [he has] gone slightly o'er low steps and [is] now mounted where powers are [his] retainers," "a scholar, and a ripe and good one, exceeding wise, fair-spoken, and persuading," yet one who is "ever double both in his words and meaning," and "a man of unbounded stomach, ever ranking himself with princes, one that by suggestion tied all the kingdom."

CRANMER, Archbishop of Canterbury, a meek, patient, honest churchman, and foil to Wolsey.

KATHERINE OF ARRAGON, Queen of King Henry, who "like a jewel has hung twenty years about his neck, yet never lost her lustre," "a true humble wife at all times," and, in general, "so good a lady that no tongue could ever pronounce dishonor of her." "That man i' the world who shall report he has a better wife, let him in nought be trusted."

ANNE BULLEN, her maid of honor, afterwards Queen, "a dainty one," and "the goodliest woman that ever lay by man."

THE DUKE OF BUCKINGHAM, the "mirror of all courtesy," "learn'd and a most rare speaker; to Nature none more bound," opposed by Wolsey, and, unlike him, loved by the Commons.

LORD ABERGAVENNY, his son-in-law,
THE DUKE OF NORFOLK,
THE DUKE OF SUFFOLK,
THE EARL OF SURREY,
THE LORD CHAMBERLAIN,
THE LORD CHANCELLOR, successor to Wolsey,
LORD SANDYS (also called SIR WILLIAM SANDYS),
SIR HENRY GUILDFORD,
SIR THOMAS LOVELL,
SIR ANTHONY DENNY,
SIR NICHOLAS VAUX,

} gentlemen of the court.

CARDINAL CAMPEIUS, papal legate.

GARDINER, Bishop of Winchester.

THE BISHOP OF LINCOLN.

CAPUCIUS, ambassador from the Emperor Charles V to Queen Katherine.

DOCTOR BUTTS, King Henry's physician.

BRANDON, and a sergeant-at-arms.

GARTER-KING-AT-ARMS.

CROMWELL, faithful servant of Wolsey.

HENRY VIII

SURVEYOR to the Duke of Buckingham, a false servant.
GRIFFITH, gentleman-usher of Queen Katherine.
PATIENCE, woman-in-waiting of Queen Katherine.
AN OLD LADY, friend of Anne Bullen.
A PORTER and his man.
Lords, Ladies, Bishops, Secretaries, Scribes, Door-keepers, Officers, Guards, Criers, Pages, Attendants, and Spirits.

Scene of the Action: London, Westminster, Kimbolton.

Act I

Some time after the return of King Henry from his meeting with the French King at the Field of the Cloth of Gold, some English nobles, including the Duke of Buckingham, discuss the splendor and the futility of that event, and remark upon the growing power of the ambitious Cardinal Wolsey, and his influence over the King. Against the advice of his friends, Buckingham is about to expose Wolsey to the King, when they are interrupted by officers who arrest Buckingham and his son-in-law, Lord Abergavenny, on charges of high treason. Judging that Wolsey is behind the accusation, the honest Duke, on hearing the names of the witnesses against him, is convinced that the Cardinal has bribed them. The good Katherine interrupts the King's affairs to plead on behalf of the people against the oppression of certain unjust taxes and to warn him of the bitter discontent and suffering that have arisen in consequence. Mildly rebuking the Cardinal, the King graciously repeals the laws and pardons all who have resisted them, but Wolsey takes care that the people shall believe that the laws were revoked through his influence. The Queen also intercedes for Buckingham, pointing out that his principal accuser is the Duke's surveyor, who has been dismissed from office on the complaints of the tenants, but the King is unconvinced. To a banquet at York Place, Cardinal Wolsey has invited "a sweet society of fair ones," and there the King, who makes one of a party of masquers, disguised as shepherds, for the first time meets Anne Bullen and dances with her.

Act II

At the trial of Buckingham, it is clear that the trumped-up charges of treason all grow out of the fact that he is next in line to the throne, should the King die without an heir. Nobly forgiving his accusers, the Duke is led to execution. Meanwhile, since meeting Anne Bullen, the King's tender conscience is troubling him with increased vigor over scruples, suggested originally by Wolsey, that his marriage with Katherine, his brother Arthur's widow, is unholy. He publicly shows his favor to Anne by creating her Marchioness of Pembroke with a thousand pounds a year. When Katherine is called to a public trial for divorce before Wolsey and a papal legate as judges, she declares her devotion and fidelity to the King during their twenty years of marriage, refuses to be judged by Wolsey, whom she accuses of instigating the divorce, and appeals directly to the Pope. Wolsey appeals to the King to exonerate him before the court, and Henry not only does so, but even gives his own version of the origin of his fears and the anguish which they have caused him.

Act III

Dismayed that the King's affections are directed at a Protestant when he had hoped for an alliance with France by a royal marriage with the Duchess of Alençon, Wolsey sends a message to Rome to delay the divorce. He even takes Katherine's side secretly and offers her his aid, but she distrusts him. One day by chance, some private papers belonging to the Cardinal are delivered to the King, among them both a copy of the incriminating letter to Rome and an inventory of his wealth great enough to make even a king envious. Confronted with these evidences of his duplicity and worldly ambition, and deprived of his offices, Wolsey bids a touching farewell to his faithful servant Cromwell, delivers his possessions to the crown, and retires from the court. Soon after, "full of repentance" for his ambition and vanity, and under arrest for treason, he dies at Leicester. Meanwhile, the King has married Anne Bullen in secret.

Act IV

Cranmer, the Archbishop of Canterbury, because of the King's conscientious scruples and the non-appearance of the

Queen at a trial, annuls the marriage with Katherine of Arragon, who is given the title of Princess Dowager and a residence at Kimbolton. There, while the new Queen is being crowned, she lies ill, attended by her faithful servants, Griffith and Patience. As she sleeps, beautiful, golden-faced spirits of peace, clad in white robes, appear to her in a vision, congee to her, and crown her with garlands. Soon after, having commended her daughter, Mary, and her attendants to the King's mercy, she dies.

Act V

Wolsey's place as an influence over the King is taken by Cranmer, and the nobles, complaining that he is "a most arch heretic, a pestilence that does infect the land," organize an opposition against him. The King, however, convinced of his truth and integrity, permits his council to bring the Archbishop to trial, but gives him a ring of authority to protect him. Kept waiting in an anteroom with lackeys and footmen, and otherwise treated with disrespect, the Archbishop saves himself from imprisonment in the Tower only by presenting the King's ring. Henry, who has been an unseen witness of his indignities, sharply reprimands the nobles, and commands them to treat the Archbishop with friendliness. He then shows Cranmer the marked favor of asking him to stand as godfather at the baptism of the little Princess Elizabeth, whose birth has just been announced. At the christening, the Archbishop speaks an eloquent prophecy of the glory this infant will some day bring to England:

> "In her days every man shall eat in safety,
> Under his own vine, what he plants, and sing
> The merry songs of peace to all his neighbors . . . .
> She shall be, to the happiness of England,
> An aged princess, many days shall see her,
> And yet no day without a deed to crown it."

Tragedies

Titus Andronicus

Dramatis Personæ

TITUS ANDRONICUS, a noble Roman, "patron of virtue, Rome's best champion," and victorious general against the Goths.

LUCIUS,
QUINTUS,
MARTIUS,
MUTIUS, } sons of Titus Andronicus.

YOUNG LUCIUS, a "tender sapling," son of Lucius Andronicus, and grandson of Titus.

MARCUS ANDRONICUS, tribune of the people, and brother of Titus.

PUBLIUS, son of Marcus the Tribune.

SATURNINUS, treacherous son of the late Emperor of Rome and afterwards declared Emperor.

TAMORA, revengeful captive Queen of the Goths and later Roman Empress.

ALARBUS,
DEMETRIUS,
CHIRON, } sons of Tamora.

AARON, a villainous Moor with a "fiend-like face," beloved by Tamora.

BASSIANUS, honest brother of Saturninus, betrothed and later husband of Lavinia.

LAVINIA, "Rome's rich ornament," daughter of Titus Andronicus and beloved of Bassianus; "Lucrece was not more chaste."

AEMILIUS, a noble Roman.

SEMPRONIUS,
CAIUS,
VALENTINE, } kinsmen of Titus Andronicus.

A NURSE and a black child, offspring of Aaron and Tamora.

A CLOWNISH COUNTRYMAN.

Senators, Tribunes, Officers, Soldiers, Attendants, Goths, and Romans.

Scene of the Action: Rome and the country near it.

Act I

Returning to Rome in triumph from the Gothic wars, Titus Andronicus brings with him as captives, Tamora, Queen of the Goths and her three sons, one of whom, in spite of his mother's tears, is sacrificed by the Andronici to appease the souls of their slain brothers. As a reward for his victories, the imperial crown is offered to Titus, but he refuses it and supports instead the claim of "proud Saturnine," elder son of the former Emperor, and accepts his proposal that he make Titus' daughter, Lavinia, his Empress. Bassianus, younger brother of Saturninus, however, declares that Lavinia is engaged to him, and with the support of her brothers, abducts her to prevent the marriage. So angry and so just is Titus at this breach of faith to the new Emperor that he kills one of his own sons for blocking his pursuit of the runaways. Saturninus, meanwhile, has gazed with favor upon Tamora, and seizing the first opportunity of dishonoring Titus, calls him traitor, and chooses the Gothic queen as his bride. Dissembling her bitter desire to avenge the death of her son, the ruthless Tamora urges Saturninus to receive Titus and his sons into favor again, to forgive Bassianus, and in secret to plot with her the general's downfall.

Act II

While hunting in the wood, Aaron, the Moorish lover of Tamora, hears her sons, Demetrius and Chiron, quarreling over their lust for Lavinia, and incites them each to ravish her in turn; they insure her silence by tearing out her tongue and cutting off her hands. During the hunt also, Bassianus and Lavinia in a lonely bower discover Tamora and Aaron at their love-making. Afraid that they will report to the Emperor, Tamora calls her sons and pretends that Bassianus and Lavinia have insulted her and threatened her with torture. The sons kill Bassianus and throw his body into a pit, and, deaf to Lavinia's pleas that she also be slain, Tamora permits them to drag her off to ravishment. Soon afterward, led by the treacherous Aaron, two of Titus' sons, Martius and Quintus, fall into the pit where Bassianus' body is concealed, and the Emperor accuses them of the murder.

Act III

Regardless of Titus' pleading, the judges sentence Titus' sons to death, and banish a third, Lucius, for attempting to rescue them. Aaron the Moor, however, treacherously brings Titus word that the Emperor will spare their lives if Marcus, Lucius, or Titus will but chop off one of his hands and send it to him as evidence of good faith. While the brother and the son are contending as to which shall make the sacrifice, old Titus with Aaron's aid cuts off his own hand and sends it to the Emperor, but the hand, together with his sons' heads, is scornfully sent back to him. Titus vows vengeance, and orders his banished son to hie to the Goths and raise an army there.

Act IV

In spite of her mutilation, Lavinia manages to convey to her father and her uncle the full story of her wrongs. With her stumps she turns the pages of the book of Ovid's *Metamorphoses* until she finds the tragic tale of Philomela, and holding a stick in her mouth, she writes in the sand the names of Chiron and Demetrius. Feigning madness, Titus sends weapons to Chiron and Demetrius, addresses messages to the gods, fastens them to arrows and shoots them in the Roman streets, and even sends a letter to the Emperor. Meanwhile, Tamora gives birth to a blackamoor, Aaron's child, which the evil brothers wish to kill; but he defends it, kills the nurse and the mid-wife to insure secrecy, arranges for the substitution of a white baby which may be presented to the Emperor as his, and takes his son to the Goths to be reared. News reaches Rome that Lucius is advancing on the city with a huge army, and fearing his popularity, Tamora has Saturninus arrange a parley with the general at Titus' house, in the hope that she can thus separate him from his army.

Act V

Accompanied by her two sons, Tamora in disguise presents herself as Revenge to the supposedly mad Titus. When she returns to tell the Emperor of her joke and accompany him to the banquet, Titus cuts the throats of the villains, as Lavinia catches their blood in a basin, and at the feast serves them up to the Empress baked in a pie. In the general holocaust that follows, Titus slays Lavinia to end her shame and then stabs Tamora; Saturninus kills Titus; and Lucius, Saturninus. Lucius then tells the people the true story of his father's tragedy and is proclaimed Emperor, while Aaron, the breeder of these crimes, is condemned to death by torture.

Romeo and Juliet

Dramatis Personæ

CAPULET,
MONTAGUE, } heads of two families in Verona who are at variance with each other.

LADY MONTAGUE,
LADY CAPULET, } their wives.

ROMEO, heir of the Montagues and a "virtuous and well governed youth" who, as the play opens, is suffering, however, from a sentimental infatuation for a disdainful mistress whom he promptly forgets upon meeting Juliet. "Though his face be better than any man's, yet his leg excels all men's; and for a hand, and a foot, and a body, though they be not to be talked on, yet they are past compare. He is not the flower of courtesy, but, I'll warrant him, as gentle as a lamb."

JULIET, daughter of the Capulets.

MERCUTIO, kinsman of the Prince; witty and realistic foil to the sentimental Romeo; "a gentleman . . . that loves to hear himself talk, and will speak more in a minute than he will stand to in a month."

BENVOLIO, a peacemaker, nephew of Montague and friend of Romeo.

TYBALT, nephew of Capulet and foil to Benvolio; a "couragcous captain of compliments," and a trained fencer who "fights by the book of arithmetic."

PARIS, a young nobleman, "a man of wax," kinsman of the Prince, and suitor for Juliet's hand; favored by Capulet." "An eagle . . . hath not so green, so quick, so fair an eye as Paris hath."

FRIAR LAURENCE, a Franciscan, confidant of Romeo; a genial herbalist and a true friend ever ready with good counsel and assistance.

NURSE, coarse confidante of Juliet and foil to Friar Laurence as an adviser.

ESCALUS, Prince of Verona.

FRIAR JOHN, messenger for Friar Laurence.

AN APOTHECARY, a seller of poisons, and as a scientist, foil to Friar Laurence.

BALTHASAR, servant of Romeo.

SAMPSON,
GREGORY, } servants of Capulet.

ABRAHAM, servant of Montague.

PETER, attendant of Juliet's Nurse.

Musicians, Maskers, Pages, Watchmen, Officers, Citizens, and Attendants.

Scene of the Action: Verona and Mantua.

151

Act I

In "fair Verona" a fresh outbreak of the ancient feud between the Montagues and Capulets causes the Prince to order all brawls to cease under penalty of death. Romeo, heir of the Montagues, fancies himself deeply in love with the fair, but disdainful Rosaline. To cure him, Benvolio, his friend, persuades him to go masked to a ball given by old Capulet, in order that he may compare Rosaline with other beauties and vows to make him think his "swan a crow." There he is attracted by a girl whose beauty teaches the "torches to burn bright," and is dismayed to learn from a servant that she is Juliet, daughter of the Capulets. Juliet, too, upon enquiring after Romeo's name, confesses to herself that her only love has sprung from her only hate. Meanwhile, the fiery Tybalt recognizes Romeo, but is sternly forbidden by old Capulet to do a guest any harm, and vows to settle the score later.

Act II

Having slipped away from his friends, Romeo lingers in Capulet's garden under Juliet's window, and overhears her confess to the stars that she loves him. He reveals his presence to her, and in an ardent love scene, they resolve to be married secretly. Next day, Juliet sends her nurse, of whom she has made a confidante, to make final arrangements, and the wedding is performed at the cell of Friar Laurence, Romeo's friend, who hopes by this alliance to turn their "households' rancor to pure love."

Act III

Returning from his wedding, Romeo comes upon his friends, Benvolio and Mercutio, in altercation with Tybalt, who has been seeking Romeo because of his intrusion at the ball. Tybalt does his best to pick a fight, but Romeo, remembering that now Tybalt is his kinsman, turns his insults aside and refuses to quarrel. Mercutio, however, who does not understand Romeo's softness, takes the quarrel upon himself, and when Romeo and Benvolio try to beat down their weapons is slain by Tybalt. Aroused by the death of his best friend, Romeo throws aside his lenity, slays Tybalt, and flees as the angry citizens begin to gather. The Prince banishes the offender, who in despair has taken refuge in Friar Laurence's cell. There he receives a ring from the grief-stricken Juliet, with a message that he visit her at night. By means of a rope ladder Romeo climbs to Juliet's chamber and at dawn flees to Mantua. Meanwhile, Juliet's parents, knowing nothing of her marriage to Romeo and thinking that all her grief is for her cousin's death, seek to alleviate her sorrow by insisting that she marry at once Paris, a kinsman of the Prince.

Act IV

In despair, Juliet consults Friar Laurence, who advises her to seem to agree to the marriage with Paris, and gives her a sleeping potion, which for a time will cause her to appear as dead. Instead of being married to Paris, she will be borne to the Capulet's burial vault, and by the time she awakes, Romeo will have had the opportunity to return and take her way to Mantua. Juliet, who would rather die than marry Paris, courageously follows the Friar's instructions.

Act V

By an accident the Friar's letter does not reach Romeo, and he hears of Juliet's death from another source. Resolute in his despair, he too procures a sleeping potion—a deadly one—from an apothecary, and returns to Verona at night. As he is opening the Capulet tomb, he is interrupted by Paris, who has come to strew his beloved's grave with flowers, and is obliged to kill him. At Juliet's side, Romeo drinks his poison and dies. Just as Friar Laurence arrives to release her, Juliet awakes, and realizing Romeo's error, kills herself with his dagger. At the tomb, over these sacrifices to their enmity, Montague and Capulet clasp hands and are at last reconciled.

Julius Caesar

Dramatis Personæ

JULIUS CAESAR, who "doth bestride the narrow world like a Colossus," but who has in his last years the "falling sickness" and is spoiled by success and adulation, ruled by superstition, and is at once ambitious and fearful.

CALPURNIA, Caesar's wife, who worships and fears him.

MARCUS BRUTUS, one of the leading conspirators against Caesar, who "sits high in all the people's hearts," an idealist of character so pure that he could suspect no stain in any man; worthy of the epitaph of his greatest enemy:

> "This was the noblest Roman of them all . . . .
> His life was gentle, and the elements
> So mixed in him that Nature might stand up
> And say to all the world, 'This was a man!' "

PORTIA, Brutus' "true and honorable wife," who would not dwell "in the suburbs of [his] good pleasure."

CAIUS CASSIUS, another of the leading conspirators, Brutus' brother-in-law and foil, as direct and practical as Brutus is idealistic and visionary; moved by envy in his hatred of Caesar and possessed of "an itching palm." "Yond Cassius has a lean and hungry look, he thinks too much; such men are dangerous. . . . He reads much, he is a great observer, and he looks quite through the deeds of men."

CASCA, another conspirator, a "sour" aristocrat who hates the "sweaty nightcaps . . . and . . . stinking breath" of "the tag-rag people," but who is "quick metal . . . in execution of any bold or noble enterprise."

TREBONIUS,
LIGARIUS,
DECIUS BRUTUS, } other conspirators against Caesar.
METELLUS CIMBER,
CINNA,

MARCUS ANTONIUS, "well beloved of Caesar," "a masker and a reveler," but withal "a shrewd contriver," a stirring orator, and a valiant warrior; leader of the opposition against the conspirators; foil to Brutus.

OCTAVIUS CAESAR, grandnephew and heir of Julius Caesar, young, cold-hearted, and politic leader of the army against the conspirators, and member with Antony and Lepidus of the triumvirate formed after the death of his uncle.

M. AEMILIUS LEPIDUS, third member of the triumvirate, "a tried and valiant soldier," but "a slight unmeritable man, meet to be sent on errands," "a barren-spirited fellow," of whom the other two members talk "but as a property."

CICERO,
PUBLIUS, } senators.
POPILIUS LENA,

FLAVIUS,
MARULLUS, } tribunes who are opposed to Caesar.

LUCILIUS,
TITINIUS,
MESSALA, } friends and followers of Brutus and Cassius.
YOUNG CATO,
VOLUMNIUS,

VARRO,
CLITUS,
CLAUDIUS,
STRATO, } servants of Brutus.
LUCIUS,
DARDANIUS,

PINDARUS, servant of Cassius.
ARTEMIDORUS OF CNIDOS, a teacher of Rhetoric.
CINNA, "Cinna the poet . . . not Cinna the conspirator."
ANOTHER POET.
A SOOTHSAYER.
Senators, Citizens, Guards, Attendants, etc.

Scene of the Action: Rome; the neighborhood of Sardis; the neighborhood of Philippi.

Act I

The return of Julius Caesar to Rome "in triumph over Pompey's blood" rejoices "the common herd" but releases against him a conspiracy of nobles who fear the results of his growing ambition, signalized by his being offered the crown thrice by his henchman Mark Antony at the feast of the Lupercalia. Cassius, the most active of the intriguers, plots with Casca, Cinna, and others to "win the noble Brutus to [their] party" so that this nobleman's name and known purity of character may cover their own more sordid motives. Meanwhile, a soothsayer has publicly warned Caesar to "beware the Ides of March."

Act II

Meeting by night at the home of Brutus, Cassius—his brother-in-law—and the other conspirators play upon his better nature until he consents to join them. He advises them, however, to be "sacrificers, but not butchers," to "carve Caesar as a dish fit for the gods," and "for Mark Antony, think not of him." Much as he loves his wife Portia, he avoids at first telling her of the conspiracy; Ligarius, however, learns of it and comes to pledge his loyalty to Brutus. On the night before the conspiracy is to mature, all nature is disturbed, the augurers return unfavorable reports to Caesar's request for a prophecy, and his wife Calpurnia has an ill-omened dream in which she sees his statue running blood, and Romans bathing in it. At her solicitation he decides not to stir out of his house; but Decius Brutus, one of the conspirators, calls upon him, reinterprets dream and portents favorably, and, with the other plotters flocking around them, conducts him through the streets and to the Capitol.

Act III

In vain does the soothsayer who has warned him before remind him that although the Ides of March have come, they have not gone, and in vain does Artemidorus the Rhetorician attempt to present him with a scroll revealing the plot, for Caesar carries it in his hand unopened to his death. In the Capitol, Trebonius entices Mark Antony away while Metellus Cimber presents to Caesar a petition for the recall of his brother from banishment. Casca, Brutus, and the other conspirators crowd up as though to second the request, and when Caesar refuses, first Casca, then the others stab him. "Et tu Brute," he cries, as he sees his friend among his enemies,

> "And, in his mantle muffling up his face,
> Even at the base of Pompey's statue,
> Which all the while ran blood, great Caesar fell."

The fox-like Antony pretends to submit to the conspirators, but subtly obtains from the trusting Brutus permission to address the citizens at Caesar's funeral. After Brutus has declaimed to the people that he has helped kill Caesar "not that [he] loved Caesar less but that [he] loved Rome more," the eloquent Antony, keeping the letter but not the spirit of his agreement not to assail the conspirators in his speech, shows "sweet Caesar's wounds" and stirs the rabble to such mutiny that they rush out to "burn [Caesar's] body in the holy place and with the brands fire the traitors' houses." After having set this mischief afoot, Antony himself goes to join Octavius Caesar and Lepidus that the three may plot further against the conspirators, who have been forced by the uproar to flee from Rome.

JULIUS CAESAR

Act IV

Antony and Octavius, having agreed to combine forces against Cassius and Brutus, set out in pursuit of the conspirators, who are in camp near Sardis. Brutus and Cassius quarrel violently over Brutus' charge that his brother-in-law has been "much condemned to have an itching palm," but the two finally drown all unkindness in a bowl of wine, and when Brutus tells his fellow general that the noble Portia has killed herself on hearing of the union of Octavius and Antony against them, Cassius is so contrite that he allows Brutus to persuade him against his more soldierly judgment to leave the safety of the hills around Sardis and meet the advancing enemy on the plains of Philippi. That night the ghost of Caesar enters Brutus' tent to tell him that they will meet again at Philippi.

Act V

On the plains of Philippi, a parley between the opposing generals having resulted only in an exchange of recriminations, the armies join battle. Against the forces led by Octavius, Brutus has an early success, but on the other wing the legions of Antony press back those of Cassius. Finding himself hard pushed, Cassius sends Titinius to learn "whether yond troops are friend or enemy." Far off the eager watchers see Titinius apparently pulled from his horse by his opponents, and without waiting for a verified report, Cassius orders his servant Pindarus to kill him, and dies with the words "Caesar, thou art revenged, even with the sword that kill'd thee." But Titinius has really met Messala, sent by Brutus to report to Cassius that Octavius is overthrown. They find the general dead, and Titinius nobly follows his master. Too pressed by his enemies to give his brother-in-law more than a passing epitaph and to exclaim "O Julius Caesar, thou art mighty yet! Thy spirit walks abroad, and turns our swords in our own proper entrails," Brutus tries "fortune in a second fight." But he is defeated and left with a few "poor remains of friends." One of these does Brutus the final service of holding the sword while he runs upon it and dies with the words "Caesar, now be still." And thus the conquerors find that this "noblest Roman of them all" did not yield to bondage but "only overcame himself."

Hamlet, Prince of Denmark

Dramatis Personæ

HAMLET, Prince of Denmark, son of the former and nephew of the present king, the "melancholy Dane;" a "sweet prince," "the glass of fashion and the mould of form;" a scholar, gentleman, and idealist, thrust by fate and by social demands into the rôle of bloody avenger which his soul abhors. "He was likely, had he been put on, to have proved most royally."

CLAUDIUS, King of Denmark, an "incestuous, murderous, damned Dane," "a vice of kings, . . . a cutpurse of the empire and the rule, . . . a king of shreds and patches;" as contrasted with his murdered brother, "Hyperion to a satyr."

GERTRUDE, weak-willed Queen of Denmark and mother of Hamlet: "frailty, thy name is woman!"

HORATIO, faithful friend and confidant of Hamlet, "a man that Fortune's buffets and rewards hath ta'en with equal thanks, . . . not passion's slave;" "more an antique Roman than a Dane."

ROSENCRANTZ, GUILDENSTERN, } disloyal friends of Hamlet, "adders fang'd," who would "play upon" him as upon a pipe, and "pluck out the heart of [his] mystery;" foils to Horatio.

POLONIUS, conceited and dull Lord Chamberlain, who thinks that spying is the highest form of state-craft, a "wretched, rash, intruding fool."

LAERTES, hot-headed and impetuous son of Polonius, who shows his sister "the steep and thorny way to heaven, whiles, like a puff'd and reckless libertine, himself the primrose path of dalliance treads;" foil to Hamlet.

OPHELIA, daughter of Polonius and sister of Laertes, beloved by Hamlet but slave to social convention and her father's will.

FORTINBRAS, capable and well-balanced Prince of Norway, "puffed with divine ambition;" foil to Hamlet.

OSRIC, a court "water-fly" and fop, who speaks only "golden words" and who has "only got the tune of the time and outward habit of encounter; a kind of yesty collection."

VOLTIMAND, CORNELIUS, } Danish courtiers sent as ambassadors to the court of Norway.

MARCELLUS, BERNARDO, } Danish officers on guard at the castle.

FRANCISCO, a Danish soldier.

REYNALDO, the patient and long-suffering servant of Polonius.

GHOST OF HAMLET'S FATHER, of "fair and warlike form," "arm'd . . . from top to toe."

A Clownish Grave-digger and his Assistant.
A "churlish Priest."
A Norwegian Captain.
Ambassadors from England.
Strolling Players who perform at the Danish court.
Lords, Ladies, Officers, Soldiers, Sailors, Messengers, and Attendants.

Scene of the Action: Denmark, mainly at the royal castle at Elsinore.

Act I

Hamlet, Prince of Denmark, is summoned from his studies at the University of Wittenberg to the Danish court at Elsinore by news of his royal father's death. His sorrow is deepened by his mother's hasty marriage to his uncle, the crafty Claudius, who has seized the throne and is attempting to prevent the Norwegian prince, Fortinbras, from invading Denmark to recover territory lost when his father was killed in battle with the late king. Claudius permits Laertes, son of the lord chamberlain Polonius, to return to the University of Paris, but orders Hamlet to remain at the Danish court. For counsel the Prince can turn to no one but his friend Horatio, for his mother sides with the King, and Ophelia, the daughter of Polonius, whom he loves, has promised her father that she will reject his suit. Hamlet's distraction is increased by the report of Horatio and two officers that the ghost of his father stalks the battlements of the castle, and in a terrifying encounter with the spectre he learns the dreadful truth: his uncle has killed his father, and he is himself faced with the terrible duty of avenging the murder.

Act II

The insanity which Hamlet feigns as a screen leads the over-confident Polonius to believe that the Prince is mad because Ophelia has repulsed his advances. Of this, however, the King is not convinced, and sets Rosencrantz and Guildenstern to spy upon Hamlet and learn the truth. The Prince plots to "catch the conscience of the King" by having a company of strolling players present before him a murder-play containing episodes which resemble those of the actual killing of his father. In the meantime the King has accepted Fortinbras' promise not to invade Denmark but has granted him permission to march through the country in an invasion of Poland.

Act III

Rosencrantz and Guildenstern and the lord chamberlain having failed utterly to discover the true cause of Hamlet's distraction, Claudius determines to send him to England with the two spies. The presentation of the murder-play so disturbs the King that he leaves the hall, but, in spite of Hamlet's conviction of his uncle's guilt, he can not make up his mind to kill him when he encounters him alone at prayer. Almost immediately afterwards when his mother is upbraiding him for his conduct, he turns upon her, her cry for help is echoed from behind the curtain, and, thrusting his rapier at an intruder who he thinks is the King, Hamlet kills the spying Polonius. The Ghost appears to Hamlet again but not to the Queen, who is convinced, for the moment, of her son's insanity; but he persuades her henceforth not to take sides against him.

Act IV

Hamlet's mischance in killing Polonius hastens his departure to England. He escapes, however, aboard a pirate vessel, and on landing in Denmark sends letters of his arrival to both Horatio and the King. In the meantime, the death and secret burial of Polonius have driven Ophelia insane and have led her impetuous brother, called upon, like Hamlet, to avenge a father's death, hotheadedly to invade the castle at the head of a mob. Claudius turns Laertes' wrath against Hamlet, and the two plot to kill the Prince with a poisoned foil in what is to pass for a fencing match between the young men. Laertes is confirmed in his wickedness by the news that Ophelia has been drowned.

Act V

At the burial of Ophelia, the distracted Hamlet, who had not learned before of her death, grapples with Laertes in her grave, and the two are separated with difficulty. Later Hamlet reveals

to Horatio that on the ship he stole from the two spies sealed
orders for his death at the hands of the English, and that he
substituted other orders for the execution of Rosencrantz and
Guildenstern. When the challenge from Laertes arrives, Hamlet
recognizes in Laertes' sorrow the parallel of his own, but he
agrees, nevertheless, to a friendly contest, and the two meet in
the presence of the court. Laertes wounds Hamlet with the en-
venomed foil, and in the scuffle they exchange weapons, and the
Prince wounds Laertes. Drinking to her son's success, the Queen
unwittingly swallows poisoned wine which Claudius has prepared
for Hamlet. As they are dying, Gertrude and Laertes reveal the
villainy of the monarch, and Hamlet kills the monster with the
poisoned rapier. From the hands of Horatio he wrests the
poisoned cup, begging his friend to live to clear his wounded name.
As Hamlet dies, the English ambassadors come in to report the
execution of the spies, and Fortinbras, the opportunist, marching
back to Norway from Poland, arrives to claim the kingdom and
to restore order to the distracted country.

Troilus and Cressida

Dramatis Personæ

TROILUS, "the Prince of Chivalry," youngest son of Priam, King of Troy, "yet matchless, firm of word," "his heart and hand both open and both free;" "never did young man fancy with so eternal and so fix'd a soul."

CRESSIDA, daughter of Calchas and beloved of Troilus; "there's language in her eye, her cheek, her lip, nay, her foot speaks; her wanton spirits look out at every joint and motive of her body."

PANDARUS, a "honey-sweet lord," uncle of Cressida and go-between for the lovers.

DIOMEDES, a Greek captain, and "a false-hearted rogue."

HECTOR, noble champion of the Trojans, and son of King Priam.

ACHILLES, champion of the Greeks, but "over-proud and under-honest, in self-assumption greater than in the note of judgment."

AJAX, another Greek champion, but "a beef-witted lord," "into whom nature hath so crowded humors, that his valor is crushed into folly, his folly sauced with discretion."

PRIAM, King of Troy.

PARIS,
DEIPHOBUS, } other sons of Priam.
HELENUS,

MARGARELON, a bastard son of Priam.

AENEAS,
ANTENOR, } Trojan commanders.

CALCHAS, a Trojan priest, taking part with the Greeks, and father of Cressida.

AGAMEMNON, commander-in-chief of the Greek forces.

MENELAUS, his brother, wronged husband of Helen.

ULYSSES,
NESTOR, } Greek commanders.
PATROCLUS,

THERSITES, a deformed, "scurvy, railing knave, a very filthy rogue," "whose gall coins slanders like a mint."

CASSANDRA, a prophetess, daughter of Priam.

HELEN, formerly wife of Menelaus, and now wife of Paris.

ANDROMACHE, wife of Hector.

ALEXANDER, servant of Cressida.

Greek and Trojan Soldiers, Servants, and Attendants.

Scene of the Action: Troy and the Greek camp before it.

162

Act I

Leaping "o'er the vaunt and firstlings of those broils," the drama opens during a truce in the eighth year of the siege of Troy by the Greeks. Troilus, youngest son of Priam, King of Troy, is madly in love with Cressida, a beautiful Trojan girl, and has engaged her uncle, Pandarus, to arrange a meeting with her. Cressida, who is really attracted by Troilus, pretends indifference in order not to seem too easily won. In the Greek camp, the generals realize that their efforts are rendered ineffective by lack of unity, which the wise Ulysses attributes to insubordination, particularly that of the great Achilles, who, drunk on his own fame, has grown "dainty of his worth" and spends his time with Patroclus, lolling in his tent, mocking at the efforts of the rest. A Trojan deputation, headed by Aeneas, brings a challenge from Hector to any Greek who will meet him in single combat. Perceiving that the challenge, though couched in general terms, is really meant for Achilles, the Greek generals determine to spite him by selecting their champion by lot and contriving to have the choice fall upon the "dull, brainless Ajax."

Act II

In Troy a council of Priam and his sons considers the Greek conditions of peace, namely, the return of Helen and the payment of an indemnity. Hector favors such an agreement, thinking Helen not worth all she has cost, but his more romantic younger brothers, Troilus, Paris, and Helenus, argue against him, and in spite of the prophetic warnings of their sister Cassandra, they agree to reject the truce and seek more glory in the war. In the Greek camp, Achilles pretends to be ill and refuses to see a deputation of the generals, whereupon they flatter Ajax's vanity and arouse him to fight with Hector. In the meantime, the scurrilous Thersites rails against everything and everyone.

Act III

Pandarus at last arranges an assignation for Troilus and Cressida, who swear to be eternally faithful to each other. Meanwhile, Calchas, Cressida's father, who, though a Trojan priest, has been serving with the Greeks, asks the Greek generals to exchange their Trojan prisoner, Antenor, for his daughter. The generals continue to snub Achilles, and when he speaks to Ulysses about it, he hears that a hero cannot rest upon past deeds and that only perseverance keeps honor bright. "A woman impudent and mannish grown is not more loath'd than an effeminate man in time of action," and Achilles at last begins to see that his reputation is in danger. Hence, he sends Thersites to Ajax with a request that he invite Hector and the Trojan lords unarmed to a feast in his tent and procure safe conduct for them from Agamemnon.

Act IV

The Trojans agree to the exchange of Cressida for Antenor, and Diomedes is sent to conduct the lady back to the Greek camp. Bemoaning the cruel fate of war, the lovers part at dawn and exchange pledges of fidelity. Troilus promises to bribe the Greek sentries and visit her often, and, noting that Diomedes is already openly admiring Cressida, threatens him with death if anything happens to her. Just as the duel between Hector and Ajax begins, Diomedes and Cressida reach safety, and with her vows to Troilus scarce uttered, she bestows a round of kisses on the Greeks who welcome her. The fight between the champions soon comes to an end, however, for Hector refuses to continue, on the ground that Ajax is his kinsman, and declaring a truce, Greeks and Trojans in friendly spirit go to a feast in Achilles' tent.

Act V

After the feast, Troilus, guided by Ulysses, seeks out Calchas' tent that he may find Cressida, and from his hiding place sees her making love with Diomedes and giving her new lover the token which Troilus himself had heard her swear ever to keep. In the fierce fighting the next day, stung by such perfidy, Troilus seeks out Diomedes, just as his counterpart, Menelaus, seeks out Paris, but with no serious results. Hector, too, joins the battle, scorning the warnings of his sister Cassandra and his wife Andromache, and kills Patroclus, the intimate friend of Achilles. Aroused from his lethargy, Achilles at last takes to the field, and finding Hector unarmed and resting, orders his Myrmidons to slay him in defiance of all honor and drags his body around the city tied to his horse's tail. As Aeneas sadly leads the Trojan forces from the field, Troilus encounters Pandarus and spurns him, leaving that obscene cynic to speak the epilogue.

Othello, The Moor of Venice

Dramatis Personæ

OTHELLO, a Moorish nobleman and soldier of fortune, "inclined into the vale of years," now in the service of the Venetian state as general against the Turks; "great of heart," "honorable and valiant," "of a free and open nature, that thinks men honest that but seem to be so," and thus easy victim to "the green-eyed monster . . . jealousy."

DESDEMONA, Brabantio's "gentle" daughter and "true and loving," wife of Othello; "a maiden never bold, of spirit so still and quiet that her motion blush'd at herself;" "a most fresh and delicate creature," "the sweetest innocent that e'er did lift up eye," she remained "chaste and heavenly true" to her jealous husband. ("An inviting eye, and yet methinks right modest.")

IAGO, a young Venetian, Othello's ancient, or ensign, outwardly "a man . . . of honesty and trust," but actually a machiavellian villain without conscience; a "viper," an "inhuman dog" of cold, egoistic, intellectual powers of evil.

CASSIO, a Florentine, Othello's lieutenant, "handsome, young," upright and honorable, who regarded his reputation as the immortal part of him, but whose weakness was wine, women, and song; dupe and foil of Iago. "He hath a person and a smooth dispose to be suspected, fram'd to make women false."

EMILIA, Iago's wife and Desdemona's loyal waiting-woman, who refuses to "charm [her] tongue" but boldly denounces villainy in terms "as liberal as the north."

RODERIGO, a foolish young Venetian with more money than brains, a "silly gentleman" and "sick fool," whose love for Desdemona makes him the easy dupe and tool of Iago.

BIANCA, Cassio's mistress, "a creature that dotes on Cassio."

BRABANTIO, a Venetian senator, Desdemona's heart-broken father.

GRATIANO, Brabantio's brother.

LODOVICO, Brabantio's kinsman, "a proper man, a very handsome man."

MONTANO, the "trusty and most valiant servitor" of the Duke of Venice, who preceded Othello as Governor of Cyprus.

THE DUKE OF VENICE.

A Clownish Servant of Othello.

Senators, Officers, Gentlemen, Messengers, Musicians, a Herald, a Sailor, Attendants, etc.

Scene of the Action: Venice and a seaport in Cyprus.

Act I

Othello, a Moorish nobleman and soldier of fortune, unconsciously evokes the spirit of evil in the villainous Iago, a young Venetian who serves as his ancient or ensign, by choosing as his lieutenant, not Iago but the Florentine, Michael Cassio. Partly to be avenged for this slight but principally because of a satanic delight in doing evil to feed his own wicked pleasure, Iago determines to bring about the downfall of the Moorish general and his new officer; but he screens the blackness of his heart behind a seemingly frank and open bearing and to all he remains the "honest Iago." Othello himself is of so noble and unsuspecting a nature that he plays easily into the hands of the villain. He has long been the welcome guest of Brabantio, a Venetian senator, who with his fair daughter Desdemona has listened eagerly to the guest's tales of high adventure until the maiden came to "love [him] for the dangers [he] has pass'd, and [he] loved her that she did pity them." Othello and Desdemona are secretly married; and Iago's first plot against him is to arouse her father at night with the report of the elopement. To screen himself in this scurvy trick, he uses as a tool a foolish young Venetian, one Roderigo, a rejected suitor of Desdemona. When the embittered Brabantio appeals to the Duke of Venice against Othello, charging the Moor with having won his daughter by sorcery, he learns that the Venetian Senate is on the point of sending the general to Cyprus to protect that island against the invasion of a Turkish fleet. Desdemona not only refuses to give up her husband and return to her father, but even begs the Duke to permit her to accompany him to Cyprus. Othello commissions Iago, "a man . . . of honesty and trust," to bring Desdemona after him; and Iago persuades the foolish Roderigo to put money in his purse, accompany him, and not give up hope of enjoying Desdemona. To himself he resolves to find a way of both getting Cassio's place and satisfying his hate of Othello. The broken-hearted father, however, sows in the Moor's heart the first evil seeds of what is to become a poison-tree:

> "Look to her, Moor, if thou hast eyes to see;
> She has deceived her father, and may thee."

Act II

Off the coast of Cyprus the same wild storm that delays the arrival of the voyagers from Venice drives off the battered Turkish fleet, leaving to the new governor Othello only the pleasant task of ordering a general rejoicing. To keep the merry-making within bounds, Othello appoints Cassio officer of the guard. A chance greeting between this guileless young man and Desdemona confirms in Iago's nimble brain the wicked scheme of plotting to make Othello believe that his wife has been unfaithful with the lieutenant. He gets Cassio drunk, primes Roderigo to pick a quarrel with him, and himself arouses the general, who at once reduces the unhappy lieutenant to the ranks. In his shame Cassio falls readily into Iago's suggestion that he beg Desdemona to intercede in his behalf. It is the villain's trap.

Act III

Cassio's quite natural unwillingness to have Othello discover him while he is talking with Desdemona, gives Iago an opportunity to hint to the Moor that Cassio is stealing away "guilty-like, seeing [him] coming" and to insinuate further that. Desdemona's plea that her husband restore the former officer to favor is prompted by her guilty passion for the young man. Thus Iago villainously injects into the Moor's mind and heart the virus of jealousy, while seeming to be most unwilling even to suggest evil; and the tortured Othello demands proofs. One such "proof" comes by chance into Iago's hand in the form of a handkerchief, an early courting gift from Othello to his wife, which she has lost, and which Iago's wife Emilia, Desdemona's waiting-woman, has found. This Iago leaves secretly in Cassio's room, and the former lieutenant, finding it, gives it to his mistress Bianca to copy. Meanwhile, Iago has told Othello that he has seen Cassio with the handkerchief, and when Desdemona cannot produce it upon her husband's demands, the general is convinced of her guilt and swears with the wicked ensign a deep oath of vengeance upon his innocent wife and Cassio.

Act IV

To convince Othello still further of his wife's guilt, Iago places the Moor where he overhears Cassio deriding Bianca but apparently alluding to Desdemona, and sees Cassio's mistress scornfully return the handkerchief to him. Completely convinced, Othello accepts Iago's suggestion that he strangle Desdemona while the ensign is to kill Cassio. Iago's eagerness to bring his plot to a conclusion is increased by the arrival from Venice of

Desdemona's kinsman Lodovico with letters from the Duke recalling Othello and appointing Cassio as his successor in Cyprus. Maddened by his wife's innocent remark to Lodovico that she would do much to reconcile her husband and the newly appointed governor, "for the love [she bears] Cassio," Othello strikes her and orders her out of his sight. He refuses to believe Emilia's testimony to his wife's chastity but openly "bewhores" the abused lady, so innocent of wrong that she even begs the wicked creator of it all to help her "win [her] lord again." To consummate his villainy Iago persuades his dupe Roderigo to waylay and kill Cassio. Meanwhile, Desdemona sings a swan-song—"Sing willow, willow, willow,"—and retires after having dismissed Emilia with the assertion that she would not abuse her lord "for all the world."

Act V

The ambushed Roderigo wounds Cassio; and, defending himself, Cassio stabs the Venetian. Iago runs Cassio through the leg, and the victim's cry for help brings Lodovico and others. To cover his own villainy and to silence Roderigo Iago then stabs him as though to kill the assailant of Cassio; and he also throws suspicion upon Bianca, with whom Cassio has supped that night. Meantime, in the castle, Othello, after refusing to believe Desdemona's protestations of complete innocence, smothers her in her bed. To Emilia, who enters to report Roderigo dead but Cassio only wounded, he confesses the murder despite the heavenly lie with which the dying lady denies his guilt; and the waiting-woman's cries bring Lodovico, Iago, and others. Othello's justification of his black deed by an allusion to Cassio's possession of Desdemona's handkerchief, leads Emilia—as yet unaware of her husband's villainy—to reveal the truth, and to stop her mouth Iago kills her. Further evidence of the villain's guilt is found in letters in the pockets of the slain Roderigo. Othello wounds but fails to kill the "damned slave." Then, after begging that he be reported to the Venetian Senate as "one that loved not wisely but too well," he stabs himself and dies with a kiss on the cold lips of his innocent lady. Cassio's first duty as lord governor is to order the "Spartan dog" Iago to torture and execution.

King Lear

Dramatis Personæ

LEAR, King of Britain, "a very foolish, fond old man, fourscore and upward," who is headstrong and "full of changes," yet "every inch a king," and "more sinned against than sinning."

GONERIL, } his unnatural elder daughters, "the shame of ladies," "she-foxes,"
REGAN, } "gilded serpents," "tigers, not daughters."

CORDELIA, his youngest daughter, the "unpriz'd precious maid," who lacks "that glib and oily art to speak and purpose not." "Her voice was ever soft, gentle, and low; an excellent thing in woman."

THE EARL OF GLOUCESTER, like Lear, a credulous, rash old man.

EDGAR, his elder legitimate son, "whose nature is so far from doing harms that he suspects none."

EDMUND, his bastard son, "a most toad-spotted traitor," "rough and lecherous."

THE DUKE OF ALBANY, "a man of milky gentleness," Goneril's "mild husband."

THE DUKE OF CORNWALL, wicked husband of Regan, a man "whose disposition . . . will not be rubb'd nor stopped."

THE DUKE OF BURGUNDY,
THE KING OF FRANCE, } rival suitors for the hand of Cordelia.

THE EARL OF KENT, a "noble and true-hearted" courtier, whose plain honest speech, like Cordelia's, sometimes results in evil for the old King to whom he is devoted. "He cannot flatter, he; an honest mind and plain, he most speak truth."

THE FOOL, "a pretty knave," Lear's "bitter, all-licensed" jester, also devoted to Lear and Cordelia, but one whose words are "a pestilent gall" to the old King.

OSWALD, Goneril's steward, "a serviceable villain," whose "easy-borrowed pride dwells in the fickle grace of her he follows," "a knave; a rascal; an eater of broken meats; a base, proud, shallow, beggarly, three-suited, hundred-pound, filthy, worsted-stocking knave; a lily-livered, action-taking, whoreson, glass-gazing, superserviceable, finical rogue; one-trunk-inheriting slave; one that would be a bawd in way of good service, and is nothing but the composition of knave, beggar, coward, and pander."

CURAN, a courtier.

An old tenant of Gloucester's.

A Doctor.

Knights, Captains, Heralds, Soldiers, and Attendants.

Scene of the Action: Britain.

Act I

Lear, King of Britain, wishes to retire after many years as ruler, and divides his kingdom among his three daughters. When the moment for the actual distribution of the territory is at hand, he somewhat childishly proposes to make his gifts dependent upon each daughter's declaration of love for him. The two eldest, Goneril, wife of the Duke of Albany, and Regan, wife of the Duke of Cornwall, are over-fulsome in their protestations, and the old King is highly pleased. As he turns expectantly to Cordelia, the youngest, to hear what she shall say "to draw a third more opulent than [her] sisters," he is hurt by her simple and sincere expression of duty and affection. Enraged at her apparent coolness, he casts her off completely, arranges to live with each of her elder sisters in turn, and presents Cordelia dowerless to her suitors. Burgundy rejects her. However, the King of France perceives her honest worth and takes her as his wife. When the Earl of Kent, a faithful but outspoken courtier, tries to come "between the dragon and his wrath," he is banished, and the wrong-headed angry old King totters out of his palace, leaving his elder daughters to stand together against their father's capriciousness. At the same time, the Earl of Gloucester, like Lear, wrongs a dutiful child and raises an undeserving one to power. Deceived by the apparent sincerity of his crafty bastard son, Edmund, who has forged a villainous letter to deprive his noble brother Edgar of his birthright, Gloucester is convinced that Edgar is plotting to murder him for his estates. Instead of going into exile, the faithful Kent returns in disguise to become a protecting servant of his old master and arrives just as Goneril, with her steward, Oswald, is beginning to treat her father with disrespect, by reducing his retinue and criticizing his followers. Cursing his eldest daughter, the old King orders his horses and departs immediately for Regan's, sending Kent ahead with an announcement of his coming.

Act II

With more lies and hypocrisy, Edmund completes his father's conviction that Edgar is an unfilial villain, just as Cornwall and

Regan arrive for a visit at Gloucester's castle. For a minor offence, actually the result of devotion to his master, Regan and her husband put Kent, the King's messenger, into the stocks. There he is found by the old King, who is accompanied only by his loving, but bitter, fool, who loses no opportunity of reminding his master of his folly in giving away his kingdom. In a stormy scene, Regan, to whom Oswald has delivered a letter from Goneril, refuses to take in her old father until he has made apology to her sister. When Goneril herself arrives, and Lear perceives that the daughters are in league to heap further indignities upon him, he sets out into the wild night with his fool.

Act III

Meanwhile, there are rumors of growing discord between Albany and Cornwall, and of an army from France secretly making its way to England. On the stormy heath, Lear, with his fool, hurls his defiance at the elements, and, joined by Kent, seeks refuge in a hovel which is already occupied by Edgar, who has adopted the disguise of poor, mad Tom o' Bedlam. There Gloucester, risking the fury of the daughters who have shut his castle gates, finds the trio and at length persuades the old King, whose mind has become unbalanced, to find shelter in a farmhouse. There in his madness, at a mock trial, Lear arraigns his daughters, with the fool and poor Tom as judges. Just as Kent has about composed him to rest, Gloucester hurries back with word that the daughters are plotting against the King's life, and that he must be taken with all speed to Dover, where he has reason to believe friends will receive them. While this has been happening, Gloucester's unnatural son has likewise been plotting the ruin and death of his father. To Cornwall, Edmund furnishes evidence that Gloucester has been assisting Cordelia's invasion and is sympathetic to the King. Then he leaves the castle so that the sisters may feel free to punish their host, even to putting out his eyes. Cornwall, however, is mortally stabbed by a frenzied servant who resists his cruelty to Gloucester.

Act IV

In the open country, Edgar, the wronged son, finds his blind father led by an old tenant and hears the pathetic confession of his mistaken wrath. Without revealing himself, Edgar becomes his father's guide, and humoring him in his desire to go to the cliffs of Dover so that he may end his life, contrives a ruse by which the old man thinks he has fallen from the cliff but miraculously escaped death. In a similar manner, Cordelia finds her poor mad father fantastically dressed with wild flowers, and cares for him so tenderly that when he first awakes, he, too thinks that he has miraculously been snatched from death. Meanwhile, Albany denounces his wife for her fiendish cruelty, the sisters add lust for Edmund to their crimes, Cornwall dies of his wound, and Edmund becomes commander-in-chief of the English forces.

Act V

Albany joins armies with Edmund, not because of sympathy with his cause, but solely because of his duty to protect Britain from a foreign foe, and in the battle the French are defeated. Lear and Cordelia become Edmund's prisoners, and under pretext of protecting them, but actually to prevent Albany from treating them kindly, Edmund sends them to prison and issues a secret order for their execution. Envious of Regan's widowhood and jealous of her love for Edmund, Goneril poisons her sister and then stabs herself when her own adultery is found out. Meanwhile, Edgar has made himself known to his blind old father, who dies of a broken heart. On Edgar's charge, Albany arrests Edmund for capital treason, and in a formal combat Gloucester's noble son maintains his accusation against the villain and gives him a mortal wound. Lear's happy reunion with Cordelia is also short-lived. Too late the repentant Edmund countermands his order against the King and his daughter. Lear tries to protect her, but Cordelia is hanged, and the broken-hearted father dies trying to revive her. In the end, Edgar, Kent, and Albany are left to mourn for the dead.

Macbeth

Dramatis Personæ

DUNCAN, the "gracious" King of Scotland, who bore "his faculties . . . meek," and was "clear in his great office."

MACBETH, general in the King's army who usurps the throne; despite his "vaulting ambition" and his "black and deep desires," he is full "o' the milk of human kindness," and "cabin'd, cribb'd, confined, bound in to saucy doubts and fears"— never able completely to silence the rebukes of his conscience. [His] "way of life is fallen into the sear, the yellow leaf; and that which should accompany old age, as honor, love, obedience, troops of friends, [he] must not look to have."

LADY MACBETH, the wife of Macbeth, whose conscience wars against her resoluteness, and whose words are bolder than her deeds; while pretending to be unsexed and hard, she cannot prevent her heart from becoming "sorely charged" with her crimes, and the woman in her ultimately dethrones the man.

BANQUO, another general in the King's army, who possesses a "royalty of nature," a "dauntless temper of his mind," and "a wisdom that doth guide his valor;" and who would keep his "bosom enfranchised and allegiance clear;" foil and high-minded rival to Macbeth.

FLEANCE, Banquo's son.

MACDUFF, a Scottish thane, a "noble, wise, judicious" "child of integrity," the grand opposite of Macbeth.

LADY MACDUFF, and her young son.

MALCOLM, King Duncan's elder son, who leads the uprising against Macbeth.

DONALBAIN, King Duncan's younger son.

LENNOX,
ROSS,
MENTEITH,   } noblemen of Scotland.
ANGUS,
CAITHNESS,

SIWARD, Earl of Northumberland, and general of the English forces against Macbeth, "an older and a better soldier none."

SIWARD'S SON, who was "God's soldier" and who "died like a man."

SEYTON, one of Macbeth's officers.

HECATE, queen of Hades and mistress of the witches' charms.

THREE WITCHES, "so wither'd and so wild in their attire," the "weird sisters," agents of Fate, "secret, black, and midnight hags," "juggling fiends . . . that keep the word of promise to our ear, and break it to our hope."

An English Doctor, a Scotch Doctor, a Gentlewoman attending Lady Macbeth, a Sergeant, a Porter, an Old Man, Apparitions, Murderers, Lords, Gentlemen, Officers, Soldiers, Messengers, and Attendants.

Scene of the Action: Scotland, chiefly at Macbeth's castle, and England.

MACBETH

Act I

Macbeth and Banquo, brave and noble generals in the army of the gracious King Duncan of Scotland, have been successful in putting down a rebellion led by Macdonwald and the thane of Cawdor, and the fame of their glorious deeds reaches the King before they do. While crossing a heath, they are met by three witches, who hail Macbeth as thane of Glamis, thane of Cawdor, and king hereafter. When Banquo also demands a prophecy, the witches tell him that he shall beget kings though he be none. The uncanny creatures vanish, but part of their prophecy is immediately confirmed when two noblemen coming from the King greet Macbeth with the title of the rebel thane of Cawdor, who has been condemned to death. This part fulfillment of the prophecy and King Duncan's advancement of his son Malcolm to the title of Prince of Cumberland combine to steel Macbeth to plot the King's death. In Lady Macbeth he finds a fellow plotter more resolute than he, and when Duncan and his sons come as guests to Macbeth's castle, fate seems to have played into the hands of the ambitious nobleman and his wife.

Act II

Banquo, stirred by the witches' prophecy that his descendants will be kings, fights down the temptation to hasten the event, but Macbeth, on the contrary, takes advantage of the opportunity afforded by the King's visit to his castle, and with the help of his wife, who screws her husband's "courage to the sticking place," and drugs the grooms of the King's bedchamber, he stabs the sleeping monarch to death. When the foul murder is discovered on the morrow, Macbeth simulates great grief and indignation, and to divert suspicion from himself he kills the grooms as though enraged by their denial of the deed. Malcolm and Donalbain, the King's sons, fear a like fate and flee the country; and Macbeth, as next of kin, is crowned King.

Act III

Knowing that the noble Banquo suspects him of the murder of Duncan, and jealous of the general because of the witches' prophecy that his descendants will be kings, Macbeth invites him to a state banquet as though to honor him, but has him and his son waylaid by murderers near the banquet-hall; Banquo is slain, but his son Fleance escapes. At the banquet, surrounded by his thanes, the tyrant King praises the absent Banquo, and the ghost of the murdered man enters and, seen only by Macbeth, takes a seat at the board. In his terror at this apparition, the King utters words which lead the noblemen to suspect his guilt; and to cover her husband's revelations, the Queen dismisses the assembly in confusion. Word comes to the nobles that Malcolm has been joined in England by Macduff, one of the most powerful of the Scottish lords. Macbeth has come generally to be regarded as a blood-thirsty tyrant; and on the barren heath Hecate, Queen of Evil, meets with the three witches to plot the King's further downfall.

Act IV

When Macbeth visits the witches in their hellish cavern and begs them to prophesy his fate, they answer his demands by a show of apparitions. The first is of an armed head, which warns him to beware Macduff, the second is of a bloody child, which promises that "none of woman born shall harm Macbeth;" the third is of a child crowned, with a tree in his hand, which promises him safety until Birnam Wood shall move against him. By these visions his fears are allayed, but his eye-balls are then seared by a show of eight kings and the smiling ghost of Banquo, who points to them as his descendants. As he leaves the witches' cavern, the news comes to him of Macduff's flight to England, and in revenge he has the thane's wife and children murdered. In England, Malcolm, after first having tested Macduff's loyalty, welcomes his aid in recovering the throne of Scotland, and the resolution of both is hardened by the terrible news that the Lady Macduff and her children have been savagely butchered by the tyrant.

Act V

In Macbeth's castle of Dunsinane, Lady Macbeth, her mind sore charged with her sins, walks and talks in her sleep, revealing to her doctor and her gentlewoman the crimes in which she and her husband have engaged. Macbeth is torn between caring for his wife and preparing to repel the English invaders, whose approach has been reported. The English forces under Malcolm and Siward, Earl of Northumberland, combine with the Scottish forces near Birnam Wood, and to conceal their numbers and their movements Malcolm orders each soldier to cut and carry a bough. Thus Macbeth is told that Birnam Wood *is* moving against him. With this message comes also the report that the Queen has died —perhaps "by self and violent hands." Despondent, the King rushes to battle, resolved to die with harness on his back. He kills young Siward, son of the English general, and then comes face to face with Macduff, the man whom he has most avoided. Macbeth's last dependence upon the witches' charms evaporates when his opponent tells him that he is not of woman born but was "from his mother's womb untimely ripp'd." Fighting hopelessly but desperately the tyrant falls before the avenger's sword. At the feet of Malcolm Macduff lays the usurper's head, and is the first to hail the young monarch as King of Scotland.

Antony and Cleopatra

Dramatis Personæ

CLEOPATRA, "a lass unparallel'd" and "a morsel for a monarch," "whom everything becomes, to chide, to laugh, to weep," but who is nevertheless "the serpent of old Nile," "cunning past man's thought." "Age cannot wither her, nor custom stale her infinite variety."

MARK ANTONY, "the noble ruin of her magic," "a rarer spirit never did steer humanity, but you, gods, will give us faults to make us men." "His taints and honors wage equal in him;" "his soldiership is twice the other twain." }

OCTAVIUS, the hard, emotionless, "scarce bearded Caesar," "the Jupiter of men;" foil to Antony. } Triumvirs, "the triple pillars of the world."

M. AEMILIUS LEPIDUS, a sufferer from the "green-sickness," and a power of little importance. }

SEXTUS POMPEIUS, leader of the naval power.

OCTAVIA, sister of Caesar and wife of Antony, "of a holy, cold, and still conversation," "a statue rather than a breather," and hence, a foil to Cleopatra. "I do think she's thirty."

CANIDIUS, lieutenant-general to Antony.

DOMITIUS ENOBARBUS,
VENTIDIUS,
EROS,
SCARUS, } friends and followers of Antony.
DERCETAS,
DEMETRIUS,
PHILO,

TAURUS, lieutenant-general to Octavius Caesar.

MAECENAS,
AGRIPPA,
DOLABELLA,
PROCULEIUS, } friends and followers of Caesar.
THYREUS,
GALLUS,

MENAS,
MENECRATES, } friends and followers of Pompey.
VARRIUS,

CHARMIAN,
IRAS, } maids-of-honor attending Cleopatra.

178

ANTONY AND CLEOPATRA

ALEXAS,
MARDIAN, a eunuch, } attendants upon Cleopatra.
SELEUCUS,
DIOMEDES,

SILIUS, an officer in Ventidius' army.
EUPHRONIUS, a schoolmaster, ambassador from Antony to Caesar.
A SOOTHSAYER.
A CLOWNISH COUNTRYMAN.
Officers, Soldiers, Messengers, and Attendants.

Scene of the Action: Alexandria, Rome, Athens, Messina, Misenum,
Actium, and various other parts of the Roman Empire.

Act I

In Alexandria at the frivolous Egyptian court, the Roman
general, Mark Antony, wastes his time in lascivious wassails,
while his followers who have known him in better days, gossip
about the spell which Cleopatra, Queen of Egypt, exerts over him
and the changes her influence has brought about. News from
Rome of unrest threatening the triumvirate, of the defiance of
young Pompey, who has gathered a sea power to avenge his
father, and at last of the death of Fulvia, Antony's wife, finally
arouse the Roman to break his strong Egyptian fetters and return
home. Accordingly, with mingled coquettishness and self-pity,
Cleopatra lets him go, but sends daily messengers after him to
find out how he fares.

Act II

Antony's Roman journey causes some surprise both to Caesar
and to Pompey. After some sharp plain speaking on both sides,
Antony and Octavius agree to overlook their jealousies and slights
of one another and to cement their new friendship by a marriage
between Octavia, Caesar's sister, and Antony. Together, they
negotiate their differences with Pompey, and seal this triple friendship with a royal feast aboard one of Pompey's galleys off
Misenum. During the drunken revels, though sorely tempted by
his admiral Menas, Pompey nobly rejects an opportunity of taking
advantage of his tipsy enemies and making himself lord of all the
world. Antony, on the other hand, is convinced by a soothsayer
that his fortunes cannot prosper side by side with Caesar's, dis-

179

patches Ventidius on a campaign into Parthia, and turns his eyes again to the Eastern Empire, while Enobarbus prophesies the inevitable result of this apparent peace. Antony "will to his Egyptian dish again. Then shall the sighs of Octavia blow the fire up in Caesar; and . . . that which is the strength of their amity shall prove the immediate author of their variance." Meanwhile, in Egypt the news of Antony's marriage so infuriates Cleopatra that she threatens with violence the very messenger who brings the word.

Act III

Later, hearing a description of Octavia's reserve, her short stature, her low forehead, round face, and soft voice, Cleopatra takes heart in the hope that Antony's new wife cannot hold him long. Ventidius' campaign in Parthia is successful, and Antony, accompanied by Octavia, bids farewell to Rome and hastens to Athens. He is hardly there before news from Rome makes clear that the old rivalry between Caesar and himself is not over. Octavius has renewed the war against Pompey, without giving Antony an opportunity to share in the glory; he has made a prisoner of Lepidus and removed him from the triumvirate; and he has otherwise slighted his associate. At Octavia's suggestion, therefore, Antony permits her to return to Rome in an attempt to smooth over their difficulties. Before her arrival, however, word reaches Rome that Antony has returned to Egypt and is publicly heaping honors upon Cleopatra and proclaiming her sons kings. Hence, it is not difficult for Octavius to persuade himself and his sister that Antony has cast her off and that the small train with which she travelled—solely for convenience—is but an added insult. The rift between the two rulers, therefore, is complete, and Octavius with all speed prepares for war against Antony. Against the advice of his officers, and solely because Octavius dares him to do it, Antony completely casts aside his advantage by land and determines to fight his rival by sea at Actium. As Queen of Egypt, Cleopatra accompanies Antony on the expedition and even leads her fleet into the fight, but just when the tide of battle might have turned to either's advantage, Cleopatra, "the breese upon her, like a cow in June, hoists sails and flies," with Antony following.

Though his dotage has lost him the world, the shamed Antony forgives the Queen, and sends Euphronius, a lowly schoolmaster, to negotiate with Caesar. Antony's request to live in either Egypt or Athens is denied, but Cleopatra's for the crown of the Ptolemies is granted, provided that she either drive Antony out or put him to death. Antony's reply is a foolish challenge to personal combat. Meanwhile, Caesar sends Thyreus, a noble ambassador, to win Cleopatra from Antony by flattery and promises, and this envoy is about to succeed, when Antony discovers him, has him whipped, and sends him back with a defiant message. When he upbraids the Queen for her lack of honor, she easily wins him back, and Antony determines to fight to the finish.

Act IV

Octavius, of course, laughs at Antony's challenge to a duel, while, one by one, the followers of Antony, thinking their fortunes lost, desert to Caesar. Even Enobarbus goes, but when Antony generously sends his treasure after him, he is overcome with self-reproach and dies, apparently of a broken heart. During the night, through supernatural music, Antony's soldiers know that Hercules, Antony's guardian spirit, has left him. On the opening day of the battle, however, Antony is at first victorious on land, but later a second ignoble flight of the Egyptian fleet brings disaster. Realizing that "this false soul of Egypt" is responsible for his disgrace, and suspecting that she "pack'd cards with Caesar," and played him false. Antony turns his wrath upon Cleopatra, determined to kill her. The Queen, however, takes refuge in her monument and tries to play upon his emotions by sending him word that having lost his love, she has taken her life and died with his name on her lips. In despair, Antony determines to follow her and begs Eros to strike him dead, but his faithful follower kills himself in preference. Antony then falls upon his own sword, just as Cleopatra, fearing the result her message might have had, sends word that she is alive. Antony asks to be taken to her, and reconciled with the Queen, dies in her arms.

Act V

News of Antony's death moves Octavius deeply, but his praise for his dead rival is interrupted by a messenger from the conquered Queen. Caesar sends fair promises, but fearing that she might take her life and so defeat him of a complete triumph, he sets a guard to keep close watch over her. Perceiving that with all her wiles she is no match for Caesar, who is flattering her merely that she may grace his triumphal procession in Rome, Cleopatra at last appreciates the nobility of Antony. Dressed in the queenly robes she wore when first she met him on the Cydnus, she takes a deadly asp which a countryman has smuggled in to her in a basket of figs, applies it to her breast, and dies. Her devoted women, Iras and Charmian, die with her. Beginning his triumph, Caesar orders her burial in the same grave with Antony, adding that "no grave upon the earth shall clip in it a pair so famous."

Timon of Athens

Dramatis Personæ

TIMON OF ATHENS, an "honorable, complete, free-hearted gentleman," "the very soul of bounty" whose "large fortune . . . subdues and properties to his love and tendance all sorts of hearts." He is "brought low by his own heart, undone by goodness," and turns misanthrope.

APEMANTUS, a churlish commentator, most "opposite to humanity," who "does neither affect company, nor is he fit for't." At first he is the foil to Timon and later the shallow, cynical parallel to his deeper misanthropy.

LUCIUS,
LUCULLUS, Timon's "trencher-friends," "summer birds," "cap-and-knee slaves,"
SEMPRONIUS, who feed on his bounty and deny him in his need.
VENTIDIUS,

FLAVIUS, the "true and honest" steward of Timon.

ALCIBIADES, an Athenian captain who also suffers from the ingratitude of mankind, but whose practical capacity for compromise makes him the foil to Timon.

TIMANDRA,
PHRYNIA, mistresses of Alcibiades.

FLAMINIUS,
SERVILIUS, servants of Timon.
LUCILIUS,

PHILOTUS,
TITUS,
LUCIUS, servants of Timon's creditors.
HORTENSIUS,

SERVANTS of VARRO and ISIDORE, usurers.

CAPHIS, servant of a senator.

A POET, a PAINTER, a JEWELLER, and a MERCHANT.

AN OLD ATHENIAN.

THREE STRANGERS.

A PAGE.

A FOOL.

CUPID and AMAZONS for a masque.

Lords, Senators, Officers, Soldiers, Banditti, and Attendants.

Scene of the Action: Athens and the wood in the vicinity.

Act I

Surrounded by fair-weather flatterers, Timon of Athens, a wealthy nobleman, is a generous friend, a considerate master, a lavish patron of the arts, and an extravagant entertainer. "No meed, but he repays sevenfold above itself; no gift to him but breeds the giver return exceeding all use of quittance." On the other hand, Apemantus, a churlish plain-dealer hated by every one for his chiding, ridicules Timon's blindness and warns him against his friends. Flavius, Timon's steward, who has reasons to worry because of his master's unbridled extravagance, also tries to warn him of his impending ruin, but the joy of giving is too great for Timon to listen to him or to give a thought to himself.

Act II

Before long, several of Timon's wealthy creditors become fearful of his solvency and send their agents to collect their loans. The importunities of these men at length force Timon to listen to the faithful Flavius, who proves to him that he owes more than twice what he possesses. Knowing that he has given unwisely but not ignobly, Timon refuses to believe that friends who are "feast-won" are "fast-lost." Accordingly, he dispatches servants to Lucullus, Lucius, and Sempronius, whom he has showered with gifts, and to Ventidius, whom he once relieved from debtors' prison, with requests for small loans. The first premonition to Timon of the ingratitude he may expect comes when Flavius reports his ill success in borrowing from the Athenian Senate.

Act III

One by one, Timon's friends deny him. Lucullus tries to bribe the servant to say he was out, Lucius regrets the ill-chance that finds him unprovided with means to help, and Sempronius professes to be hurt that Timon should apply to him only after others have refused. His eyes opened at last to the worthlessness of these parasites. Timon resolves to invite them to one more banquet. When they all appear with faint excuses for denying his messengers, Timon serves them with covered dishes of warm water, which he throws in their faces, and drives them out of his house with curses. Meanwhile, in the Senate, Alcibiades, famous general and the firm but truly impecunious friend of Timon, encounters another manifestation of Athenian ingratitude. Merely because he pleads too persistently against the death sentence imposed upon a brave soldier who has served Athens faithfully, Alcibiades himself is banished by the angry Senators. Cursing their injustice and lack of consideration for his services, Alcibiades, however, resolves to collect his discontented troops and strike at Athens.

Act IV

With bitter curses against all mankind, the misanthropic Timon shakes the dust of Athens from his feet and goes into voluntary exile in a cave near the sea. There, while digging for roots to gnaw, he finds buried treasure. Soon after, Alcibiades, with his army of discontents and his two mistresses, Timandra and Phrynia, happens to pass that way and speaks the first sincere words Timon has heard. Though his soldiers are deserting because he lacks money to pay them, Alcibiades offers Timon gold. When he hears that the expedition is marching against Athens, Timon shares his treasure with the general and his mistresses, mixing his gifts with bitter curses all the while. In his cave, also, he is visited by the misanthropic Apemantus and matches his deep, passionate railing to the churlish nature of the cynical philosopher. Word of Timon's new-found treasure soon brings other visitors. To two thieves, Timon gives some of his gold and such bitter praise of thievery that they are almost converted from their profession. Here, too, he is found by his steward Flavius, who has sought him for love and not for gain. At first Timon curses him for being like the rest, but at last, touched by his devotion, acknowledges him as the one honest man who redeems mankind. To him he gives a huge sum on condition that he never visit him again nor show charity to any one.

Act V

Believing that Timon's wretchedness is but a pose adopted to test his friends, a self-seeking poet and a painter also visit Timon, professing old friendship, but he gives them nothing but curses. Even the Athenian Senate sends a delegation soliciting his aid against Alcibiades and promising him even greater dignities than those he has renounced, but Timon expresses his utter indifference as to what fate befalls the city. Alcibiades, on the other hand, is more willing to conciliate. Before Athens he arbitrates his wrongs with the citizens and is permitted to enter the town on his promise to spare the innocent and avenge himself only upon his enemies and Timon's. But as this just and peaceable agreement is reached, word is brought that Timon has died in his cave.

Coriolanus

Dramatis Personæ

CAIUS MARCIUS, afterwards surnamed CORIOLANUS, "a soldier even to Cato's wish," and a modest hero who "hath deserved worthily of his country," but one who lacks tact, and "ill-school'd in bolted language," refuses to placate "the mutable, rank-scented many." "His nature is too noble for this world; he would not flatter Neptune for his trident; or Jove for's power to thunder."

MENENIUS AGRIPPA, "a humorous patrician, and one that loves a cup of hot wine with not a drop of allaying Tiber in it," "a perfecter giber for the table than a necessary bencher in the Capitol," but an old and true friend of Coriolanus, trusted by the people, and hence, foil to Coriolanus.

VOLUMNIA, mother of Coriolanus, and in large measure the moulder of his character, "in anger, Juno-like."

VIRGILIA, gentle wife of Coriolanus, and foil to Volumnia.

YOUNG MARCIUS, son of Coriolanus.

VALERIA, a friend of Volumnia and Virgilia.

TITUS LARTIUS,
COMINIUS,
} fellow generals with Coriolanus against the Volsces.

SICINIUS VELUTUS,
JUNIUS BRUTUS,
} "a pair of strange ones," tribunes of the people and enemies of Coriolanus. "When [they] speak best unto the purpose, it is not worth the wagging [their] beards." "They lie deadly that tell [they] have good faces."

TULLUS AUFIDIUS, general of the Volsces and rival in glory to Coriolanus, who hates and admires him.

Roman and Volscian Senators, Patricians, Citizens, Aediles, Lictors, Soldiers, Servants, Guards, Conspirators, and Attendants.

Scene of the Action: Rome Corioli, Antium, and their neighborhoods.

Act I

During a famine in Rome, the citizens rebel against the patrician senate, and especially against Caius Marcius, a noble but haughty general. Menenius Agrippa tries to reason with the mob by pointing out that the senate has cared for the plebeians like fathers, that it is not responsible for the hard times, and that all of the members of the state must be united in harmony. Marcius, on the other hand, holds them in contempt and bluntly upbraids them for their presumption. While he is in the midst of his speech, he is summoned to battle against the Volsces, who are in arms under Tullus Aufidius, Marcius' great rival, whom he hates and admires. Volumnia, the mother of Marcius, is proud of her son's opportunity for glory in the war and certain of his success, but his quiet and gentle wife, Virgilia, fearing for his safety, prefers to remain in retirement until his return. During the siege of Corioli, the Romans are at first repulsed, until Marcius, cursing his craven troops, alone pursues the fleeing Volsces through their gates. Spurred by his incredibly heroic deeds, the Romans take the city, and in their enthusiasm for their modest leader, who cannot endure praise and refuses to share the spoils, they crown him with the oaken garland and hail him by the title of "Coriolanus."

Act II

Meanwhile, the plebeians have been granted several tribunes, two of whom, Sicinius and Brutus, hate Marcius and hope to see his fall. Coriolanus returns to Rome in triumph and is met by his gentle wife and his proud mother, who rejoices in the wounds he bears as a proof of his manhood. In recognition of his services to Rome, the Senate nominates him to the office of Consul, and, distasteful as it is to him, Coriolanus bows to the custom which requires that candidates stand in the Forum, display their wounds, and humbly beg the votes of the citizens. His evident contempt for the commonalty, however, repels the people, but he nevertheless gains their support. While he is changing the ostentatious candidate's robe for garments more to his liking, Brutus and Sicinius subtly convince the fickle plebeians that Coriolanus as Consul would deprive them of their liberties, and they hurry to the Capitol, not to invest him with his office, but to repent their election.

Act III

Enraged by the ingratitude of "the mutable rank-scented many," Coriolanus is so outspoken that the tribunes call him traitor and only with difficulty can the popular Menenius prevent his being torn to pieces in the streets. While they demand their general's death, Menenius undertakes to have him make amends. Accordingly, at the urging of his friends, who fear for the safety of Rome, and particularly of Volumnia, Coriolanus swallows his indignities and makes a humble appearance before the people in the Forum. The malicious accusations of the tribunes, however, make him forget his promises, and he tactlessly loses his temper again. As a result, he is banished, and, cursing Rome, he leaves it defenceless before its threatening enemies.

Act IV

Outside the city gates Coriolanus takes leave of his family and friends, and, disguised as a beggar, goes to Antium where his rival, Aufidius, is raising a new army against Rome. Amazed that Coriolanus should be so misprized by his country, Aufidius shows him every outward sign of friendship and makes him equal in command with himself. Together they advance upon Rome, to the utter consternation of the citizens. Aufidius, however, dislikes Coriolanus' assured manner and envies his popularity with the troops, knowing that the Roman is over-shadowing his own greatness. But he bides his time for vengeance upon his old rival.

Act V

When the army reaches the gates of Rome, first Comenius and then Menenius go out to plead for the city, but Coriolanus refuses to recognize his old friends and is deaf to all entreaties. Only when his mother, accompanied by Virgilia, Valeria, and young Marcius, kneel before him, does he relent. Relying upon Aufidius, who was present at the interview, to justify him before the Volsces, Coriolanus withdraws the troops and returns to Corioli. There, Aufidius calls him traitor and accuses him of cheating the Volsces out of a victory, and in the confusion arising out of Coriolanus' tactless reminder to the crowd of the havoc he once wrought in Corioli, he is stabbed by hired conspirators. Once his rival is dead, Aufidius is struck with sorrow and resolves to do honor to the greatness of his memory.

Everyday Expressions From Shakespeare

"So are you to my thought as food to life."—Sonnet 75

The influence of Shakespeare's work in the theatre and in literature, as every one knows, is both widespread and important. But his mark is also upon the very vocabulary which we use daily, and many common expressions which have now attained the dignity of unidentified quotations have had their origin in his plays. The following is but "an inventory to particularize their abundance":

HAMLET
flaming youth
in my mind's eye
to the manner born
hoist by his own petard
the glass of fashion
the primrose path
it smells to heaven
there's the rub
the dog will have his day
method in his madness
brevity is the soul of wit
cudgel thy brains
as easy as lying
the whips and scorns of time
more matter and less art
neither a borrower nor a lender be
this mortal coil
yeoman's service

OTHELLO
a chronicle of small beer
the green-eyed monster
pomp and circumstance
who steals my purse steals trash
a round unvarnished tale
a foregone conclusion
not wisely but too well
the seamy side
wear my heart on my sleeve
balmy slumbers

A MIDSUMMER NIGHT'S DREAM
single blessedness
a lion among the ladies

JULIUS CAESAR
it was Greek to me
an itching palm
master spirits
a dish fit for the gods
a lean and hungry look
masters of their fates
the dogs of war

I HENRY IV
give the devil his due
tell truth and shame the devil
come betwixt the wind and his nobility
hearts of gold
the better part of valor is discretion

2 HENRY IV
he has eaten me out of house and home
the weaker vessel

MACBETH
make assurance doubly sure
the crack of doom
the milk of human kindness
a sorry sight
the wine of life
applaud to the very echo

MUCH ADO ABOUT NOTHING
merry as the day is long
with fear and trembling
good men and true
a valiant trencher man

Everyday Expressions From Shakespeare

AS YOU LIKE IT
that was laid on with a trowel
too much of a good thing
this working day world
much virtue in "if"
good wine needs no bush
an ill-favoured thing, but mine own

ROMEO AND JULIET
what's in a name?
the public haunt of men
a fool's paradise
pink of courtesy

KING JOHN
paint the lily
elbow room
cold comfort

KING LEAR
every inch a king
more sinned against than sinning
the wheel is come full circle

CORIOLANUS
to flutter the dove cotes
to die by inches

ANTONY AND CLEOPATRA
my salad days
I wish you joy o' the worm
it beggared all description

THE TWO GENTLEMEN OF VERONA
to make a virtue of necessity
a woman's reason
home keeping youth have ever homely
wits

THE MERRY WIVES OF WINDSOR
as good luck would have it
throw cold water on it

TWELFTH NIGHT
like Patience on a monument
a carpet knight

LOVE'S LABOR LOST
play fast and loose
out of the question
a marvellous good neighbor, and
a very good bowler

I HENRY VI
halcyon days

2 HENRY VI
the main chance

3 HENRY VI
a nine days' wonder

THE MERCHANT OF VENICE
my own flesh and blood
a harmless necessary cat
a Daniel come to judgement
it's a wise father that knows his own
child

RICHARD II
a spotless reputation

THE COMEDY OF ERRORS
something in the wind

TROILUS AND CRESSIDA
one touch of nature makes the whole
world kin

THE TAMING OF THE SHREW
my cake is dough
there's small choice in rotten apples
let the world slide

THE TEMPEST
misery acquaints a man with strange
bedfellows
we are such stuff as dreams are made
on

THE WINTER'S TALE
a snapper-up of unconsidered trifles

Book-Titles From Shakespeare

"O that I had a title good enough to keep him company!"
—The Merchant of Venice, II, iv

Still another evidence that Shakespeare's wit is potent yet is the frequent use by modern authors of terse quotations, rich in connotation from the plays, as titles for their books. A complete collection of Shakespearean book-titles would number many hundreds, and the following selection makes no pretence to completeness. Most of those listed are recent, but a few older titles have been included:

"Two truths are told
As happy prologues to the swelling act
Of the imperial theme." (*Macbeth*, I, iii)

KNIGHT, G. WILSON: *The Imperial Theme.*

"Vaulting ambition, which o'erleaps itself
And falls on the other [side]." (*Macbeth*, I, vii)

MIDDLETON, ELLIS: *Vaulting Ambition.*

"There's husbandry in Heaven; their candles are all out." (*Macbeth*, II, i)

WILLCOCKS, M. P.: *Husbandry in Heaven.*

"Sleep that knits up the ravell'd sleave of care." (*Macbeth*, II, ii)

MUNDAY, M. C.: *The Ravelled Sleeve.*

"What, will the line stretch out to the crack of doom?" (*Macbeth*, IV, i)

EDWARDS, HUGH: *Crack of Doom.*

"To-morrow, and to-morrow, and to-morrow,
Creeps in this petty pace from day to day
To the last syllable of recorded time;
And· all our yesterdays have lighted fools
The way to dusty death. Out, out, brief candle!
Life's but a walking shadow, a poor player
That struts and frets his hour upon the stage
And then is heard no more. It is a tale
Told by an idiot, full of sound and fury,
Signifying nothing." (*Macbeth*, V, v)

BARRY, P.: *To-morrow and To-morrow*; PINKERTON, B.: *This Petty Pace*; TOMLINSON, H. M.: *All Our Yesterdays*; ROBBINS, C.: *Dusty Death*; HUXLEY, A.: *Brief Candles*; WHITE, E. W.: *Walking Shadows*; CHILD, H.: *A Poor Player*; MACAULAY, R.: *Told by an Idiot*; FAULKNER, W.: *The Sound and the Fury.*

"A little more than kin, and less than kind." (*Hamlet*, I, ii)

SEAFORTH, C.: *More than Kin*; DOBIE, C. C.: *Less than Kind.*

"Do not, as some ungracious pastors do,
Show me the steep and thorny way to Heaven,
Whilst, like a puff'd and reckless libertine,
Himself the primrose path of dalliance treads
And recks not his own rede." (*Hamlet*, I, iii)

GOOLDEN, BARBARA: *The Primrose Path.*

"This above all: to thine own self be true,
And it must follow, as the night the day,
Thou canst not then be false to any man." (*Hamlet*, I, iii)

FORD, L.: *False to Any Man.*

"There needs no ghost, my lord, come from the grave to tell us this." (*Hamlet*, I, v)

ADAM, R.: *There Needs No Ghost.*

"What a piece of work is a man! . . . In action how like an angel! In apprehension how like a god!" (*Hamlet*, II, ii)

MacDONNELL, A. G.: *How Like an Angel;* STOUT, REX: *How Like a God.*

"To die; to sleep. To sleep? Perchance to dream! Ay, there's the rub." (*Hamlet*, III, i)

LUYTENS, MARY: *Perchance to Dream.*

"And by a sleep to say we end
The heartache and the thousand natural shocks
That flesh is heir to." (*Hamlet*, III, i)

KIRSTEIN, LINCOLN: *Flesh Is Heir.*

"For who would bear the whips and scorns of time?" (*Hamlet*, III, i)

GILES, NORMAN: *The Whips of Time.*

"The law's delay,
The insolence of office, and the spurns
That patient merit of the unworthy takes."
(*Hamlet*, III, i)

NORTHROP, W. B. and J. B.: *The Insolence of Office: The Story of the Seabury Investigations.*

"The undiscovered country from whose bourne No traveller returns." (*Hamlet*, III, i)

McKENNA, S.: *The Undiscovered Country;* AUSLANDER, J.: *No Traveller Returns.*

"For some must watch, while some must sleep, So runs the world away." (*Hamlet*, III, ii)

WHITE, E. L.: *Some Must Watch.*

" 'Tis now the very witching time of night
When churchyards yawn and hell itself breathes out
Contagion to this world." (*Hamlet*, III, ii)

THOMAS, A.: *The Witching Hour;* ASQUITH, CYNTHIA: *When Churchyards Yawn.*

"Look here, upon this picture, and on this, The counterfeit presentment of two brothers."
(*Hamlet*, III, iv)

HOWELLS, W. D.: *A Counterfeit Presentment.*

"You cannot call it love, for at your age The heyday in the blood is tame."
(*Hamlet*, III, iv)

GOODWIN, GERRINT: *The Heyday in the Blood.*

"There's rosemary, that's for remembrance."
(*Hamlet*, IV, v)

WILSON, M. R.: *Rosemary for Remembrance.*

"When sorrows come, they come not single spies, But in battalions." (*Hamlet*, IV, v)

VACHELL, H. A.: *When Sorrows Come.*

"There is no ancient gentleman but gardeners, ditchers, and grave makers; they hold up Adam's profession." (*Hamlet*, V, i)

MEADE, J. R.: *Adam's Profession.*

"The cat will mew and dog will have his day."
(*Hamlet*, V i)

JACKSON, F.: *The Cat Will Mew.*

"The rest is silence." (*Hamlet*, V, ii)

SHARTEN-ANTINK, C. and M.: *The Rest Is Silence.*

"The fault, dear Brutus, is not in our stars
But in ourselves that we are underlings."
(*Julius Caesar*, I, ii)

BARRIE, J. M.: *Dear Brutus;* MARSHALL, M. M.: *Not in Our Stars.*

"Cry 'Havoc,' and let slip the dogs of war."
(*Julius Caesar*, III, i)

YEATS-BROWN, F.: *Dogs of War.*

"There is a tide in the affairs of men
Which, taken at the flood, leads on to fortune;
Omitted, all the voyage of their life
Is bound in shallows and in miseries."
(*Julius Caesar*, IV, iii)

WILDE, P.: *There Is a Tide;* TURNER, J. H.: *The Affairs of Men;* SMITH, E. L.: *Tides in the Affairs of Men;* LAMBERT, D.: *Taken at the Flood.*

"It is too rash, too unadvis'd, too sudden,
Too like the lightning, which doth cease to be
Ere one can say it lightens."
(*Romeo and Juliet*, II, ii)

CHAMBERS, D.: *Too Like the Lightning.*

"Hist, Romeo, hist! O, for a falconer's voice
To lure this tassel-gentle back again."
(*Romeo and Juliet*, II, ii)

MANNIN, ETHEL: *The Falconer's Voice.*

"The imagined happiness that both
Receive in either by this dear encounter."
(*Romeo and Juliet*, II, vi)

HALL, BARBARA: *Dear Encounter.*

" 'Tis not so deep as a well, nor so wide as a church-door; but 'tis enough, 'twill serve."
(*Romeo and Juliet*, III, i)

PARKER, DOROTHY: *Not so Deep as a Well.*

"A plague o' both your houses!"
(*Romeo and Juliet*, III, i)

ANDERSON, MAXWELL: *Both Your Houses.*

"O, I am Fortune's fool!"
(*Romeo and Juliet*, III, i)

SABATINI, R.: *Fortune's Fool.*

"Night's candles are burnt out, and jocund day
Stands tiptoe on the misty mountain tops."
(*Romeo and Juliet*, III, v)

BERRY, W. R.: *Night's Candles;* FEVEREL, T. R.: *Jocund Day.*

"It was the nightingale, and not the lark."
(*Romeo and Juliet*, III, v)

FORD, FORD MADOX: *It Was the Nightingale.*

"O churl! drunk all, and left no friendly drop
To help me after?" (*Romeo and Juliet*, V, iii)

WADE, HENRY: *No Friendly Drop.*

"A fool, a fool! I met a fool i' the forest,
A motley fool." (*As You Like It*, II, vii)

ALDINGTON, R.: *A Fool i' the Forest: a Phantasmagoria.*

"One man in his time plays many parts,
His acts being seven ages."
(*As You Like It*, II, vii)

GLASGOW, ELLEN: *One Man in His Time.*

"Then the whining school-boy, with his satchel
And shining morning face, creeping like snail
Unwillingly to school." (*As You Like It*, II, vii)

ALLARDICE, ANNE: *Unwillingly to School.*

BOOK-TITLES FROM SHAKESPEARE

"Then a soldier . . .
Seeking the bubble reputation
Even in the cannon's mouth."
(*As You Like It*, II, vii)

WREN, PERCIVAL CHRISTO-PHER: *Bubble Reputation.*

"Men have died from time to time and worms
have eaten them, but not for love."
(*As You Like It*, IV, i)

SEYMOUR, BEATRICE KEAN: *But Not for Love.*

"Summer's lease hath all too short a date."
(*Sonnet* 18)

CUNYNGHAME, DOROTHY: *Summer's Lease.*

"Till whatsoever star that guides my moving
Points on me graciously with fair aspect,
And puts apparel on my tatter'd loving,
To show me worthy of thy sweet respect."
(*Sonnet* 26)

BOTTOME, PHYLLIS: *Tatter'd Loving.*

"When, in disgrace with Fortune and men's eyes."
(*Sonnet* 29)

CRONYN, G.: *Fortune and Men's Eyes.*

"If this be error and upon me proved, I never
writ, nor no man ever loved." (*Sonnet* 116)

ASKWITH, BETTY: *If This Be Error.*

"Two loves I have of comfort and despair."
(*Sonnet* 144)

PITMAN, OWEN: *Two Loves I Have.*

"In the dark backward and abysm of time."
(*The Tempest*, I, ii)

NEVINSON, H. W.: *In the Dark Backward.*

"Misery acquaints a man with strange bedfellows."
(*The Tempest*, II, ii)

SOUTAR, ANDREW: *Strange Bedfellows.*

"This is the tune of our catch play'd by the
picture of Nobody." (*The Tempest*, III, ii)

OWENS, PHILIP: *Picture of Nobody.*

"We are such stuff
As dreams are made on, and our little life
Is rounded with a sleep." (*The Tempest*, IV, i)

O'BRIEN, KATHLEEN: *Our Little Life.*

"O brave new world,
That has such people in 't!" (*The Tempest*, V, i)

HUXLEY, ALDOUS: *Brave New World.*

"Journeys end in lovers' meeting,
Every wise man's son doth know."
(*Twelfth Night*, II, iii)

TYNAN, KATHARINE: *Lovers' Meeting.*

"Dost thou think, because thou art virtuous,
there shall be no more cakes and ale?"
(*Twelfth Night*, II, iii)

MAUGHAM, W. S.: *Cakes and Ale.*

"O, fellow, come, the song we had last night.
Mark it, Cesario, it is old and plain.
The spinsters and the knitters in the sun
And the free maids that weave their thread with
bones do use to chant it. It is silly sooth."
(*Twelfth Night*, II, iv)

"OCTAVE THANET": *Knitters in the Sun.*

"Daylight and champaign discovers no more."
(*Twelfth Night*, II, v)

YOUNG, G. M.: *Daylight and Champaign.*

"Thus the whirligig of time brings in his revenges." (*Twelfth Night*, V, i)

MURRAY, D. C.: *Time's Revenges.*

"Served the lust of my mistress' heart and did the act of darkness with her."
(*King Lear*, III, iv)

BISHOP, JOHN PEALE: *Act of Darkness.*

"Keep thy foot out of brothels, thy hand out of plackets, thy pen from lenders' books, and defy the foul fiend." (*King Lear*, III, iv)

COLLIER, J.: *Defy the Foul Fiend.*

"As flies to wanton boys, are we to the gods, They kill us for their sport." (*King Lear*, IV, i)

OKE, RICHARD: *Wanton Boys.*

"Ay, every inch a king:
When I do stare, see how the subject quakes."
(*King Lear*, IV, vi)

PILAR, PRINCESS, and CHAPMAN-HUSTON, DESMOND: *Every Inch a King.*

"When we are born, we cry that we are come To this great stage of fools." (*King Lear*, IV, vi)

MERRICK, LEONARD: *This Stage of Fools.*

"Thou art a soul in bliss; but I am bound Upon a wheel of fire." (*King Lear*, IV, vii)

KNIGHT, G. WILSON: *The Wheel of Fire.*

"Men must endure
Their going hence, even as their coming hither;
Ripeness is all." (*King Lear*, v, ii)

LINKLATER, ERIC: *Ripeness Is All.*

"The wheel is come full circle."
(*King Lear*, V, iii)

COLLIER, J.: *Full Circle.*

"It is excellent
To have a giant's strength; but it is tyrannous
To use it like a giant."
(*Measure for Measure*, II, ii)

KING, BASIL: *The Giant's Strength.*

"But man, proud man,
Drest in a little brief authority."
(*Measure for Measure*, II, ii)

ULRICH, MABEL: *Man, Proud Man;* DANVERS-WALKER, A.: *Brief Authority.*

"There may be in the cup
A spider steep'd, and one may drink, depart,
And yet partake no venom, for his knowledge
Is not infected; but if one present
The abhorr'd ingredient to his eye, make known
How he hath drunk, he cracks his gorge, his sides
With violent hefts." (*The Winter's Tale*, II, i)

SHEARING, JOSEPH: *The Spider in the Cup.*

"A merry heart goes all the day
Your sad tires in a mile-a."
(*The Winter's Tale*, IV, iii)

SWINNERTON, FRANK: *The Merry Heart.*

(An allusion to the character who peddles ballads in *The Winter's Tale*, IV, iv)

ROLLINS, HYDER E.: *The Pack of Autolycus.*

"The web of our life is of a mingled yarn, good and ill together."
(*All's Well that Ends Well*, IV, iii)

HERRICK, ROBERT: *The Web of Life*; JOHN, M. W.: *Mingled Yarn.*

"My salad days,
When I was green in judgement."
(*Antony and Cleopatra*, I, v)

HAWKES, C. P.: *Salad Days.*

"Let's have one other gaudy night."
(*Antony and Cleopatra*, III, xiii)

SAYERS, DOROTHY L.: *Gaudy Night.*

"Give me my robe, put on my crown; I have Immortal longings in me."
(*Antony and Cleopatra*, V, ii)

LEIGH, URSULA: *Give Me My Robe.*

"And you, good yeoman,
Whose limbs were made in England, show us here The mettle of your pasture." (*Henry V*, III, i)

ALLEN, JAMES LANE: *The Mettle of the Pasture.*

"Come, your answer in broken music; for thy voice is music and thy English broken; therefore, queen of all, Katharine, break thy mind to me in broken English." (*Henry V*, V, ii)

MacTAGGART, MORNA: *Broken Music.*

"Still have I borne it with a patient shrug, For sufferance is the badge of all our tribe."
(*The Merchant of Venice*, I, iii)

SACHAR, A. L.: *Sufferance Is the Badge.*

"The quality of mercy is not strained.
It droppeth as the gentle rain from heaven Upon the place beneath."
(*The Merchant of Venice*, IV, i)

CLARKE, I. C.: *As the Gentle Rain*; BEHRMAN. S. N.: *Rain from Heaven.*

"The moon shines bright. In such a night as this, When the sweet wind did gently kiss the trees And they did make no noise, in such a night Troilus methinks mounted the Troyan walls And sigh'd his soul toward the Grecian tents, Where Cressida lay that night."
(*The Merchant of Venice*, V, i)

DEUTSCH, BABETTE: *In Such A Night*

"The man that hath no music in himself, Nor is not mov'd with concord of sweet sounds, Is fit for treasons, stratagems, and spoils."
(*The Merchant of Venice*, V, i)

WHITE, WILLIAM ALLEN: *Stratagems and Spoils: Stories of Love and Politics.*

"How far that little candle throws his beams! So shines a good deed in a naughty world."
(*The Merchant of Venice*, V, i)

GLENN, I.: *Little Candle's Beams.*

"Fie, fie, how wayward is this foolish love, That, like a testy babe, will scratch the nurse And presently, all humbled, kiss the rod!"
(*The Two Gentlemen of Verona*, I, ii)
"Wilt thou, pupil-like,
Take the correction, mildly kiss the rod, And fawn on rage with base humility?"
(*Richard II*, V, i)

YATES, EDMUND: *Kissing the Rod.*

Bibliography

The following list of books is intended merely to suggest to the reader the best editions of Shakespeare and some of the more important critical works of recent years which will be useful in a study of the plays. It is not in any sense complete. Many of the volumes referred to below contain bibliographies and thus point the way to further study.

EDITIONS OF SHAKESPEARE'S PLAYS

One-volume Editions:

The New Cambridge Edition of the Complete Plays and Poems of William Shakespeare, edited by William Allan Neilson and Charles Jarvis Hill, The Houghton Mifflin Company.

The Globe Edition, edited by W. G. Clark and W. A. Wright, The Macmillan Company.

The Oxford Edition, edited by W. J. Craig, Oxford University Press. (Also issued in three volumes.)

The Shakespeare Head Edition, edited by A. H. Bullen, Basil Blackwell.

The Kittredge Edition, edited by George Lyman Kittredge, Ginn and Company.

Mr. William Shakespeare's Comedies, Histories, and Tragedies. A photographic facsimile of the First Folio edition, prepared by Helge Kökeritz and Charles Tyler Prouty, Yale University Press.

The Sisson Edition, edited by Charles Jasper Sisson, Harper and Brothers.

Editions in More than One Volume:

The Tudor Shakespeare, edited by William Allan Neilson and A. H. Thorndike, 40 small volumes, The Macmillan Company.

The Yale Shakespeare, edited by Members of the Department of English, Yale University, 40 small volumes, Yale University Press.

The New Shakespeare, edited by Sir Arthur Quiller-Couch and Sir J. Dover Wilson, Cambridge University Press. (In progress.)

Selected Plays of Shakespeare, edited by Karl J. Holzknecht and Norman E. McClure, 4 volumes, The American Book Company. (Twenty-four plays and the sonnets with introductions and notes.)

The New Variorum Shakespeare, edited by H. H. Furness and H. H. Furness, Jr., The J. B. Lippincott Company. (A reference edition with exhaustive notes, in which about half the plays have appeared. Since the death of H. H. Furness, Jr., the work is being carried forward by a committee of the Modern Language Association.)

BOOKS ON THE LIFE OF SHAKESPEARE

LEWIS, B. ROLAND (ed.), The Shakespeare Documents: Facsimilies, Translations, and Commentary, 2 volumes, Stanford University Press, 1941.

LEE, SIR SIDNEY, A Life of William Shakespeare, The Macmillan Company, rev. ed. 1925.

ADAMS, JOSEPH QUINCEY, A Life of William Shakespeare, The Houghton Mifflin Company, 1923. (These two biographies are now considered standard.)

Bibliography

SMART, J. S., Shakespeare: Truth and Tradition, Longmans, Green, and Company, 1928.
(A study of Shakespeare's surroundings and a scrutiny of fact and tradition about him.)

RALEIGH, SIR WALTER, Shakespeare (English Men of Letters Series), The Macmillan Company, 1907.

ALDEN, RAYMOND MACDONALD, Shakespeare (Master Spirits of Literature Series), Duffield and Company, 1922.

WILSON, J. DOVER, The Essential Shakespeare, Cambridge University Press, 1930.
(Three excellent general studies of Shakespeare and his work as well as biographies.)

CHAMBERS, SIR EDMUND K. and WILLIAMS, CHARLES, A Short Life of Shakespeare with the Sources, Oxford University Press, 1933.
(An abridgment of Chambers' William Shakespeare: A Study of Facts and Problems (1930) mentioned below.)

FRIPP, EDGAR I., Shakespeare—Man and Artist, 2 volumes, Oxford University Press, 1938.
(A series of studies, biographical and literary, dealing with Shakespeare's Stratford friends, his acquaintance with children, medicine, music, the law, etc. and discussing the legends about Shakespeare.)

REESE, M. M., Shakespeare: His World and His Work, St. Martin's Press, 1953.
(A fresh account of the man, his life, and his art, against the background of the world in which he lived and worked.)

BOOKS ON THE ELIZABETHAN AGE

Shakespeare's England: An Account of the Life and Manners of his Age, 2 volumes, Oxford University Press, 1916.
(An excellent work containing chapters upon every phase of Elizabethan life, all written with especial attention to Shakespeare's plays.)

ROWSE, A. L., The England of Elizabeth, The Macmillan Company, 1951. The Expansion of Elizabethan England, The Macmillan Company, 1955.
(Lively accounts of the structure of Elizabethan society and the expansion of that society, both by the state and by individual enterprise.)

BYRNE, M. ST. CLARE, Elizabethan Life in Town and Country, The Houghton Mifflin Company, 1925. (Revised edition, 1934.)
(A pleasantly written account of the daily life of ordinary Elizabethan people.)

Life in Shakespeare's England: A Book of Elizabethan Prose, compiled by J. Dover Wilson, Cambridge University Press, 1911.

England in Shakespeare's Day, edited by G. B. Harrison, Harcourt, Brace and Company, 1928.
(Two books of classified extracts from the works of Shakespeare and his contemporaries illustrating the manners and customs of his age.)

SCHELLING, FELIX E., English Literature during the Lifetime of Shakespeare, Henry Holt and Company, 1910. (Revised edition 1927.)
(Shakespeare's work seen in relation to the literature surrounding it.)

SHEAVYN, PHOEBE, The Literary Profession in the Elizabethan Age, Manchester, 1909.
(Authorship and the conditions amid which it was pursued as a profession in Shakespeare's day.)

BOOKS ON THE ELIZABETHAN DRAMA AND THEATRE

HARBAGE, ALFRED, Annals of English Drama: 975-1700. An Analytical Record of All

Plays, Extant or Lost, Chronologically Arranged and Indexed by Authors, Titles, Dramatic Companies, University of Pennsylvania Press, 1940.

SCHELLING, FELIX E., Elizabethan Playwrights: A Short History of the English Drama from Medieval Times to the Closing of the Theatres in 1642, Harper and Brothers, 1925.

(A study of the flourish of the drama of which Shakespeare's plays were a part by one of the foremost authorities on the subject.)

BOAS, F. S., An Introduction to Tudor Drama, Oxford University Press, 1933.

(A volume written for the reader who, without specialized knowledge, wishes to understand the dramatic conditions which had their flowering in Shakespeare.)

CREIZENACH, WILHELM, The English Drama in the Age of Shakespeare, The J. B. Lippincott Company, 1916.

(A translation of a section of the author's Geschichte des neueren dramas.)

PARROTT, THOMAS MARC, and BALL, ROBERT HAMILTON, A Short View of Elizabethan Drama. Together with some account of its principal playwrights and the conditions under which it was produced, Scribners, [1943].

FARNHAM, WILLARD, The Medieval Heritage of Elizabethan Tragedy, University of California Press, 1936.

(The debt of Elizabethan drama to the Middle Ages.)

BOAS, F. S., Shakespeare and his Predecessors, Scribners, 1896.

(Especial stress is laid upon the indebtedness of Shakespeare to the work of the earlier Elizabethans.)

Elizabethan Plays Written by Shakespeare's Friends, Colleagues, Rivals, and Successors, D. C. Heath and Company, [1933].

Elizabethan and Stuart Plays, edited by Charles Read Baskervill, Virgil B. Heltzel, and Arthur H. Nethercot, Henry Holt and Company, [1934].

English Drama, 1580-1642, edited by C. F. Tucker Brooke and N. B. Paradise, D. C. Heath and Company, 1933.

(Good collection of plays by Shakespeare's contemporaries.)

HOLZKNECHT, KARL J., Outlines of Tudor and Stuart Plays, 1497-1642, Barnes and Noble, 1947.

(Critical synopses of more than 80 plays.)

ADAMS, JOSEPH QUINCEY, Shakespearean Playhouses: A History of English Theatres from the Beginnings to the Restoration, The Houghton Mifflin Company, 1917.

(A history of Elizabethan playing places from the days of the innyards to 1642.)

ADAMS, JOHN CRANFORD, The Globe Playhouse: Its Design and Equipment, Harvard University Press, 1942.

(The best account of Shakespeare's theatre.)

THORNDIKE, A. H., Shakespeare's Theatre, The Macmillan Company, 1916.

(A survey of information about the theatres of Shakespeare's time, with some account of dramatic companies, government regulation, actors, and acting.)

LAWRENCE, W. J., The Physical Conditions of the Elizabethan Public Playhouse, Harvard University Press, 1927.

(A treatise on the structure and conventions of the theatre and the stage.)

BALDWIN, T. W., The Organization and Personnel of the Shakespearean Company, Princeton University Press, 1927.

(A scholarly study of the laws and customs governing the organization of an Elizabethan company.)

A Series of Papers on Shakespeare and the Theatre . . . by Members of the Shakespeare Association, Oxford University Press, 1927.

(Among the articles are the following:

BIBLIOGRAPHY

HAINES, C. M., The Development of Shakespeare's Stagecraft.

HARRISON, G. B., Shakespeare's Actors.

ISAACS, J., Shakespeare as a Man of the Theatre.

NOBLE, RICHMOND, Shakespeare's Songs and the Stage.

COWLING, G. H., Shakespeare and the Elizabethan Stage.

BYRNE, M. ST. CLARE, Shakespeare's Audience.

All emphasize the influence of theatrical conditions upon Shakespeare.)

SPRAGUE, ARTHUR COLBY, Shakespeare and the Audience: A Study in the Technique of Exposition, Harvard University Press, 1935.

(Shakespeare's technique as it was determined by the special conditions of his theatre.)

HARBAGE, ALFRED, Shakespeare's Audience, Columbia University Press, 1941.

(An interpretation of evidence on the size, social composition, behavior, and esthetic and intellectual capacity of Shakespeare's audience.)

BOOKS ON SHAKESPEARE'S WORK

HOLZKNECHT, KARL J., The Backgrounds of Shakespeare's Plays, American Book Company, 1950.

(Chapters on Shakespeare's dramatic art and what lies behind it—the social, literary, theatrical, and philosophical antecedents which determine the modern reader's appreciation and understanding.)

A Companion to Shakespeare Studies, edited by Harley Granville-Barker and G. B. Harrison, The Macmillan Company, 1934.

(A collection of essays—each by a special student—on various phases of Shakespearean study: his national and social background, his dramatic art, the drama of his time, his sources, his text, Shakespearean criticism and scholarship, etc.)

BAKER, GEORGE PIERCE, The Development of Shakespeare as a Dramatist, The Macmillan Company, 1907.

(A study of Shakespeare as a practical playwright writing for a particular theatre, company, and public.)

MATTHEWS, BRANDER, Shakespere as a Playwright, Scribners, 1913.

BRADLEY, A. C., Shakespearean Tragedy, The Macmillan Company, 1904.

(The nature of tragedy as Shakespeare knew and applied it.)

CAMPBELL, LILY B., Shakespeare's Tragic Heroes: Slaves of Passion, Cambridge University Press, 1930; reprinted 1952 by Barnes & Noble, Inc.

(A study of his tragedies in relation to the philosophy of his day.)

CHARLTON, H. B., Shakespearian Tragedy, Cambridge University Press, 1948.

(Studies of Shakespeare's more popular tragedies.)

CHARLTON, H. B., Shakespearian Comedy, The Macmillan Company, 1938.

(A series of studies of Shakespeare's comic art.)

PARROTT, THOMAS MARC, Shakespearian Comedy, Oxford University Press, 1949.

(The only full analysis of Shakespearian comedy, as found in the tragedies and histories as well as in the lighter plays.)

GORDON, GEORGE, Shakespearian Comedy and Other Studies, Oxford University Press, [1944].

(Several papers on aspects of comedy.)

CAMPBELL, OSCAR JAMES, Shakespeare's Satire, Oxford University Press, 1943.

ANDERS, H. R. D., Shakespeare's Books: A Dissertation on Shakespeare's Reading and the Immediate Sources of His Works, Berlin, 1904.

(The best compendium of books with which Shakespeare is known to have been acquainted, but it devotes little attention to his use of them.)

COLLIER, J. P., and HAZLITT, W. C., Shakespeare's Library: A Collection of the Romances, Novels, Poems, and Histories Used by Shakespeare in the Composition

of His Works, Second Edition, 6 volumes, London, 1875.
(A reprint of all the important sources except Holinshed's Chronicles.)

Fairy Tales, Legends, and Romances Illustrating Shakespeare and other Early English Writers, edited by W. C. Hazlitt, London, 1875.

The Shakespeare Classics, Being the Sources and Originals of Shakespeare's Plays, under the General Editorship of Sir Israel Gollancz, London, 1907—:

1. The Chronicle History of King Leir, edited by Sir Sidney Lee (1909)
2. The Taming of a Shrew, edited by F. S. Boas (1908)
3-4. Shakespeare's Plutarch, edited by C. F. Tucker Brooke, 2 volumes (1909)
5. Sources and Analogues of a Midsummer Night's Dream, edited by Frank Sidgwick (1908)
6. Lodge's Rosalynde, edited by W. W. Greg (1907)
7. Greene's Pandosto, edited by P. G. Thomas (1907)
8. Brooke's Romeus and Juliet, edited by J. J. Munro (1908)
9. The Troublesome Reign of King John, edited by F. J. Furnivall and J. J. Munro (1908)
10. The Menaechmi: The Latin Text together with the Elizabethan Translation, edited by W. H. D. Rouse (1912)
11. Rich's Apolonius and Silla, edited by Morton Luce (1912)
12. The Sources of Hamlet, edited with Essays on the Legend by Sir Israel Gollancz (1926)

Shakespeare's Holinshed: The Chronicle and the Historical Plays Compared by W. G. Boswell-Stone, London, 1896. (Revised edition, 1907).
(A reprint of the passages used by Shakespeare.)

Holinshed's Chronicle as Used in Shakespeare's Plays, edited by Allardyce and Josephine Nicoll, Everyman Library, 1927. (Based on Boswell-Stone's work.)

SCHELLING, FELIX E., The English Chronicle Play: A Study in the Popular Historical Literature Environing Shakespeare, The Macmillan Company, 1902.

MARRIOT, J. A. R., English History in Shakespeare, E. P. Dutton and Company, 1918.
(A study of Shakespeare's use of history emphasizing the broad underlying themes of the history plays.)

TILLYARD, E. M. W., Shakespeare's History Plays, The Macmillan Company, 1946.
(A study of the philosophical, historical, and literary background of Shakespeare's chronicle plays.)

CAMPBELL, LILY B., Shakespeare's Histories, "Mirrors" of Elizabethan Policy, Huntington Library, 1947.
(An interpretation of the English history plays in relation to the modes of living, thinking, and playwriting of the day, and as reflections of Elizabethan domestic and foreign policy.)

MACCALLUM, M. W., Shakespeare's Roman Plays and Their Background, The Macmillan Company, 1910. (A study of Shakespeare's use of classical materials.)

LAWRENCE, W. W., Shakespeare's Problem Comedies, The Macmillan Company, 1931.
(Analyses in the light of his inheritance from the Middle Ages.)

TILLYARD, E. M. W., Shakespeare's Problem Plays, University of Toronto Press, 1949.
(Studies of Hamlet, Troilus and Cressida, All's Well, and Measure for Measure.)

TILLYARD, E. M. W., Shakespeare's Last Plays, Chatto and Windus, 1938.
(A study of Cymbeline, The Winter's Tale, and The Tempest.)

STOLL, E. E., Shakespeare Studies: Historical and Comparative in Method, The Macmillan Company, 1927.

STOLL, E. E., Art and Artifice in Shakespeare: A Study in Dramatic Contrast and Illusion, Cambridge University Press, 1933. Reprinted by Barnes & Noble, Inc., 1951.
(Attempts to arrive at what Shakespeare meant to his own day.)

BIBLIOGRAPHY

NOBLE, RICHMOND, Shakespeare's Use of Song with the Text of the Principal Songs, Oxford University Press, 1923.

NOBLE, RICHMOND, Shakespeare's Biblical Knowledge and Use of the Book of Common Prayer, as exemplified in the Plays of the First Folio, The Macmillan Company, 1935.

SPURGEON, CAROLINE F. E., Shakespeare's Imagery and What it Tells Us, The Macmillan Company, 1935.
(An examination of Shakespeare's poetic images and figures of speech, more valuable for the data accumulated than the inferences drawn from them.)

EVANS, E. IFOR, The Language of Shakespeare's Plays, Methuen, [1952].
(Shakespeare's use of words in the theatre.)

Aspects of Shakespeare, Oxford University Press, 1933.
(A reprint of nine British Academy Lectures on Shakespeare.)

RIDLEY, M. R., Shakespeare's Plays: A Commentary, E. P. Dutton and Company, 1938. (A book of brief critical comment.)

SPENCER, HAZLETON, The Art and Life of William Shakespeare, Harcourt, Brace and Company, 1940.
(Shakespeare's life, his medium, and critical analysis of each play.)

SMITH, LOGAN PEARSALL, On Reading Shakespeare, Harcourt, Brace and Company, 1933. (A pleasantly written account for the general reader.)

BOOKS OF REFERENCE

JAGGARD, WILLIAM, Shakespeare Bibliography. A Dictionary of Every Known Issue of the Writings of Our National Poet and of Recorded Opinion Thereon in the English Language, Stratford-on-Avon, 1911.
(729 triple-columned pages.)

HALLIDAY, F. E., A Shakespeare Companion, 1550-1950, Gerald Duckworth and Company, 1952.
(A handbook, not only to Shakespeare, but also to the Elizabethan theatrical world and to the history of Shakespeare's work both on the stage and in the study.)

SUGDEN, E. H., A Topographical Dictionary to the Works of Shakespeare and His Fellow Dramatists, Manchester University Press, 1925; distributed by Barnes and Noble.
(A dictionary of information about place names in the Elizabethan drama, with a map of Elizabethan London.)

EBISCH, WALTHER, and SCHUCKING, L. L., A Shakespeare Bibliography, Oxford University Press, 1931. Supplement for the year 1930-1935, Oxford University Press, 1937.

CHAMBERS, E. K., William Shakespeare: A Study of Facts and Problems, 2 volumes, Oxford University Press, 1930.
(A scholarly treatment of the problems in Shakespeare's biography, his theatre, his text, the dates of his plays, etc.)

A New and Complete Concordance or Verbal Index to Words, Phrases, and Passages, in the Dramatic Works of Shakespeare, compiled by John Bartlett, The Macmillan Company, 1894.

A Shakespeare Glossary, edited by C. T. Onions, Oxford University Press, 1911.
(Revised edition, 1919.) (The best handy Shakespeare dictionary.)

ABBOTT, E. A., A Shakespeare Grammar: An Attempt to Illustrate Some of the Differences between Elizabethan and Modern English, The Macmillan Company, 1869. (Still the best treatment of Shakespeare's language.)

AN INDEX OF CHARACTERS AND PLACES IN
SHAKESPEARE'S PLAYS

This Index records only those characters which are specifically named, which have a part in the action, or which are in some other way distinguished. Characters merely referred to are not listed, and the host of "Ladies, Gentlemen, Officers, and Attendants" have not been indexed. Page references are to the appropriate lists of *Dramatis Personæ* where the character is described. Place-names are distinguished from the names of characters by *italics*. Only those which indicate the setting of the action or which appear on one of the maps are listed. Places outside of England merely referred to in the dialogue are omitted. The maps on pages 5, 102, 104, however, indicate not only Shakespeare's scenes, but, with a few insignificant exceptions, other places referred to by him, and localities, principally in London, to which a reader of Shakespeare may wish to refer.

Aaron, *TAnd.*, p. 148.
Abergavenny, Lord, *H8*, *p.* 142.
Abhorson, *M for M*, *p.* 80.
Abraham, *R&J*, p. 151.
Achilles, *T&C*, p. 162.
Actium, A&C, p. 179.
Adam, *AYLI*, p. 70.
Adrian, *Temp.*, p. 96.
Adriana, *C of E.* p. 43.
Aegeon, *C of E.* p. 43.
Aemilia, *C of E*, p. 43.
Aemilius, *TAnd.*, p. 148.
Aeneas, *T&C*, p. 162.
Agamemnon, *T&C*, p. 162.
Agincourt, H5, Map, p. 102.
Agrippa, *A&C*, p. 178.
Agrippa, Menenius, *Cor.*, p. 187.
Aguecheek, Sir Andrew, *TN*, p. 74.
Ajax, *T&C*, p. 162.
Alarbus, *TAnd.*, p. 148.
Albany, Duke of, *KL*, p. 170.
Alcibiades, *T of A*, p. 183.
Aldersgate, Maps, p. 5, 104.
Aldgate Street, Maps, p. 5, 104.
Alençon Duc d', *1H6*, p. 125.
Alexander, *T&C,* p. 162.
Alexandria, A&C, p. 179.
Alexas, *A&C*, p. 179.
Alice, *H5*, p. 122.
Aliena, character assumed by Celia, *AYLI*, p. 70.
Alonso, *Temp.*, p. 96.
Amazons, *T of A*, p. 183.
Amiens, *AYLI*, p. 70.
Andromache, *T&C*, p. 162.
Andronicus, see Lucius; Lucius, Young; Marcus; Martius; Mutius; Publius; Quintus; Titus.
Angelo, *C of E*, p. 43.
Angelo, *M for M*, p. 80.
Angiers, KJ, 1H6, Map, p. 102.

Angus, *Macb.*, p. 174.
Anne, Lady, *R3*, p. 137.
Antenor, *T&C,* p. 162.
Antigonus, *WT*, p. 92.
Antioch, Per., p. 84.
Antiochus, *Per.*, p. 84.
Antiochus' Daughter, *Per.*, p. 84.
Antipholus of Ephesus, *C of E*, p. 43.
Antipholus of Syracuse, *C of E.*, p. 43.
Antium, Cor., p. 187.
Antonio, *M of V*, p. 54.
Antonio, *M Ado*, p. 66.
Antonio, *Temp.*, p. 96.
Antonio, *TG of V*, p. 47.
Antonio, *T N*, p. 74.
Antony, Mark, *JC*, p. 154; *A&C*, p. 178.
Apemantus, *T of A*, p. 183.
Apothecary, *R&J*, p. 151.
Archibald, see Douglas, Earl of.
Archidamus, *WT*, p. 92.
Arden, Forest of, AYLI, p. 70.
Ariel, *Temp.*, p. 96.
Armado, Don Adriano de,*LLL*, p. 40.
Artemidorus of Cnidos, *JC*, p. 155.
Arthur, *KJ*, p. 106.
Arviragus, *Cym.*, p. 87.
Ashford, 2H6, Map, p. 102.
Asmath, *2H6*, p. 130.
Athenian, An Old, *T of A*, p. 183.
Athens, A & C, p. 179; *T of A*, p. 183; *MND*, p. 50.
Audrey, *AYLI*, p. 70.
Aufidius, Tullus, *Cor.*, p. 187.
Aumerle, Duke of, *R2*, p. 110.
Autolycus, *WT*, p. 92.
Auvergne, Countess of, *1H6*, p. 126.

Bagot, *R2*, p. 110.
Balthasar, *M of V*, p. 55.
Balthasar, character assumed by Portia, *M of V*, p. 54.

Balthazar, *C of E,* p. 43.
Balthazar, *M Ado,* p. 66.
Balthazar, *R&J,* p. 151.
Bangor, 1H4, Map. p. 102.
Bankside, Map, p. 104.
Banquo, *Macb.,* p. 174.
Baptista Minola, *T of S,* p. 58.
Bardolph, *1H4,* p. 114; *2H4,* p. 118; *H5,* p. 121; *MW of W,* p. 62.
Bardolph, Lord, *2H4,* p. 117.
Barkloughly Castle, R2, Map, p. 102.
Barnardine, *M for M,* p. 80.
Burnet, 3H6, Map, p. 102.
Bassanio, *M of V,* p. 54.
Basset, *1H6,* p. 125.
Bassianus, *TAnd.,* p. 148.
Bastard of Orleans, *1H6,* p. 125.
Bates, *H5,* p. 121.
Baynard's Castle, R3, Map, p. 104.
Beatrice, *M Ado,* p. 66.
Beaufort, Henry, Bishop of Winchester, and later Cardinal, *1H6,* p. 125; *2H6,* p. 129.
Beaufort, Thomas, see Exeter.
Bedford, Duke of, *H5,* p. 121; *1H6,* p. 125.
Belarius, *Cym.,* p. 87.
Belch, Sir Toby, *TN,* p. 74.
Belmont, M of V, p. 55.
Benedick, *M Ado,* p. 66.
Benvolio, *R&J,* p. 151.
Berkeley, *R3,* p. 138.
Berkeley, Lord, *R2,* p. 110.
Bernardo, *Haml.,* p. 158.
Bertram, *AWEW,* p. 77.
Bevis, George, *2H6,* p. 129.
Bianca, *Oth.,* p. 166.
Bianca, *T of S,* p. 58.
Bigot, Lord, *KJ,* p. 106.
Biondello, *T of S,* p. 58.
Birnam Wood, Macb., Map, p. 102.
Biron, *LLL,* p. 40.
Bishopsgate Street, Maps, p. 5, 104.
Blackfriars, H8, Map, p. 104.
Blackfriars Theatre, (1596), p. 5.
Blackheath, H5, 1H6, Map, p. 104.
Blanch of Spain, *KJ,* p. 106.
Blunt, *2H4,* p. 117.
Blunt, Sir James, *R3,* p. 137.
Blunt, Sir Walter, *1H4,* p. 113.
Boar's Head Tavern, 1H4, 2H4, Map, 104.
Boatswain, *Temp.,* p. 96.
Bohemia, WT, p. 92.
Bolingbroke, Henry, *R2,* p. 110.
Bolingbroke, Roger, *2H6,* p. 130.
Bona, *3H6,* p. 134.
Borachio, *M Ado,* p. 66.
Bosworth Field, R3, Map, p. 102.
Bottom, *MND,* p. 50.
Boult, *Per.,* p. 84.
Bourbon, Duke of, *H5,* p. 122.
Bourchier, Cardinal, Archbishop of Canterbury, *R3,* p. 138.
Boyet, *LLL,* p. 40.
Brabantio, *Oth.,* p. 166.
Brakenbury, Sir Robert, *R3,* p. 138.
Brandon, *H8,* p. 142.
Brandon, Sir William, *R3,* p. 137.
Bridewell, H8, Map, p. 104.
Bridgnorth, 1H4, Map, p. 102.
Bristol, R2, Map, p. 102.

Britain, Cym., p. 87.
Brook, Master, character assumed by Ford, *MW of W,* p. 62.
Burgh, Hubert de, *KJ,* p. 106.
Brutus, Decius, *JC,* p. 154.
Brutus, Junius, *Cor.,* p. 187.
Brutus, Marcus, *JC,* p. 154.
Buckingham, Duke of, *2H6,* p. 129.
Buckingham, Duke of, *H8,* p. 142.
Buckingham, Duke of, *R3,* p. 137.
Bucklersbury, MW of W, Map, p. 104.
Bullcalf, *2H4,* p. 118.
Bullen, Anne, *H8,* p. 142.
Burgundy, Duke of, *H5,* p. 122; *1H6,* p. 125.
Burgundy, Duke of, *KL,* p. 170.
Burton, 1H4, Map, p. 102.
Bury St. Edmunds, KJ, 2H6, Map. p. 102.
Bushy, *R2,* p. 110.
Butts, Doctor, *H8,* p. 142.

Cade Jack, *2H6,* p. 129.
Cadwal, character assumed by Arviragus, *Cym,* p. 87.
Caesar, Julius, *JC,* p. 154.
Caithness, *Macb.,* p. 174.
Caius, *TAnd.,* p. 148.
Caius, Dr., *MW of W,* p. 62.
Calais, H5, Map, p. 102.
Calchas, *T&C,* p. 162.
Caliban, *Temp.,* p. 96.
Calpurnia, *JC,* p. 154.
Cambridge, H5, 1H6, 2H6, Map. p. 102.
Cambridge, Earl of, *H5,* p. 121.
Camillo, *WT,* p. 92.
Campeius, Cardinal, *H8,* p. 142.
Canidius, *A&C,* p. 178.
Canterbury, H5, KJ, H8, Map. p. 102.
Canterbury, Archbishop of, *H5,* p. 121.
Canterbury, Archbishop of, see Bourchier, Cranmer.
Caphis, *T of A,* p. 183.
Capucius, *H8,* p. 142.
Capulet, *R&J,* p. 151.
Capulet, Lady, *R&J,* p. 151.
Carlisle, R2, Map. p. 102.
Carlisle, Bishop of, *R2,* p. 110.
Casca, *JC,* p. 154.
Cassandra, *T&C,* p. 162.
Cassio, *Oth.,* p. 166.
Cassius, Caius, *JC,* p. 154.
Catesby, Sir William, *R3,* p. 137.
Cato, Young, *JC,* p. 155.
Celia, *AYLI,* p. 70.
Ceres, spirit representing, *Temp.,* p. 96.
Cerimon, *Per.,* p. 84.
Cesario, character assumed by Viola, *TN,* p. 74.
Charing Cross, 1H6, Map, p. 104.
Charles, *AYLI,* p. 70.
Charles, Dauphin and later King of France, *1H6,* p. 125.
Charles VI, King of France, *H5,* p. 121.
Charmian, *A&C,* p. 178.
Charterhouse, see *Chartreux.* Map. p. 104.
Chatham, 2H6, Map. p. 102.
Chatillon, *KJ,* p. 107.
Chartreux (Charterhouse), H8, Map. p. 104.
Cheapside, 2H6, Map. p. 104.
Chiron, *TAnd.,* p. 148.

Index

Cicero, *JC*, p. 154.
Cimber, Metellus, *JC*, p. 154.
Cinna, *JC*, p. 154.
Cinna, the Poet, *JC*, p. 155.
Clarence, George, Duke of, *3H6*, p. 133; *R3*, p. 137.
Clarence, Thomas, Duke of, *2H4*, p. 117.
Clarence, young son and daughter of, *R3*, p. 138.
Claudio, *M for M*, p. 80.
Claudio, *M Ado*, p. 66.
Claudius, *Haml.*, p. 158.
Claudius, *JC*, p. 155.
Clement's Inn, *2H4*, Map, p. 104.
Cleomenes, *WT*, p. 92.
Cleon, *Per.*, p. 84.
Cleopatra, *A&C*, p. 178.
Clerk of Chatham, *2H6*, p. 130.
Clifford, Lord, *2H6*, p. 129; *3H6*, p. 133.
Clifford, Young, *2H6*, p. 129.
Citus, *JC*, p. 155.
Cloten, *Cym.*, p. 87.
Clown, *WT*, p. 92.
Clownish Countryman, *A&C*, p. 179; *TAnd.*, p. 148.
Cobham, Eleanor, see Gloucester, Duchess of.
Cobweb, *MND*, p. 50.
Colville, Sir John, *2H4*, p. 117.
Cominius, *Cor.*, p. 187.
Conrade, *M Ado*, p. 66.
Constable of France, *H5*, p. 122.
Constance, *KJ*, p. 106.
Cordelia, *KL*, p. 170.
Corin, *AYLI*, p. 70.
Coriolanus, *Cor.*, p. 187.
Corioli, *Cor.*, p. 187.
Cornelius, *Cym.*, p. 87.
Cornelius, *Haml.*, p. 158.
Cornwall, Duke of, *KL*, p. 170.
Costard, *LLL*, p. 40.
Court, *H5*, p. 121.
Courtezan, *C of E*, p. 43.
Coventry, *R2*, *1H4*, *3H6*, Map, p. 102.
Crab, *TG of V*, p. 47.
Cranmer, Archbishop of Canterbury, *H8*, p. 142.
Cressida, *T&C*, p. 162.
Cripplegate, Map, p. 104.
Cromwell, *H8*, p. 142.
Crosby Place, *R3*, Map, p. 104.
Cupid, *T of A*, p. 183.
Curan, *KL*, p. 170.
Curio, *TN*, p. 74.
Curtain Theatre (1577), p. 5.
Curtis, *T of S*, p. 58.
Cymbeline, *Cym.*, p. 87.
Cymbeline, Queen of, *Cym.*, p. 87.
Cyprus, *Oth.*, p. 166.

Dardanius, *JC*, p. 155.
Dartford, *2H6*, Map. p. 102.
Daventry, *1H4*, Map, p. 102.
Davy, *2H4*, p. 118.
Deiphobus, *T&C*, p. 162.
Demetrius, *A&C*, p. 178.
Demetrius, *MND*, p. 50.
Demetrius, *TAnd.*, p. 148.
Denmark, *Haml.*, p. 159.
Dennis, *AYLI*, p. 70.
Denny, Sir Anthony, *H8*, p. 142.
Derby, Lord Stanley, Earl of, *R3*, p. 137.

Dercetas, *A&C*, p. 178.
Desdemona, *Oth.*, p. 166.
Diana, *AWEW*, p. 77.
Diana, *Per.*, p. 84.
Dick the Butcher, *2H6*, p. 129.
Diomedes, *A&C*, p. 179.
Diomedes, *T&C*, p. 162.
Dion, *WT*, p. 92.
Dionyza, *Per.*, p. 84.
Doctor, *KL*, p. 170.
Doctor, English, *Macb.*, p. 174.
Doctor, Scotch, *Macb.*, p. 174.
Dogberry, *M Ado*, p. 66.
Dolabella, *A&C*, p. 178.
Donalbain, *Macb.*, p. 174.
Doncaster, *1H4*, Map, p. 102.
Dorcas, *WT*, p. 92.
Dorset, Marquis of, *R3*, p. 137.
Douglas, Archibald, Earl of, *1H4*, p. 113.
Dover, *KL*, Map. p. 102.
Dromio of Ephesus, *C of E*, p. 43.
Dromio of Syracuse, *C of E*, p. 43.
Duke of Florence, *AWEW*, p. 77.
Duke of Milan, *TG of V*, p. 47.
Duke of Orleans, *H5*, p. 122.
Duke of Venice, *M of V*, p. 54.
Duke of Venice, *Oth.*, p. 166.
Duke Senior, *AYLI*, p. 70.
Dull, *LLL*, p. 40.
Dumain, *LLL*, p. 40.
Duncan, *Macb.*, p. 174.
Dunsinane, *Macb.*, Map, p. 102.

Eastcheap, *1H4*, *2H4*, Map, p. 104.
Edgar, *KL*, p. 170.
Edmund, *KL*, p. 170.
Edmund of Langley, see York.
Edmund, Earl of Rutland, see Rutland.
Edward, later Edward IV, *2H6*, p. 129; *3H6*, p. 133; *R3*, p. 137.
Edward, Prince of Wales, *3H6*, p. 133.
Edward, Prince of Wales, later Edward V, *R3*, p. 137.
Egeus, *MND*, p. 50.
Eglamour, *TG of V*, p. 47.
Elbow, *M for M*, p. 80.
Elinor, Queen, *KJ*, p. 106.
Elizabeth, Queen, *R3*, p. 137.
Elsinore, *Haml.*, p. 159.
Eltham, *1H6*, Map, p. 102.
Ely, *H5*, *R3*, Map, p. 102.
Ely, Bishop of, *H5*, p. 121.
Ely, John Morton, Bishop of, *R3*, p. 137.
Ely Place, *R2*, *R3*, Map, p. 104.
Emilia, *Oth.*, p. 166.
Emilia, *WT*, p. 92.
Enobarbus, Domitius, *A&C*, p. 178.
Ephesus, *C of E*, p. 43; *Per.*, p. 84.
Eros, *A&C*, p. 178.
Erpingham, Sir Thomas, *H5*, p. 121.
Escalus, *M for M*, p. 80.
Escalus, *R&J*, p. 151.
Escanes, *Per.*, p. 84.
Essex, Earl of, *KJ*, p. 107.
Euphronius, *A&C*, p. 179.
Evans, Sir Hugh, *MW of W*, p. 62.
Exeter, *R2*, *H5*, *1H6*, *R3*, Map, p. 102.
Exeter, Duke of, *H5*, p. 121.
Exeter, Duke of, *3H6*, p. 133.
Exeter, Thomas Beaufort, Duke of, *1H6*, p. 125.

206

Index

Fabian, *TN*, p. 74.
Falstaff, Sir John, *1H4*, p. 114; *2H4*, p. 117; *MW of W*, p. 62.
Fang, *2H4*, p. 118.
Fastolfe, Sir John, *1H6*, p. 125.
Father that has killed his son, *3H6*, p. 134.
Faulconbridge, Lady, *KJ*, p. 106.
Faulconbridge, Philip, *KJ*, p. 106.
Faulconbridge, Robert, *KJ*, p. 106.
Feeble, *2H4*, p. 118.
Fenton, *MW of W*, p. 62.
Ferdinand, *LLL*, p. 40.
Ferdinand, *Temp.*, p. 96.
Feste, *TN*, p. 74.
Fidele, character assumed by Imogen, *Cym*, p. 87.
Finsbury, *1H4*, Map, p. 104.
Fish Street *2H6* Map, p. 104.
Fitzwater, Lord, *R2*, p. 110.
Flaminius *T of A*, p. 183.
Flavius, *JC*, p. 154.
Flavius, *T of A*, p. 183.
Fleance, *Macb.*, p. 174.
Fleet Prison, *2H4*, Map, p. 104.
Fleet River, Maps, p. 5, 104.
Flint Castle, *R2*, Map, p. 102.
Florence, *AWEW*, p. 77.
Florizel, *WT*, p. 92.
Fluellen, *H5*, p. 121.
Flute, *MND*, p. 50.
Fool, *KL*, p. 170.
Ford, *MW of W*, p. 62.
Ford, Mistress, *MW of W*, p. 62.
Forres, *Macb.*, Map. p. 102.
Fortinbras, *Haml.*, p. 158.
Fortune Theatre (1600), p. 5.
Francisca, *M for M*, p. 80.
Francisco, *Haml.*, p. 158.
Francisco, *Temp.*, p. 96.
Frederick, *AYLI* p. 70.
Friar Francis, *M Ado*, p. 66.
Friar John, *R&J*, p. 151.
Friar Laurence, *R&J*, p. 151.
Friar Lodowick, character assumed by Duke Vincentio, *M for M.*, p. 80.
Froth, *M for M.*, p. 80.

Gadshill, *1H4*, Map, p. 102.
Gadshill, *1H4*, p. 114.
Gallus, *A&C*, p. 178.
Ganymede, character assumed by Rosalind, *AYLI*, p. 70.
Gardiner, Bishop of Winchester, *H8*, p. 142.
Gargrave, Sir Thomas, *1H6*, p. 125.
Garter King-at-Arms, *H8*, p. 142.
Gaultree Forest, *2H4*, Map, p. 102.
Gaunt, John of, *R2*, p. 110.
George, Duke of Clarence, see Clarence.
Gertrude, *Haml.*, p. 158.
Ghost of Hamlet's father, *Haml.*, p. 158.
Glansdale, Sir William, *1H6*, p. 125.
Glendower, Owen, *1H4*, p. 113.
Globe Theatre (1599), p. 5.
Gloucester, *KL*, Map, p. 102.
Gloucester, Earl of, *KL*, p. 170.
Gloucester Duchess of, *R2*, p. 110.
Gloucester, Eleanor Cobham, Duchess of, *2H6*, p. 129.
Gloucester, Humphrey, Duke of, *2H4* p. 117; *H5*, p. 121; *1H6*, p. 125; *2H6*, p. 129.

Gloucester, Richard, Duke of, later Richard III, *2H6*, p. 129; *3H6*, p. 133; *R3*, p. 137.
Gobbo, Launcelot, *M of V*, p. 54.
Gobbo, Old, *M of V*, p. 55.
Goffe, Matthew, *2H6*, p. 129.
Goneril, *KL*, p. 170.
Gonzalo, *Temp.*, p. 96.
Governor of Harfleur, *H5*, p. 122.
Governor of Paris, *1H6*, p. 126.
Gower, *2H4*, p. 117.
Gower, *H5*, p. 121.
Gower, *Per.*, p. 84.
Gracechurch Street, Maps, p. 5, 104.
Grandpré, *H5*, p. 122.
Gratiano, *M of V*, p. 54.
Gratiano, *Oth.*, p. 166.
Gravediggers, *Haml.*, p. 159.
Gray's Inn, Map, p. 104.
Green, *R2*, p. 110.
Gregory, *R&J*, p. 151.
Grey, Lord, *R3*, p. 137.
Grey, Sir Thomas, *H5*, p. 121.
Gremio, *T of S*, p. 58.
Griffith, *H8* p. 143.
Grumio, *T of S*, p. 58.
Guiderius, *Cym.*, p. 87.
Guildenstern, *Haml.*, p. 158.
Guildford, Sir Henry, *H8*, p. 142.
Guildhall, *R3*, Map, p. 104.
Gurney, James, *KJ*, p. 107.

Hal, Prince, see Henry, Prince.
Hamlet, *Haml.*, p. 158.
Harcourt, *2H4*, p. 117.
Harfleur, *H5*, Map, p. 102
Hastings, Lord, *2H4*, p. 117.
Hastings, Lord, *3H6*, p. 133.
Hastings, Lord, *R3*, p. 137.
Hecate, *Macb.*, p. 174.
Hector, *T&C*, p. 162.
Helen, *Cym.*, p. 87.
Helen, *T&C*, p. 162.
Helena, *AWEW*, p. 77.
Helena, *MND*, p. 50.
Helenus, *T&C*, p. 162.
Helicanes. *Per.*, p. 84.
Henry, Prince, *KJ*, p. 107.
Henry, Prince, *1H4*, p. 113; *2H4*, p. 117.
Henry IV, *1H4*, p. 113; *2H4*, p. 117.
Henry V, *H5*, p. 121.
Henry VI, *1H6*, p. 125; *2H6*, p. 129; *3H6*, p. 133.
Henry VII. see Richmond, Henry.
Henry VIII, *H8*. p. 142.
Herbert, Sir Walter, *R3*, p. 137.
Hermia, *MND*, p. 50.
Hermione, *WT*, p. 92.
Herne the Hunter, character assumed by Falstaff, *MW of W*, p. 62.
Hero, *M Ado*, p. 66.
Hexham, *3H6*, Map, p. 102.
Hippolyta, *MND*, p. 50.
Holborn, *R3*, Map, p. 104.
Holland, John, *2H6*, p. 129.
Holmedon, *1H4*, Map. p 102.
Holofernes, *LLL*, p. 40.
Hope Theatre (1613), p. 5.
Horatio, *Haml.*, p. 158.
Horner, Thomas, *2H6*, p. 130.
Hortensio, *T of S*, p. 58.

Hortensius, *T of A*, p. 183.
Host of the Garter Inn, *MW of W*, p. 62.
Host of the Inn, *TG of V*, p. 47.
"Hotspur," see Percy, Henry.
Hume, *2H6*, p. 129.
Humphrey, Duke of Gloucester, see Gloucester.
Hymen, god of marriage, represented in *AYLI*, p. 70.

Iachimo, *Cym.*, p. 87.
Iago, *Oth.*, p. 166.
Iden, Alexander, *2H6*, p. 129.
Illyria, TN, p. 74.
Imogen, *Cym.*, p. 87.
Inverness, Macb. Map, p. 102.
Iras, *A&C*, p. 178.
Iris, spirit representing, *Temp.*, p. 96.
Isabel, *H5, p.* 121.
Isabella, *M for M* p. 80.

Jamy, *H5*, p. 121.
Jaquenetta, *LLL*, p. 40.
Jaques, *AYLI*, p. 70
Jaques de Boys *AYLI*, p. 70.
Jessica, *M of V*, p. 54.
Jeweller, *T of A*, p. 183.
Joan la Pucelle, *1H6*, p. 125.
John Don, *M Ado*, p. 66.
John, King, *KJ*, p. 106.
John of Lancaster, see Lancaster.
Jordan, Margery, *2H6*, p. 129.
Julia, *TG of V*, p. 47.
Juliet, *M for M*, p. 80.
Juliet, *R&J*, p. 151.
Juno, spirit representing, *Temp.*, p. 96.

Katharina, *T of S*, p. 58.
Katharine, Princess of France, *H5*, p. 121.
Katherine, *LLL*, p. 40.
Katherine of Arragon, Queen, *H8*, p. 142.
Kenilworth, 2H6, Map, p. 102.
Kent, Earl of, *KL*, p. 170.
Kimbolton, H8, Map, p. 102.
King of France, *AWEW*, p. 77.
King of France, *KL*, p. 170.

Lady, An Old, *H8*, p. 143.
Laertes, *Haml.*, p. 158.
Lafeu, *AWEW*, p. 77.
Lancaster, John of, *1H4*, p. 113; *2H4*, p. 117.
Langley, Edmund of, see York.
Langley, R2, Map, p. 102.
Lartius, Titus, *Cor.*, p. 187.
Launce, *TG of V*, p. 47.
Lavache *AWEW*, p. 77.
Lavinia, *TAnd.*, p. 148.
Lear, *KL*, p. 170.
Le Beau, *AYLI*, p. 70.
Leicester, R3, H8, Map, p. 102.
Lena, Popilius, *JC*, p. 154.
Lennox, *Macb.*, p. 174.
Leonardo, *M of V*, p. 55.
Leonato, *M Ado*, p. 66.
Leonatus, Posthumus, *Cym.*, p. 87.
Leonine, *Per.*, p. 84.
Leontes, *WT*, p. 92.
Lepidus, *JC*, p. 154; *A&C*, p. 178.
Lewis, Dauphin of France, *KJ*, p. 106.

Lewis, Dauphin of France, *H5*, p. 121.
Lieutenant of the Tower, *3H6*, p. 134.
Ligarius, *JC*, p. 154.
Limehouse, H8, Map, p. 104.
Lincoln, Bishop of, *H8*, p. 142.
Lincoln, H8, Map, p. 102.
Lion, rôle assumed by Snug, *MND*, p. 50.
Lodovico, *Oth.*, p. 166.
Lombard Street, see *Lumbert Street*, Map, p. 104.
London, KJ, R2, 1H4, 2H4, H5, 1H6, 2H6, 3H6, R3, H8, Map, p. 102.
London Bridge, 1H6, 2H6, Map, p. 104.
London Stone, 2H6, Map, p. 104.
London Wall, Map p. 5, 104.
Longaville, *LLL*, p. 40.
Lord Chamberlain, *H8*, p. 142.
Lord Chancellor, *H8*, p. 142.
Lord Chief-Justice of the King's Bench, *2H4*, p. 117.
Lorenzo, *M of V*, p. 54.
Louis XI, King of France, *3H6*, p. 134.
Lovel, Lord, *R3*, p. 137.
Lovell, Sir Thomas *H8*, p. 142.
Luce, *C of E*, p. 43.
Lucentio, *T of S*, p. 58.
Lucetta, *TG of V*, p. 47.
Luciana, *C of E*, p. 43.
Lucilius, *JC*, p. 155.
Lucilius, *T of A*, p. 183.
Lucio, *M for M*, p. 80.
Lucius, *JC*, p. 155.
Lucius, *T of A*, p. 183.
Lucius, Andronicus, *TAnd.*, p. 148.
Lucius, Andronicus, Young, *TAnd.*, p. 148.
Lucius, Caius, *Cym.*, p. 87.
Lucullus, *T of A*, p. 183.
Lucy, Sir William, *1H6*, p. 125.
Ludgate Hill, Map, p. 5, 104.
Ludlow, R3, Map, p. 102.
Lumbert Street (Lombard Street), *2H4* Map, p. 104.
Lychorida, *Per.*, p. 84.
Lymoges, *KJ*, p. 106.
Lysander, *MND*, p. 50.
Lysimachus, *Per.*, p. 84.

Macbeth, *Macb.*, p. 174.
Macbeth, Lady, *Macb.*, p. 174.
Macduff, *Macb.*, p. 174.
Macduff, Lady, *Macb.*, p. 174.
Macduff, son of, *Macb.*, p. 174.
Macmorris, *H5*, p. 121.
Maecenas, *A&C*, p. 178.
Malcolm, *Macb.*, p. 174.
Malvolio, *TN*, p. 74.
Mamillius, *WT*, p. 92.
Man, Isle of. 2H6, Map, p. 102.
Mantua, R&J, p. 151; *TG of V*, p. 47.
Marcellus, *Haml.*, p. 158.
Marcius, Caius, (Coriolanus), *Cor.*, p. 187.
Marcius, Young, *Cor.*, p. 187.
Marcus Andronicus, *TAnd.*, p. 148
Mardian, *A&C*, p. 179.
Margarelon, *T&C*, p. 162.
Margaret, *M Ado*, p. 66.
Margaret of Anjou, later Queen, *1H6*, p. 126; *2H6*, p. 129; *3H6*, p. 133; *R3*, p. 137.
Maria, *LLL*, p. 40.
Maria, *TN*, p. 74.

Index

Mariana, *AWEW*, p. 77.
Mariana, *M for M*, p. 80.
Marina, *Per.*, p. 84.
Marseilles, *AWEW*, p. 77.
Marshalsea Prison, *H8*, Map, p. 104.
Martext, Sir Oliver, *AYLI*, p. 70.
Martius Andronicus, *TAnd.*, p. 148.
Marullus, *JC*, p. 154
Master of the Ship, *Temp.*, p. 96.
Mayor of London, *1H6.*, p. 126.
Mayor of London, *R3*, p. 138.
Mayor of St. Albans, *2H6*, p. 130.
Mayor of York, *3H6*, p. 134.
Melun, *KJ*, p. 107.
Menas, *A&C*, p. 178.
Menecrates, *A&C*, p. 178.
Menelaus, *T&C*, p. 162.
Menteith, *Macb.*, p. 174.
Mercade, *LLL*, p. 40.
Merchant, *T of A*, p. 183.
Mercutio, *R&J*, p. 151.
Messala, *JC*, p. 155.
Messina, *A&C*, p. 179; *M Ado*, p. 66.
Misenum, *A&C*, p. 179.
Michael, *2H6*, p. 129.
Michael, Sir *1H4*, p. 113.
Middleham Castle, *3H6*, Map, p. 102.
Middle Temple Hall, *1H4*, Map, p. 104.
Milan, *TG of V*, p. 47.
Mile End Green, *2H4*, Map, p. 104.
Milford Haven, *Cym.*, *R3*, Map, p. 102.
Miranda, *Temp.*, p. 96.
Monmouth, *1H4*, Map, p. 102.
Montague, *R&J*, p. 151.
Montague, Lady, *R&J*, p. 151.
Montague, Marquis of, *3H6*, p. 133.
Mortimer's Cross, *3H6*, Map, p. 102.
Montano, *Oth.*, p. 166.
Montgomery, Sir John, *3H6*, p. 133.
Montjoy, *H5*, p. 122.
Moon, rôle assumed by Starveling, *MND*, p. 50.
Moorditch, *1H4*, Map, p. 104.
Moorfields, *H8*, Map, p. 104.
Moorgate, Map, p. 104.
Mopsa, *WT*, p. 92.
Morgan, character assumed by Belarius, *Cym.*, p. 87.
Mortimer, Edmund, *1H4*, p. 113.
Mortimer, Lady, *1H4*, p. 113.
Mortimer, Edmund, *1H6*, p. 125
Mortimer, Sir Hugh, *3H6*, p. 133.
Mortimer, Sir John, *3H6*, p. 133.
Morton, *2H4*, p. 117.
Morton, John, Bishop of Ely, see Ely.
Moth, *LLL*, p. 40.
Moth, *MND*, p. 50.
Mouldy, *2H4*, p. 118.
Mowbray, Lord, *2H4*, p. 117.
Mowbray, Thomas, *R2*, p. 110.
Mustardseed, *MND*, p. 50.
Mutius Andronicus, *TAnd.*, p. 148.
Mytilene, *Per.*, p. 84.

Nathaniel, Sir, *LLL*, p. 40.
Navarre, *LLL*, p. 40.
Nerissa, *M of V*, p. 54.
Nestor, *T&C*, p. 162.
Neville, Richard, Earl of Warwick, **see** Warwick.
Newgate, *1H4*, Map, p. 104.
Norfolk, Duke of, *3H6*, p. 133.

Norfolk, Duke of, *R3*, p. 137.
Norfolk, Duke of, *H8*, p. 142.
Northumberland, Henry Percy, **Earl of**, *R2*, p. 110; *2H4*, p. 117.
Northumberland, Lady, *2H4*, p. 117.
Northumberland, Earl of, *3H6*, p. 133.
Nurse, *R&J*, p. 151.
Nurse, *TAnd.*, p. 148.
Nym, *H5*, p. 121; *MW of W*, p. 62.

Oberon, *MND*, p. 50.
Octavia, *A&C*, p. 178.
Octavius Caesar, *A&C*, p. 178; *JC*, p. 154.
Oliver, *AYLI*, p. 70.
Olivia, *TN*, p. 74.
Ophelia, *Haml.*, p. 158.
Orlando, *AYLI*, p. 70.
Orleans, *1H6*, Map, p. 102.
Orsino, *TN*, p. 74.
Osric, *Haml.*, p. 158.
Oswald, *KL*, p. 170.
Othello, *Oth.*, p. 166.
Overdone, Mistress, *M for M*, p. 80.
Oxford, *2H4*, Map, p. 102.
Oxford, Earl of, *3H6*, p. 133.
Oxford, Earl of, *R3*, p. 137.

Padua, *T of S*, p. 58.
Page, *MW of W*, p. 62.
Page, Mistress, *MW of W*. p. 62.
Page, Anne, *MW of W*, p. 62.
Page, William, *MW of W*, p. 62.
Page, of Falstaff, *2H4*, p. 118.
Painter, *T of A*, p. 183.
Pandarus, *T&C*, p. 162.
Pandulph, Cardinal, *KJ*, p. 106.
Panthino, *TG of V*, p. 47.
Paris, *R&J*, p. 151.
Paris, *T&C*, p. 162.
Paris, *AWEW*, *H5*, *1H6*, *2H6*, *Haml.*, Map, p. 102.
Paris Garden, *H8*, Map, p. 104.
Parliament House, *3H6*, Map, p. 104.
Parolles, *AWEW*, p. 77.
Patience, *H8*, p. 143.
Patroclus, *T&C*, p. 162.
Paulina, *WT*, p. 92.
Peaseblossom, *MND*, p. 50.
Pedro, Don. *M Ado*, p. 66.
Pembroke, Earl of, *KJ*, p. 106.
Pembroke, Earl of, *3H6*, p. 133.
Pentapolis, *Per.*, p. 84.
Percy, Henry, Earl of Northumberland, see Northumberland.
Percy, Henry, "Hotspur," *1H4*, p. 113; *R2*, p. 110.
Percy, Lady, *1H4*, p. 113; *2H4*, p. 117.
Percy, Thomas, Earl of Worcester, see Worcester.
Perdita, *WT*, p. 92.
Pericles, *Per.*, p. 84.
Peter, *M for M*, p. 80.
Peter, *2H6*, p. 130.
Peter, *R&J*, p. 151.
Peter of Pomfret, *KJ*, p. 107.
Peto, *1H4*, p. 114; *2H4*, p. 118.
Petruchio, *T of S*, p. 58.
Phebe, *AYLI*, p. 70.
Philario, *Cym.*, p. 87.
Philemon, *Per.*, p. 84.
Philip, of France, *KJ*, p. 106.

209

Philippi, JC, p. 155.
Philo, *A&C,* p. 178.
Philostrate, *MND,* p. 50.
Philotus, *T of A,* p. 183.
Phrynia, *T of A,* p. 183.
Pickt-hatch, MW of W, Map, p. 104.
Pierce of Exton, *R2,* p. 110.
Pinch, *C of E,* p. 43.
Pindarus, *JC,* p. 155.
Pisanio, *Cym.,* p. 87.
Pistol, *2H4,* p. 118; *H5,* p. 121; *MW of W,* p. 62.
Players, *Haml.,* p. 159.
Poet, *JC,* p 155.
Poet, *T of A,* p. 183.
Poins, *1H4,* p. 114; *2H4,* p. 118.
Pole, William de la, Earl of Suffolk, see Suffolk.
Polixenes, *WT,* p. 92.
Polonius, *Haml.,* p. 158.
Polydore, character assumed by Guiderius, *Cym.,* p. 87.
Pomfret, KJ, Map, p. 102.
Pomfret Castle, R2, R3, Map, p. 102.
Pompeius, Sextus, *A&C,* p. 178.
Pompey, *M for M,* p. 80.
Porter, drunken, *Macb.,* p. 174.
Portia, *JC,* p. 154.
Portia, *M of V,* p. 54.
Prat, Mother, of Brainford, character assumed by Falstaff, *MW of W,* p. 62.
Priam, *T&C,* p. 162.
Priest, *Haml.,* p. 159.
Prince of Arragon, *M of V,* p. 54.
Prince of Morocco, *M of V,* p. 54.
Princess of France, *LLL,* p. 40.
Proculeius, *A&C,* p. 178.
Prospero, *Temp.,* p. 96.
Proteus, *TG of V,* p. 47.
Provost of the prison, *M for M,* p. 80
Publius, *JC,* p. 154.
Publius Andronicus, *TAnd.,* p. 148.
Puck, *MND,* p. 50.
Pyramus, rôle assumed by Bottom, *MND,* p. 50.

Quickly, Mistress, *1H4,* p. 114; *2H4,* p. 118; *H5,* p. 121; *MW of W,* p. 62.
Quince, *MND,* p. 50.
Quintus Andronicus, *TAnd.,* p. 148.

Rambures, *H5,* p. 122.
Ratcliff, Sir Richard, *R3,* p. 137.
Ravenspurgh, R2, 1H4, 3H6, Map, p. 102.
Red Bull Theatre (1605), p. 5.
Regan, *KL,* p. 170.
Reignier, Duc d'Anjou, *1H6,* p. 125.
Reynaldo, *Haml.,* p. 158.
Richard II, *R2,* p. 110.
Richard II, Queen of, *R2,* p. 110.
Richard III, see Gloucester.
Richmond, Henry Earl of, later Henry VII, *3H6,* p. 133; *R3,* p. 137.
Rivers, Lord, *3H6,* p. 134; *R3,* p. 137.
Robin, *MW of W,* p 62.
Robin Goodfellow, see Puck.
Rochester, 1H4, Map, p. 102.
Roderigo, *Oth.,* p. 166.
Rome, *A&C,* p. 179; *Cor.,* p. 187; *Cym.,* p. 87; *JC.,* p. 155; *TAnd.,* p. 148.
Romeo, *R&J,* p. 151.

Rosalind, *AYLI,* p. 70.
Rosaline, *LLL,* p. 40.
Rosencrantz, *Haml.,* p. 158.
Rose Theatre, (1587), p. 5.
Ross, *Macb.,* p. 174.
Ross, Lord, *R2,* p. 110.
Rotherham, Thomas, Archbishop of York, *R3,* p. 138.
Rouen, 1H6, Map, p. 102.
Rousillon, AWEW, p. 77.
Rousillon, Countess of, *AWEW,* p. 77.
Rugby, *MW of W,* p. 62.
Rumor, *2H4,* p. 117.
Rutland, Edmund, Earl of, *3H6,* p. 133.

St. Albans, 1H4, 2H4, 2H6, 3H6, R3, Map, p. 102.
St. George's Fields, 2H4, Map, p. 104.
St. Laurence Poultney, Parish of, H8, Map, p. 104.
St. Magnus Corner, 2H6, Map, p. 104.
St. Paul's, 2H4, Map, p. 104.
Salanio, *M of V,* p. 54.
Salarino, *M of V,* p. 54.
Salerio, *M of V,* p. 54.
Salisbury, *KJ, R2, H5, 1H6, 2H6, R3, H8,* Map, p. 102.
Salisbury, Earl of, *KJ,* p. 106.
Salisbury, Earl of, *R2,* p. 110.
Salisbury, Earl of, *H5,* p. 121.
Salisbury, Earl of, *1H6,* p. 125.
Salisbury, Earl of, *2H6,* p. 129.
Sampson, *R&J,* p. 151.
Sandal Castle, 3H6, Map, p. 102.
Sandys, Lord, (Sir William), *H8,* p. 142.
Sardis, JC, p. 155.
Saturninus, *TAnd.,* p. 148.
Say, Lord, *2H6,* p 129.
Savoy, 2H6, Map, p. 104.
Scales, Lord, *2H6,* p. 130.
Scarus, *A&C;* 178.
Scroop, Lord, *H5,* p. 121.
Scroop, Sir Stephen, *R2,* p. 110.
Scroop, Richard, Archbishop of York, *1H4,* p. 113; *2H4,* p. 117.
Sebastian, *Temp.,* p. 96.
Sebastian, *TN,* p. 74.
Sebastian, character assumed by Julia, *TG of V,* p. 47.
Seleucus, *A&C,* p. 179.
Sempronius, *TAnd.,* p. 148.
Sempronius, *T of A,* p. 183.
Servants to Varro and Isidore, usurers, *T of A,* p. 183.
Severn River, 1H4, Map, p. 102.
Servilius. *T of A,* p. 183.
Seyton, *Macb.,* p. 174.
Shadow, *2H4,* p. 118.
Shallow, Robert, *2H4,* p. 118; *MW of W,* p. 62.
Shepherd, An Old, *1H6,* p 126.
Shepherd, Old. *WT,* p. 92.
Sheriff of Wiltshire. *R3,* p. 138.
Shipton Moor, see *Gaultree Forest, 2H4,* Map, p. 102.
Shoreditch, Maps, p. 5, 104.
Shrewsbury, 1H4, Map, p 102.
Shylock, *M of V,* p. 54.
Sicilia, WT, p. 92.
Silence, *2H4,* p. 118.
Silius, *A&C,* p. 179.
Silvia, *TG of V,* p. 47.

Index

Silvius, *AYLI*, p. 70.
Simonides, *Per.*, p. 84.
Simpcox, *2H6*, p. 130.
Simpcox, Wife of, *2H6*, p. 130.
Simple, *MW of W*, p. 62.
Siward, *Macb.*, p. 174.
Siward's son, *Macb.*, p. 174.
Slender, *MW of W*, p. 62.
Sly, Christopher, *T of S*, p. 58.
Smith the Weaver, *2H6*, p. 129.
Smithfield, *2H4, 2H6*, Map, p. 104.
Snare, *2H4*, p. 118.
Snout, *MND*, p. 50.
Snug, *MND*, p. 50.
Solinus, *C of E*, p. 43.
Somerset, John Beaufort, Earl and later
  Duke of, *1H6*, p. 125; *2H6*, p. 129;
  3H6, p. 133.
Somerville, Sir John, *3H6*, p. 133.
Son that has killed his father, *3H6*,
  p. 134.
Soothsayer, *A&C*, p. 179; *Cymb.*, p. 87;
  JC, p. 155.
Southampton, *H5*, Map, p. 102.
Southwark, *2H6*, Maps, p. 104.
Southwell, *2H6*, p. 129.
Speed, *TG of V*, p. 47.
Stafford Sir Humphrey, *2H6*, p. 129.
Stafford, Lord, *3H6*, p 133.
Stafford, William, *2H6*, p. 129.
Staines, *H5*, Map, p. 102.
Stanley, Sir John, *2H6*, p. 130.
Stanley, Lord, Earl of Derby, see Derby.
Stanley, Sir William, *3H6*, p. 133.
Starveling, *MND*, p. 50.
Stephano, *M of V*, p. 55.
Stephaano, *Temp.*, p. 96.
Strand, *H8*, Map, p. 104.
Strangers, Three, *T of A*, p. 183.
Stratford, Map, p. 102.
Strato, *JC*, p. 155.
Suffolk, Earl and Duke of, William de
  la Pole, *1H6*, p. 125; *2H6*, p. 129.
Suffolk, Duke of, *H8*, p. 142.
Surrey, Duke of, *R2*, p. 110.
Surrey, Earl of, *2H4*, p. 117.
Surrey, Earl of, *R3*, p. 137.
Surrey, Earl of, *H8*, p. 142.
Surveyor to the Duke of Buckingham,
  H8, p. 143.
Sutton Co'fil', *1H4*, Map, p. 102.
Swan Theatre, (1595), p. 5.
Swinstead Abbey KJ, Map, p. 102.

Talbot, John, *1H6*, p. 125.
Talbot, Lord, *1H6*, p. 125.
Tamora, *TAnd.*, p. 148.
Tamworth, *R3*, Map, p. 102.
Tarsus, *Per.*, p. 84
Taurus, *A&C*, p. 178.
Tearsheet, Doll, *2H4*, p. 118.
Temple Gardens, *1H6*, Map, p. 104.
Tenant of Gloucester's, *KL*, p. 170.
Tewkesbury, *3H6*, Map, p. 102.
Thaisa *Per.*, p. 84.
Thaliard, *Per.*, p. 84.
Thames River, Maps, p. 5, 104.
Theatre (1576), p. 5.
Thersites, *T&C*, p. 162.
Theseus, *MND*, p. 50.
Thisby, rôle assumed by Flute, *MND*,
  p. 50.

Thomas, *M for M*, p. 80.
Thomas, Duke of Clarence, see Clarence.
Thurio, *TG of V*, p. 47.
Thyreus, *A&C*, p. 178.
Timandra, *T of A*, p. 183.
Time, (Chorus), *WT*, p. 92.
Timon of Athens, *T of A*, p. 183.
Titania, *MND*, p. 50.
Titinius, *JC*, p. 155.
Titus, *T of A*, p. 183.
Titus Andronicus, *TAnd.*, p. 148.
Tom o' Bedlem, character assumed by
  Edgar, *KL*, p. 170.
Topas, Sir, character assumed by Feste,
  TN, p. 74.
Touchstone, *AYLI*, p. 70.
Tower, *R2, 1H6, 2H6, 3H6, R3, H8*,
  Map, p. 104.
Tower Hill, *H8*, Map, p. 104.
Tower Street, Map p. 104.
Towton, *3H6*, Map, p. 102.
Tranio, *T of S*, p. 58.
Travers, *2H4*, p. 117.
Trebonius, *JC*, p. 154.
Tressel, *R3*, p. 138.
Trinculo, *Temp.*, p. 96.
Troilus, *T&C*, p. 162.
Troy, *T&C*, p. 162.
Tubal, *M of V*, p. 54.
Turnball Street, *2H4*, Map, p. 104.
Tutor to Rutland, *3H6*, p. 134.
Tybalt, *R&J*, p. 151.
Tyburn, *LLL*, Map, p. 104.
Tyre, *Per.*, p. 84.
Tyrrel, Sir James, *R3*, p. 137.

Ulysses, *T&C*, p. 162.
Ursula, *M Ado*, p. 66.
Urswick, Christopher, *R3*, p. 138.

Valentine, *TAnd.*, p. 148.
Valentine, *TN*, p. 74.
Valentine, *TG of V*, p. 47.
Valeria, *Cor.*, p. 187.
Varrius, *A&C*, p. 178.
Varrius, *M for M*, p. 80.
Varro, *JC*, p. 155.
Vaughan, Sir Thomas, *R3*, p. 137.
Vaux, *2H6*, p. 130.
Vaux, Sir Nicholas, *H8*, p. 142.
Velutus, Sicinius, *Cor.*, p. 187.
Venice, *M of V*, p. 55; *Oth*, p. 166.
Ventidius, *A&C*, p. 178.
Ventidius, *T of A*, p. 183.
Verges, *M Ado*, p. 66.
Vernon, *1H6*, p. 125.
Vernon, Sir Richard, *1H4*, p. 113.
Verona, *R&J*, p. 151; *TG of V*, p. 47.
Vienna, *M for M*, p. 80.
Vincentio, *M for M*, p. 80.
Vincentio, *T of S*, p. 58.
Viola, *TN*, p. 74.
Violenta, *AWEW*, p. 77.
Virgilia, *Cor.*, p. 187.
Voltimand, *Haml.*, p. 158.
Volumnia, *Cor.*, p. 187.
Volumnius, *JC*, p. 155.

Wakefield, *2H6, 3H6*, Map, p. 102.
Wall, rôle assumed by Snout, *MND*,
  p. 50.
Warkworth Castle, *1H4, 2H4*, Map, p.
  102.

211

Index

Wart, *2H4*, p. 118.
Warwick, 3H6, Map, p. 102.
Warwick, Earl of, *2H4*, p. 117.
Warwick, Earl of, *H5*, p. 121.
Warwick, Richard Neville, Earl of, *1H6*, p. 125; *2H6*, p. 129; *3H6*, p. 133.
Westminster, 2H4, H8, Map, p. 104.
Westminster Abbey, 1H6, 2H6, R3, Map, p. 104.
Westminster, Abbot of, *R2*, p. 110.
Westminster Hall, R2, Map, p. 104.
Westmoreland, Earl of, *1H4*, p. 113; *2H4*, p. 117; *H5*, p. 121.
Westmoreland, Earl of, *3H6*, p. 133.
Whitechapel Street, Maps, p. 5, 104.
Whitefriars, R3, Map, p. 104.
Whitehall, H8, Map, p. 104.
White Hart, Southwark, 2H6, Map, p. 104.
Whitmore, Walter, *2H6*, p. 130.
Widow of Florence, *AWEW*, p. 77.
William, *AYLI*, p. 70.
Williams, *H5*, p. 121.
Willoughby, Lord, *R2*, p. 110.
Winchester, 1H6, 2H6, H8, Map, p. 102.
Winchester, Bishop of, see Beaufort, Gardiner.

Windsor, MW of W, R2, Map, p. 102.
Witches, *Macb.*, p. 174.
Wolsey, Thomas, Cardinal of York, *H8*, p. 142.
Woodville, *1H6*, p. 126.
Woodville, Elizabeth, later Queen, *3H6*, p. 133.
Worcester, KJ, R2, 1H4, 2H4, Map; p. 102.
Worcester, Thomas Percy, Earl of, *1H4*, p. 113.
Wye River, 1H4, Map, p. 102.

York, R2, 1H4, 2H4, H5, 1H6, 2H6; 3H6, R3, Map, p. 102.
York, Archbishop of, see Rotherham, Scroop.
York, Cardinal of, see Wolsey.
York, Edmund of Langley, Duke of, *R2*, p. 110.
York, Richard Plantagenet, Duke of, *1H6*, p. 125; *2H6*, p. 129; *3H6*, p. 133.
York, Richard, Duke of, *R3*, p. 137.
York, Duke of, *H5*, p. 121.
York, Duchess of, *R2*, p. 110.
York, Duchess of, *R3*, p. 137.
York Place, H8, Map, p. 104.

212

Genealogical Charts

The Houses of York and Lancaster
Claim of Henry V to the Throne of France

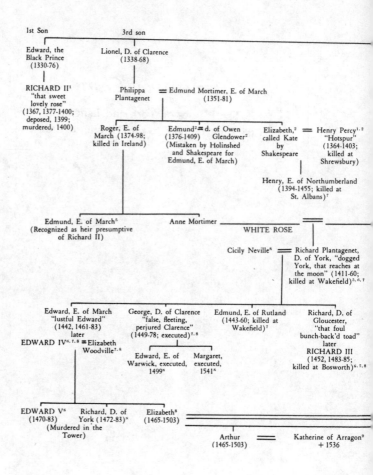

1st Son   3rd son

Edward, the
Black Prince
(1330-76)

Lionel, D. of Clarence
(1338-68)

RICHARD II[1]
"that sweet
lovely rose"
(1367, 1377-1400;
deposed, 1399;
murdered, 1400)

Philippa
Plantagenet = Edmund Mortimer, E. of March
(1351-81)

Roger, E. of
March (1374-98;
killed in Ireland)

Edmund[2] = d. of Owen
(1376-1409) Glendower[2]
(Mistaken by Holinshed
and Shakespeare for
Edmund, E. of March)

Elizabeth,[2] = Henry Percy[1,2]
called Kate   "Hotspur"
by   (1364-1403;
Shakespeare killed at
            Shrewsbury)

Henry, E. of Northumberland
(1394-1455; killed at
St. Albans)[7]

Edmund, E. of March[5]
(Recognized as heir presumptive
of Richard II)

Anne Mortimer

WHITE ROSE

Cicily Neville[8] = Richard Plantagenet,
D. of York, "dogged
York, that reaches at
the moon" (1411-60;
killed at Wakefield)[5,6,7]

Edward, E. of March
"lustful Edward"
(1442, 1461-83)
later
EDWARD IV[6,7,8] = Elizabeth
Woodville[7,8]

George, D. of Clarence
"false, fleeting,
perjured Clarence"
(1449-78; executed)[7,8]

Edmund, E. of Rutland
(1443-60; killed at
Wakefield)[7]

Richard, D. of
Gloucester,
"that foul
bunch-back'd toad"
later
RICHARD III
(1452, 1483-85;
killed at Bosworth)[6,7,8]

Edward, E. of Margaret,
Warwick, executed, executed,
1499[8]   1541[8]

EDWARD V[8] Richard, D. of
(1470-83)   York (1472-83)[8]
         (Murdered in the
         Tower)

Elizabeth[8]
(1465-1503)

Arthur
(1465-1503)

Katherine of Arragon[9]
+ 1536

THE HOUSES OF YORK AND LANCASTER

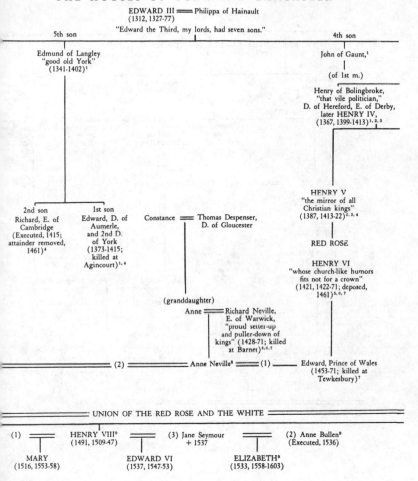

EDWARD III ══ Philippa of Hainault
(1312, 1327-77)

"Edward the Third, my lords, had seven sons."

5th son   4th son

Edmund of Langley   John of Gaunt,[1]
"good old York"
(1341-1402)[1]

                                                                        (of 1st m.)

                                                    Henry of Bolingbroke,
                                                    "that vile politician,"
                                                    D. of Hereford, E. of Derby,
                                                    later HENRY IV,
                                                    (1367, 1399-1413)[1, 2, 3]

                                                    HENRY V
                                                    "the mirror of all
                                                    Christian kings"
                                                    (1387, 1413-22)[2, 3, 4]

2nd son   1st son
Richard, E. of   Edward, D. of   Constance ══ Thomas Despenser,   RED ROSE
Cambridge   Aumerle,   D. of Gloucester
(Executed, 1415;   and 2nd D.
attainder removed,   of York   HENRY VI
1461)[4]   (1373-1415;   "whose church-like humors
                       killed at   fits not for a crown"
                       Agincourt)[1, 4]   (1421, 1422-71; deposed,
                                                                                    1461)[5, 6, 7]

                                            (granddaughter)
                                            Anne ══ Richard Neville,
                                                    E. of Warwick,
                                                    "proud setter-up
                                                    and puller-down of
                                                    kings" (1428-71; killed
                                                    at Barnet)[5, 6, 7]

═══ (2) ═══ Anne Neville[8] ═══ (1) ═══ Edward, Prince of Wales
                                        (1453-71; killed at
                                        Tewkesbury)[7]

═══ UNION OF THE RED ROSE AND THE WHITE ═══

(1) ══ HENRY VIII[9] ══ (3) Jane Seymour ══ (2) Anne Bullen[9]
       (1491, 1509-47)   + 1537   (Executed, 1536)

MARY   EDWARD VI   ELIZABETH[9]
(1516, 1553-58)   (1537, 1547-53)   (1533, 1558-1603)

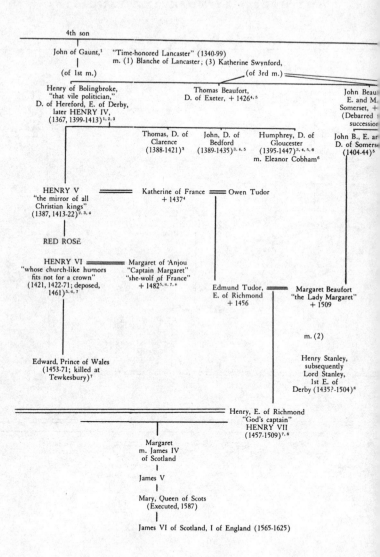

4th son
───

John of Gaunt,[1]   "Time-honored Lancaster" (1340-99)
                    m. (1) Blanche of Lancaster; (3) Katherine Swynford,
    (of 1st m.)   (of 3rd m.) ═══

Henry of Bolingbroke,   Thomas Beaufort,   John Beaufort
 "that vile politician,"   D. of Exeter, + 1426[4, 5]   E. and M.
 D. of Hereford, E. of Derby,   Somerset, +
 later HENRY IV,   (Debarred
 (1367, 1399-1413)[1, 2, 3]   succession

              Thomas, D. of   John, D. of   Humphrey, D. of   John B., E. an
              Clarence   Bedford   Gloucester   D. of Somerset
              (1388-1421)[3]   (1389-1435)[3, 4, 5] (1395-1447)[3, 4, 5, 6] (1404-44)[5]
                                               m. Eleanor Cobham[6]

HENRY V   ═══════   Katherine of France ═══ Owen Tudor
 "the mirror of all   + 1437[4]
 Christian kings"
 (1387, 1413-22)[2, 3, 4]

    RED ROSE

HENRY VI ═══════   Margaret of Anjou
 "whose church-like humors "Captain Margaret"
 fits not for a crown"   "she-wolf of France"
 (1421, 1422-71; deposed,   + 1482[5, 6, 7, 8]
 1461)[5, 6, 7]   Edmund Tudor,   ═══ Margaret Beaufort
                                                 E. of Richmond   "the Lady Margaret"
                                                 + 1456   + 1509

                                                                       m. (2)

Edward, Prince of Wales   Henry Stanley,
 (1453-71; killed at   subsequently
 Tewkesbury)[7]   Lord Stanley,
                                                                        1st E. of
                                                                        Derby (1435?-1504)[8]

═══════════════════════════════   Henry, E. of Richmond
                                    "God's captain"
                                    HENRY VII
                                    (1457-1509)[7, 8]

                 Margaret
                 m. James IV
                 of Scotland

                 James V

                 Mary, Queen of Scots
                 (Executed, 1587)

                 James VI of Scotland, I of England (1565-1625)

THE HOUSES OF YORK AND LANCASTER

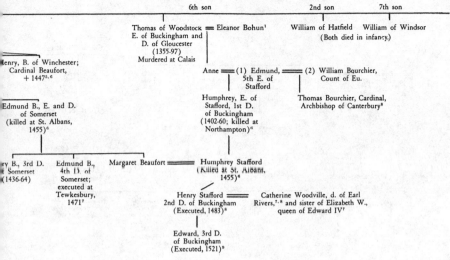

EDWARD III === Philippa of Hainault
(1312, 1327-77)

"Edward the Third, my lords, had seven sons."

	6th son	2nd son	7th son
	Thomas of Woodstock === Eleanor Bohun[1] E. of Buckingham and D. of Gloucester (1355-97) Murdered at Calais	William of Hatfield William of Windsor (Both died in infancy.)	

Henry, B. of Winchester;
Cardinal Beaufort,
+ 1447[5, 6]

Anne === (1) Edmund, === (2) William Bourchier,
5th E. of   Count of Eu.
Stafford

Edmund B., E. and D.
of Somerset
(killed at St. Albans,
1455)[6]

Humphrey, E. of   Thomas Bourchier, Cardinal,
Stafford, 1st D.   Archbishop of Canterbury[8]
of Buckingham
(1402-60; killed at
Northampton)[6]

ry B., 3rd D.   Edmund B.,   Margaret Beaufort ===== Humphrey Stafford
t Somerset   4th D. of   (Killed at St. Albans,
(1436-64)   Somerset;   1455)[6]
            executed at
            Tewkesbury,
            1471[7]

Henry Stafford ===== Catherine Woodville, d. of Earl
2nd D. of Buckingham   Rivers,[7, 8] and sister of Elizabeth W.,
(Executed, 1483)[8]   queen of Edward IV[7]

Edward, 3rd D.
of Buckingham
(Executed, 1521)[9]

KEY TO SUPERSCRIPTIONS

1. *Richard II*

2. *1 Henry IV*

3. *2 Henry IV*

4. *Henry V*

5. *1 Henry VI*

6. *2 Henry VI*

7. *3 Henry VI*

8. *Richard III*

9. *Henry VIII*

Dates of birth, accession, and death

CLAIM OF HENRY V TO THE THRONE OF FRANCE

(Dates of birth, accession, and death)

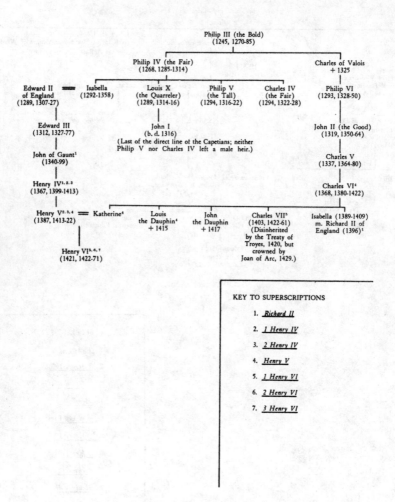

Philip III (the Bold)
(1245, 1270-85)

Philip IV (the Fair) (1268, 1285-1314) — **Charles of Valois** + 1325

Edward II of England (1289, 1307-27) ══ **Isabella** (1292-1358) — **Louis X (the Quarreler)** (1289, 1314-16) — **Philip V (the Tall)** (1294, 1316-22) — **Charles IV (the Fair)** (1294, 1322-28) — **Philip VI** (1293, 1328-50)

Edward III (1312, 1327-77)

John I (b. d. 1316)
(Last of the direct line of the Capetians; neither Philip V nor Charles IV left a male heir.)

John of Gaunt[1] (1340-99)

John II (the Good) (1319, 1350-64)

Henry IV[1,2,3] (1367, 1399-1413)

Charles V (1337, 1364-80)

Charles VI[4] (1368, 1380-1422)

Henry V[2,3,4] (1387, 1413-22) ══ **Katherine**[4] — **Louis the Dauphin**[4] + 1415 — **John the Dauphin** + 1417 — **Charles VII**[5] (1403, 1422-61) (Disinherited by the Treaty of Troyes, 1420, but crowned by Joan of Arc, 1429.) — **Isabella** (1389-1409) m. Richard II of England (1396)[1]

Henry VI[5,6,7] (1421, 1422-71)

KEY TO SUPERSCRIPTIONS

1. *Richard II*
2. *1 Henry IV*
3. *2 Henry IV*
4. *Henry V*
5. *1 Henry VI*
6. *2 Henry VI*
7. *3 Henry VI*